"A teacher's job is no longer to dispense knowle
itate learning for students whose future world i
Literacy Is Still *Not Enough* is the right book at
redouble our efforts to shift a multigenerational culture of learning that
has been preparing students for a world that is in the rearview mirror."

—Jeff Remington, National STEM Teacher Ambassador
Palmyra, PA

"Literacy is not enough! In spite of frequent critiques, schools are better
at teaching simple reading and math skills than we have ever been. It is
not enough! *Literacy Is* Still *Not Enough* shows how new fluencies drive
success at all levels and shows the way to teach children the habits of
mind that will define the new success. Well done on this rich reboot of
a classic."

—Fran Murphy, Retired Dean of Education
St. John Fisher College
Rochester, NY

"Finally, a book that not only tells 'why' we need to teach the long-
talked about 21st century learning skills, but much more critically
'how.' A masterful handbook for school leaders *and* school teachers.
Essential reading!"

—Andy Rankin, Principal
Avalon Public School
Avalon Beach, New South Wales, Australia

"This timely how-to guide is designed to help students, teachers,
and schools effectively manage the many challenges of a world experiencing the profound disruption and ongoing reconfiguration of
COVID-19 times. Learning the essential fluencies leads to the development of practical teaching and learning constructs based on modern
learning skills that will enable successful and productive global citizenship for the modern, ever changing world.

"The six fluencies are derived from an extensive review of global essential
skills lists. This is an eminently practical resource that must be used to
inform teacher training programs, which currently seem to lag behind
the education young people need to successfully navigate life in the
twenty-first century."

—Mike Frost, Director
Education and Training Consultant, Mike Frost & Associates
Hobart, Tasmania

"I have implemented the 9Ds of Solution Fluency in three different school settings with great success. My students have thrived and flourished using the carefully crafted learning progressions for inspiring real-world learning experiences."

"The initial publication of *Literacy Is Not Enough* had a profound impact on me as an educational leader, my colleagues, and my students. I am elated that Mohan, Jukes, and Schaaf updated this instructional gem."

"The content and resources are innovative and appropriately presented for educators teaching in an unpredictable and ever-changing world—a visionary resource for the future of learning."

—Dany Coelho, Principal
Waitara Public School
Wahroonga, New South Wales, Australia

"*Literacy Is* Still *Not Enough* is a provocative read that not only opens many new discussions, and addresses topics left unanswered from the past, but also provided me with strategies to move to new levels of engagement and competencies. This book is a must-read for all in education."

—Lisa Holmes, Professor of Education
Spokane Community College
Spokane, WA

"*Literacy Is* Still *Not Enough* is an important and timely book that makes a compelling case for embracing an ever-evolving understanding of what it means to be literate in today's highly visual and hyper-connected world. But beyond being a framework for establishing new foundations of literacy that meet the world where it is today, the book champions the use of authentic learning projects which are able to demonstrate relevance and context to today's learners. This book is recommended reading for educators who not only want to better prepare their students for today's landscape of communication, creativity, employment and global awareness, but to do so through projects that matter."

—Nikos Theodosakis, Speaker, Educator, and Author
Penticton, British Columbia, Canada

"This book is for any educational stakeholder who no longer believes 'the way we've always done it' is a good enough basis for an educational decision. Mohan, Jukes, and Schaaf have developed a pedagogical solution by reimagining the six modern fluencies. Their 9Ds process for real-world problem solving ensures that students are competent in the essential skills they will need after graduation.

"As an educator in an ever-changing world, this book reinforced the need for problem-focused learning. The 9Ds process for real-world problem-solving provides a road map for student success. My head was spinning with new ideas to make learning in my classroom more relevant by focusing on the six modern fluencies. My copy will be placed in an easy-to-grab location to use as a guide when designing any and all new units."

"Mohan, Jukes, and Schaaf provide a deep look into the challenges that are making it hard for students to be successful when they leave the classroom. Fortunately, they provide clear and concise steps to allow students to learn independently through the 9Ds process ensuring the development of the modern fluencies. This book is a must-read for any educator who wants to disrupt the field of education and support students in thriving beyond life in the classroom."

"The book is a helpful guide for designing units that emphasize developing higher-order independent thinking skills through explicit, organized steps, unit examples, and practical assessment strategies. The only reason I wanted to put the book down was to create fluency units that promote active, engaged, higher-level thinking in today's and tomorrow's learners."

—Becky Zayas, Academy Teacher
Forsyth County Day School
Lewisville, NC

Literacy Is *Still* Not Enough

This book is dedicated to my number one fans, biggest and unwavering supporters—my family. I can always count on them. My family has showed me what it means to love and be loved. There are no words to express my gratitude and thanks to my dad and late mum. To my late husband Mini, who showed me what the true meaning of life is. He was my rock and biggest support system. He helped make me who I am. My daughter Shona and son Sherwen are the constant in my life. I can totally count on them when life's journey gets tough. They are there on both the good days and bad days. They are always there to protect and defend me and catch my tears on days that I could flood the world. Their warm embrace, reassurance and love is my spiritual support in life. They support me in whatever I do, celebrate my successes and never judge me for who I am.

— Nicky Mohan

This book is dedicated to the memories of my parents and brother, Arthur, Margaret, and John Jukes; and to my sisters Ann and Cathy. Though we are separated by time and distance, we will always be together.

—Ian Jukes

For my wonderful family—Rachel, Connor, and Ben, for their love and support. And for my mother, Susan; my late father, Stephen; and my sister, Kristy—your guidance and patience helped me develop into the man I am today.

—Ryan L. Schaaf

We would like to send a special thank you and shout out to Arnis Burvikovs for his continuing support, encouragement, and guidance throughout the process of planning and writing this book. It has been a wonderful journey. We wish you the very best in your retirement.

Literacy Is *Still* Not Enough

Modern Fluencies for Teaching, Learning, and Assessment

Nicky Mohan

Ian Jukes

Ryan L. Schaaf

Foreword by George Saltsman

CORWIN

FOR INFORMATION

Corwin
A SAGE Company
2455 Teller Road
Thousand Oaks, California 91320
(800) 233-9936
www.corwin.com

SAGE Publications Ltd.
1 Oliver's Yard
55 City Road
London, EC1Y 1SP
United Kingdom

SAGE Publications India Pvt. Ltd.
B 1/I 1 Mohan Cooperative Industrial Area
Mathura Road, New Delhi 110 044
India

SAGE Publications Asia-Pacific Pte. Ltd.
18 Cross Street #10-10/11/12
China Square Central
Singapore 048423

Acquisitions Editor: Ariel Curry
Editorial Assistant: Caroline Timmings
Production Editor: Amy Schroller
Copy Editor: Deanna Noga
Typesetter: Hurix Digital
Proofreader: Sally Jaskold
Indexer: Integra
Cover Designer: Rose Storey

Printed in the United States of America

ISBN: 9781544381268

This book is printed on acid-free paper.

21 22 23 24 25 10 9 8 7 6 5 4 3 2 1

Contents

Chapter 3: From Literacy to Fluency: The Starting Point

Chapter 4: Modern Learning Pedagogy and the Learning Progression

Chapter 5: Modern and Future-Ready Learning Environments

PART II: An Introduction to the Modern Fluencies

Chapter 6: Teaching and Learning Using the Modern Fluencies   71

Chapter 7: Solution Fluency: Real-World Problem Solving   75

Chapter 8: Collaboration Fluency: Global Connections   101

PART III: Moving Forward

For a digital library of resources related to each chapter of *Literacy Is* Still *Not Enough*, please visit the companion website at **http://www.resources.corwin.com/ literacyisstillnotenough**.

Foreword

There is a familiar and recurring proposition that the most effective way to improve student performance is to get back to basics. This sentiment suggests that schools should emphasize "The Three Rs" of reading, 'riting, and 'rithmetic—even to the exclusion of subjects perceived as less "academic," such as art, music, or physical education. Proponents of this approach imply these three touchstones provide the educational foundation students need to be successful.

What I believe this approach misses most, and that the precursor book *Literacy Is Not Enough* so eloquently demonstrated, is that for students to be effectual in an ever changing and technologically advanced world, they require fluencies beyond the Three Rs alone. To excel in a period of rapid global progress, students need to be confident in working in diverse teams, to be creative in solving authentic problems, and be resourceful applying knowledge in real-world settings. *Literacy Is Not Enough* clearly and powerfully articulated that if we are to ignite a life-long love for learning in our students, we need to connect their education to what they care most passionately about—we need to respect students' intrinsic motivations for learning.

Since its 2011 release, the ideas and concepts presented in *Literacy Is Not Enough* are now embedded into classrooms and education systems around the world. Alongside contemporaries such as the late Sir Ken Robinson, Alvin Toffler, and Howard Gardner, a global movement took hold to rethink what the essential elements of education should be. The positive effects of this movement have now reached millions of students worldwide. Yet there is still work to do.

More than a decade ago, *Literacy Is Not Enough* urged us to prepare for an uncertain future. It prompted us to move quickly in our reforms. What I, and so many of my colleagues, didn't realize then was just how soon that future would arrive.

Looking back now, the year 2011 feels like a lifetime ago. A time before post-truth and alternative facts. A time before a global pandemic moved students into remote instruction and employees into virtual work teams. It was a time before global economic realignments and social upheaval. It was a time before the new-normal became part of our daily vocabulary.

Literacy Is Still *Not Enough* is exactly the right book at exactly the right time, not just because the world has changed, but because education has also changed. Schools have now acquired hundreds of millions of new digital devices for student use. Almost every teacher is now experienced in teaching in some type of digital learning platform. Daily virtual collaboration and video conferencing are now familiar activities for most school administrators. The debate on when the technological age will arrive in schools has ended. It's here!

For years prior to the COVID-19 pandemic, the incorporation of 21st century fluencies into the curriculum was a largely aspirational goal. Access to funding for technology and need for teacher training were logistical hurdles that slowed adoption. However, now, we possess the tools to help students use their innovation and imagination to solve real-world problems. We have the networks to enhance communication fluency and to assist student's understanding of the interconnectedness of our global society. And we also have an increased sense of responsibility to help our students find truth in a sea of conflicting information. What we didn't have, until now, is a step-by-step guide that helps educators use these technologies to incorporate modern fluencies into present-day classrooms.

Literacy Is Still *Not Enough* provides clear, sequential steps to help achieve each of the six modern fluencies in a classroom setting. It is a guide for implementation at a time when implementation is most needed. Readers will find clear and practical advice on not just why to implement, but how. This book is a must have guide for every educator regardless of who their learners are or where in the world they live.

Finally, *Literacy Is* Still *Not Enough* helps educators build a bridge between traditional and progressive learning. It helps unfold the full intellectual and creative genius of all our students. Educators are the knowledge providers for learners in the knowledge age. Education stands in the gap between the present and their future, between failure and fulfillment. I believe that it is the energy, passion, creativity, commitment, and hard work of all educators, every day that builds the bridge so our children can cross the gap from the present to the future. And as our children cross this gap so does our collective future.

As an educator, you will find this book both inspirational and practical. *Literacy Is* Still *Not Enough* is a lifeline for teachers dealing with all the pressures of the modern classroom. You will want to refer to it again and again for practical ideas about how to prepare your students for their future. But this book also acts as a catalyst for inspiration to help reimagine what education should be in a time of global transformation.

I was fortunate to cross paths with Ian Jukes, Nicky Mohan, and Ryan Schaaf in 2015, shortly after the release of their book *Reinventing Learning for the Always-On Generation: Strategies and Apps That Work.* As like-minded educators we quickly forged what would soon become one of the most rewarding and inspirational collaborations of my career. This book now extends this invitation to you. Encapsulated in these pages is the knowledge, insight, and collective experiences of three of the world's most gifted educators. *Literacy Is* Still *Not Enough* is more than a book alone. It's an invitation to collaborate with a community of global educators who have dedicated themselves to proving relevant and impactful learning for generations of students to come. I hope you will join us in this journey.

—George Saltsman
Director of Educational Innovation
Lamar University
Beaumont, TX

Preface: Evolution of the Fluencies

In 2011, we published *Literacy Is Not Enough*, which became a bestseller because it disrupted the field of instructional planning and learning (Crockett, Jukes, & Churches). The book was well received globally, translated into multiple languages, and sold more than 100,000 copies worldwide. It promoted the idea that equipping learners with traditional literacy skills—reading, writing, and arithmetic—while necessary, was no longer enough. The book suggested that if learners were to thrive academically, professionally, and personally, they needed to move beyond a primary focus on traditional literacies to an increased emphasis on modern fluencies. The fluencies are mental processes that can be learned, adapted, and applied in the context of real-world problems and challenges. The original fluencies identified in *Literacy Is Not Enough* (2011) are:

- **Solution Fluency:** the ability to solve complex problems in real time.

- **Information Fluency:** the ability to interpret information in all forms and formats to extract the essential knowledge, perceive its meaning, and use it in real-world tasks.

- **Creativity Fluency:** the ability to think creatively in both digital and non-digital environments to develop unique and useful solutions.

- Media Fluency: the ability to communicate in multiple multimedia formats.

- Collaboration Fluency: the ability to collaborate seamlessly in both physical and virtual spaces, with real and virtual partners.

- Global Digital Citizenship: the attributes of individuals and groups who are aware of and understand today's world and their place in it. They take an active role in their community and work with others to make our planet more equal, fair, and sustainable for all.

Since the book was written over 10 years ago, an ever-evolving world, the changing needs of business, and the emergence of the New Digital Landscape have dramatically altered the essential skills, knowledge, and habits of mind needed to succeed in both the modern world and our personal lives.

After extensive research and 7 years of practical application working with dozens of schools, districts, and organizations around the world, as well as constructive feedback from practicing educators, gaps were identified in the original fluency processes. To address these gaps, new innovative steps were developed and added to the processes. The fluencies were repurposed to enhance the effectiveness of the framework to better reflect the relentless social, cultural, and economic shifts occurring today. These shifts are the compelling reason why we undertook writing the new book you now hold.

Increasingly, educational systems are being mandated by the changing demands of the workforce to incorporate essential next-generation skills into their curricula. Many school systems are identifying and prioritizing these skills by creating modern profiles of graduates. These highly prized competencies include critical thinking, social-emotional learning, analytical thinking, problem solving, metacognition, creativity, innovation, collaboration, communication, growth mindset, entrepreneurialism, and global citizenship.

As a result of this new focus, learners today must not only master traditional skills such as reading, writing, and math, but they must also cultivate a very different set of skills. These new skills are essential to succeed in a culture of technology-driven automation and a highly competitive global labor market. The book outlines a practical framework for integrating these fluencies into the traditional curriculum.

The new fluencies provide a platform for authentic teaching, learning, and assessment. The term *authentic* describes instructional approaches designed to connect mandated content learners are required to learn within a real-world context. This approach helps learners see the relevance of what is being taught and how they can apply these essential skills to their daily lives. Rather than exploring hypothetical situations or memorizing isolated, fragmented content from a textbook, the fluencies empower learners to put their skills and knowledge to practical use by designing and developing solutions and creating products that will be beneficial for communities and the world at large.

How to Use This Book

Read this book the way you build a house. You can build the most beautiful home, complete with wooden floors, tinted windows, two-car garage, and massive skylights—but, if you don't start by creating a solid, stable foundation, the first time there's heavy rain, the house will get washed away. Chapters 1 through 6 represen the foundation of *Literacy Is* Still *Not Enough*. These chapters present the case for using the fluencies at the macro-level. Chapters 7 through 12 take the fluencies to the micro-level, where each of the fluencies provides a framework to help educators learn and then infuse the learning progressions into daily instructional activities.

Approaching this book is like reading a choose-your-own-adventure story. Once you read Chapters 1 through 6, you can then decide how you want to progress with reading the book. You can either read the book by starting at the beginning and reading until the end using the left-to-right, top-to-bottom, beginning-to-end, page-after-page traditional method. If that approach works for you, great! Alternatively, you can opt for the choose-your-own-adventure approach, which is a strategy that closely aligns with the way many members of the digital generations prefer to learn. Once you have read Chapters 1 through 6, you can skim or scour the table of contents or scan the book for topics you find interesting, relevant, or required. Just identify a starting point and jump right in.

For example, if you are a classroom teacher looking to incorporate problem-solving activities to engage learners, you might want to jump directly to Chapter 7, Solution Fluency: Real-World Problem Solving. This chapter provides a step-by-step guide to solving problems or challenges. This approach allows you to cover the mandated requirements while simultaneously using real-world contexts. If you are an educational leader wanting your staff to integrate creative learning activities into the curriculum, you will want to read Chapter 11, Creativity Fluency: Innovation and Imagination. This chapter provides a structured process for enhancing creativity. To facilitate team-based activities, go to Chapter 8, Collaboration Fluency: Global Connections. To help learners develop effective research skills, use Chapter 9, Information Fluency: InfoWhelm and HyperInformation.

The book has been intentionally designed to empower educators to experience the text in a way that meets the needs of their students. Whatever approach you use, the message found in *Literacy Is* Still *Not Enough* will be transformative. The time is now to better prepare students for their futures rather than our past. This book will help you make this essential leap!

Acknowledgments

The authors would like to thank the thousands of teachers who sacrificed their time and persevered through the COVID-19 pandemic to offer their students a beacon of light during such dark, uncertain times. They would also like to commend the ingenuity, creativity, and imagination of children of the digital generation. The authors would like to thank Andy Rankin, Ashlea Simonetti, and the teachers of Avalon Public School for their participation in providing such wonderful resources for the book and their tireless commitment to their students. They would also like to thank Dany Coelho, Helen Davis, Cameron Jones, Michael Strahan, and Susan Leitch for their support and commitment to this book.

Publisher's Acknowledgments

Corwin gratefully acknowledges the contributions of the following reviewers:

Virginia E. Kelsen, PhD

Dr. Ronda Mitchell

Angela M. Mosley, EdD

Dr. Tanna Nicely

Cathy Sosnowski

About the Authors

Nicky Mohan is a global citizen by choice. Born and raised in South Africa, she now shares her time between New Zealand and Canada. Dr. Mohan has been a classroom teacher, a school administrator, a university leader, a business sector manager, a co-operate trainer, an international speaker, and a global consultant and acknowledged expert in the field of instructional design. Dr. Mohan also worked as the Director of Curriculum for the 21st Century Fluency Group (Canada). She is currently the Managing Partner of the InfoSavvy Group (Canada) and Director and cofounder of SpringBoard21 (USA), international educational consulting firms. Nicky has co-written five books including the award-winning *Reinventing Learning for the Always-On Generation* and is a member of the Teacher Task Force–UNESCO core working group on The Role of AI in Education. To contact her and get to know more about her work and her team, follow @nickymohan on Twitter and visit their websites https://infosavvy21.com/ and https://www.springboard21.com/

Ian Jukes is the founder of the InfoSavvy Group, an international educational leadership consulting firm based in Canada and New Zealand. Professionally, Dr. Jukes has been a classroom teacher, teaching every grade from kindergarten to Grade 12; a school, district, and ministry leader; a university professor; a keynote speaker; and an international consultant. He has worked with clients in more than 80 countries and made more than 12,000 presentations. He has written or co-written 23 books and nine education series. His most recent books include the award-winning *Reinventing Learning for the Always-On Generation, Teaching the Digital Generations, Living on the Future Edge, Understanding the Digital Generation, Literacy Is Not Enough, A Brief History of the Future of Education,* and *LeaderShift 2020.* First and foremost, however, Ian is a passionate educational evangelist. His focus continues to be on the compelling need to restructure our educational institutions so that they become relevant to the current and future needs of the digital generation— and to prepare learners for their future and not just society's past.

Ryan L. Schaaf is an associate professor of educational technology at Notre Dame of Maryland University and a graduate faculty member for the Johns Hopkins School of Education. Before higher education, Ryan was a public school teacher, instructional leader, curriculum designer, and technology integration specialist in Maryland. In 2007, he was nominated as Maryland Teacher of the Year. Ryan enjoys facilitating workshops on online or distance learning, digital-age learning, emerging technologies and trends in education, game-based learning, and future-focused teacher preparation. His published books include *Making School a Game Worth Playing: Digital Games in the Classroom; Using Digital Games as Assessment and Instruction Tools; Reinventing Learning for the Always-On Generation: Strategies and Apps That Work; Game On: Using Digital Games to Transform Teaching, Learning, and Assessment;* and *A Brief History of the Future of Education: Learning in the Age of Disruption.* Recently, *Reinventing Learning for the Always-On Generation: Strategies and Apps That Work* earned an Independent Publisher Book Award as one of the year's best independently published titles worldwide. To learn more about Ryan's work, follow @RyanLSchaaf on Twitter or contact him at https://www.ryanschaaf.com/.

Setting the Scene for the Modern Fluencies

Highly Educated Useless People 1

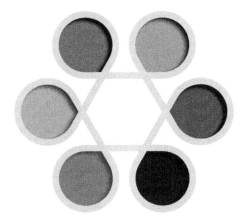

"It is possible to store the mind with a million facts and still be entirely uneducated."

—Alec Bourne

Introduction

Ian had just finished speaking at a major international conference when a delegate approached him. What the man said took Ian by complete surprise, not only because of *what* he said but also *who* he was.

"Our students are amongst the very best academic performers in the world," the speaker described the learners from his country. But he quietly added, "The problem is that most of them [the learners] couldn't think their way out of a wet paper bag even if their life depended upon it. They're nothing but highly educated, useless people."

The commentator was the Minister of Education of a very high profile, high performing country. Ian was speechless. Hmmmm . . . highly educated useless people? What was the Minister telling him?

The minister was suggesting that his nation's high-achieving learners had school smarts and, thus, could excel at academics. They had developed special abilities that allowed them to move smoothly through the school system. They had cultivated the essential skills needed to cram for and successfully complete tests. He was implying that most academically successful learners do well, in large part, because they have learned how to play the "game called school."

But in describing his country's learners as "highly educated useless people," what he was also suggesting was that while many of these learners, particularly the brainy ones, had school smarts, they did not possess what is generally known as street smarts. For him, being street smart was about having practical intelligence (Sternberg, 1985). Practical intelligence is about developing skills needed to solve real-world, real-life problems in real time. This type of intelligence requires developing the necessary higher-level thinking skills and competencies to live and work in the world beyond school. Practical intelligence skills go well beyond those needed to do well on a written examination.

Ian became curious. What were the distinctions between being school smart and street smart?

How could so many learners who performed well in school and were able to excel on tests, at the same time be so inadequately prepared for life?

After much debate around our expectations related to the who, what, why, where, when, and how of learning, we believe we finally have an answer. Our mandate is to help our children become lifelong thinkers and learners.

When children first attend primary school, they are entirely dependent on their teachers to tell them what to do, who to do it with, how to do it, when to do it, where to sit, and even for how long. The primary focus is on mastering content and learning through memorization within a tightly controlled, structured instructional environment.

In this educational landscape, mastery of content is frequently valued over thinking critically about the content. The teachers tell the learners what they need to do to pass the test, to pass the course, to pass the grade, to move to the next level, and finally to graduate. All the answers are prearranged, preformatted, and ready for absorption by those who are willing and able to play the game called school. These are the academically successful students. These are the learners who are comfortable operating in a culture of dependency—dependent on the teacher, dependent on the textbook, dependent on the test.

Then after graduation from school, having spent 13 or more years in the system, the intellectual scaffolding that has held the learners up for all their years in education is suddenly removed. When this happens, and they enter the real world, many of them fall flat on their faces. As educators, we cannot understand why our formerly well-performing learners are unable to succeed in life beyond school. We find this confusing even though, as educators, we are responsible for creating and maintaining this culture of dependency on the teacher, the textbooks, and the test. And it's not just teachers who are bewildered. Parents are also baffled when many recently graduated adult children continue living at home, needing to be supported, because of factors such as the global pandemic, social upheaval, and the precarious nature of the global economy.

In today's world, school success does not necessarily guarantee success in life. So what is the problem? The answer lies in our continued focus on ensuring compliance in our learners rather than cultivating independent thinkers, doers, and lifelong learners. Somewhere along the line, we have lost sight of the need to develop both school and life skills.

If our children are to survive, let alone thrive in a 21st century culture of technology-driven automation, abundance, and access to global labor markets, independent, creative, and divergent thinking must hold the highest currency. If our learners are to be successful in making the transition, our mission as educators must be to move from demanding the compliance of learners, to progressively shifting the responsibility for learning from the teacher to the learner.

This shift sounds simple, but in fact, it is an incredibly complex task. For this change to happen, it must occur in the hearts and minds of every single educational stakeholder, including politicians, policy designers, educational leaders, teachers, parents, and learners.

This new and different paradigm for teaching and learning is that of progressive withdrawal. The educator's job is no longer about standing up in front of their students and showing them how smart the teacher is. Rather, the educator's role is to help learners discover how smart they are and to progressively shift the burden of responsibility for learning from the teacher, where it has traditionally been, to the learner, where it truly belongs. Good teachers create positive environments for learners. Good teachers create environments where learners feel safe to share their thinking, ask probing questions, and participate intelligently in conversations.

Our responsibility must be to ensure that learners no longer need us by the time they complete school—rather like a parent. We want to

> The educator's role is to help learners discover how smart they are and to progressively shift the burden of responsibility for learning from the teacher to the learner.

ensure that our kids are independent and can stand on their own. Think of your child's first attempts to ride a bike. Many times, the bike falls over. Or when learning to walk, they lose their balance and fall to the ground. Or their Cheerios slide off the spoon as they attempt to eat.

How did we respond? Good parents don't say, "C-, you fail, 36%, you're not meeting the bicycling standards, we need to develop a rubric for walking without failing," or "We need a Common Core curriculum to help keep their food on the spoon." Of course not! What did we do? We clapped our hands, helped them up, brushed them off, wiped away their tears, and encouraged them to try again. We understood that our job as parents, as complicated and challenging as it might be (particularly during the teenage years), was to help our children be independent, able to stand on their own as they begin to make their way through life.

not a matter of either/or, we need to develop school & life skills in students

So what should we do? Do we give up on helping learners become school smart and simply focus on assisting them to become street smart? Absolutely not, we need them to be both—it is not a matter of just either/or. We must ask, what do we want our learners to be, feel, think, and do that measurably demonstrates that they are willing and prepared to step out from school into the world in which they will work, live, and play?

Definitively answering this question is not simple, given that our present-day world is profoundly complex and in a constant state of flux. We live in the age of InfoWhelm and HyperInformation, where digital content is growing exponentially in both quantity and complexity. In this shifting landscape, information is instantly available. Learners must move beyond simple mastery of content recall to develop the capacity to interpret and apply both old and new knowledge to different situations, problems, and environments.

Access to information is not the only obstacle. Learning to become a discerning and creative consumer of information is an ongoing challenge. In the new digital reality, the application of higher-order independent cognitive skills learned within the context of real-world, real-life, and real-time tasks is essential. For learning to be meaningful, students must be able to transfer previous learning to new and different situations and challenges.

We firmly believe that invoking progressive withdrawal and fostering street smarts in school-smart learners requires a significant shift in the existing educational paradigm. To enable this shift demands that we rethink the design of our schools, classrooms, and related learning environments. At the same time, we need to rethink our assumptions about instructional design, what constitutes learning, and even our definitions of what it means to be intelligent. And ultimately, we must also rethink how we assess and evaluate both instruction and learning.

Standardized tests can only measure a very narrow range of rational cognitive skills measured by bubble tests, multiple-choice questions, or fill-in-the-blank exams. Real learning is about assessing much more than simple information regurgitation. A student's competency or potential cannot be measured using a single test. That's why educators must also change the way learning is assessed to include authentic assessment using rubrics, journals, reflection, logs, feedback, feedforward, and so on.

The primary purpose of learning today must be about cultivating the essential long-term skills, dispositions, and habits of mind needed so our learners can construct their understanding of the world and how it works. These are the essential skills necessary to deal with adversity and conquer the many challenges learners will face in life. These are the skills, dispositions, and habits of mind that will last a lifetime. They are as important as, if not more important than, learning how to factor trinomials or calculate square roots. But these long-term skills are also substantially different from the content-focused knowledge and skills that were (and remain) the primary focal point of traditional education.

The bottom line is that schools must change if we are going to address the growing disconnect between being school smart and being street smart. If we are to make schools more relevant and prepare learners for the world that awaits them, there are at least five fundamental changes that need to be made.

> The primary purpose of learning today must be about cultivating the essential long-term skills, dispositions, and habits of mind needed so our learners can construct their understanding of the world and how it works.

1. *Acknowledge the New Digital Landscape*

   Schools must embrace the new reality of the online, digitized world that has been severely complicated by the COVID-19 crisis we are experiencing today. Outside of schools, the digital world has fundamentally and irrevocably altered the way we work, play, communicate, shop, and view our fellow citizens (Jukes & Schaaf, 2019).

   It must be emphasized that this is not about schools having high-speed networks or learners having constant access to laptops and handhelds. Even when high-tech resources are available, if the technologies are only used to reinforce old assumptions and practices about teaching, learning, and assessment, little will have changed. Instead, this is about developing the full spectrum of cognitive and emotional

using tech. to reinforce old ways of teaching will not solve the issue

intelligence increasingly required in the culture of the 21st century. As such, this is primarily a headware (critical thinking, problem-solving, collaboration, creativity, etc.), not hardware (laptops, tablets, smartphones, networks, etc.), issue. It is all well and good to purchase and install new technology, but in and of itself this is not enough.

2. *Facilitate and Guide Student Learning*

The New Digital Landscape allows learners access to information and learning experiences outside of schools and classrooms. Learners can access almost anything, anytime—information, music, multimedia from multiple sources. As a result, learners can determine what they want to learn—something that contradicts the traditional model where teachers primarily determine what is learned, how it's discovered, how long it's studied, what tools are used, and how the learning is assessed.

× technology allows the learner to choose what they learn = new concept

Many adults, decision-makers, and traditional educators are simply not in sync with the new digital reality of today's learners. As a result, many schools and teachers continue to use new technologies to reinforce old mindsets. The lives of today's students are very different from the lives of students for whom the existing education systems were initially developed. To ensure that our students can navigate their way through an increasingly interconnected and complex world, it is our duty to equip them with the essential skills needed to do so. What we desperately need is a balance between our world and theirs—between traditional and digital learning environments.

As you finish reading this chapter, the questions you need to be asking are, how have you modified and how will you modify your instructional assumptions and practices to address the fact that learners have fundamentally changed and continue to change? Nothing is stopping us from changing the way we learn and how we teach, but if educators haven't changed their teaching approach markedly in the past 10 years, then they are just not meeting the needs of today's students.

How have you modified and how will you modify your instructional assumptions and practices to address the fact that learners have fundamentally changed and continue to change?

3. *Change Mindsets*

We must address the shift in thinking patterns of digital learners. They live and operate in a multimedia, online, multitask, random access, color graphics, video, audio, and visual literacy world.

As Steven Johnson (2006) pointed out in *Everything Bad Is Good for You*, these skills are generally not acknowledged, valued, addressed, or emphasized in our schools. They are not accepted because these abilities do not typically reflect the mindsets and skillsets of the older generations. As we explored in depth in *Reinventing Learning for the Always-On Generation: Strategies and Apps that Work* (2015), educators must acknowledge that today's learners not only think differently but also learn differently from the way previous generations learned. Only by recognizing that our world has fundamentally and irrevocably changed will we be able to begin to reconsider and redesign learning environments, instruction, and how we assess learning.

4. *Assess Holistically*

We must broaden evaluation to encompass activities that provide a complete picture of what it means for learners to learn. As management guru Tom Peters (1986) wrote, "What gets measured gets done," and conversely, "what doesn't get measured doesn't get done." We must begin to measure more than information recall.

Dave Masters (as cited in Jukes, 2011) uses this analogy:

> "You can get a good picture of a person's health by taking their height and weight, but would you go to a doctor who only took your height and weight and said here's a complete picture of your health? The answer, of course, is no. It would require a battery of tests—urinalysis, blood tests, blood pressure, cholesterol, checking for lumps, and so on to get an accurate picture of your health."

However, many schools act like the former doctors. Learners are tested using standardized instruments that primarily measure information recall and low-level understanding of concepts. The scores are then interpreted as representing a complete picture of a learner's abilities. It is highly presumptuous to say that current test scores are a complete indicator of what learners are learning.

A full picture requires authentic assessment strategies, including portfolios of performance that demonstrate learning. Assessment must also include evidence of the application of theory to solve real-world problems, not just recall of theoretical content.

we are missing the connection of making material relevant for students real lives.

5. *Develop the Whole Learner*

Last but not least, if we hope to increase the relevancy of the learning that takes place, we must increase the connection between instruction in schools and the world outside. The critical point is that students see the relevance of what they are learning. Understanding is facilitated when learners can make a connection between the content and context as it is applied to the world outside of schools.

For this connection to occur, schools must become less insular. We need to systematically work to bring the outside world into our schools, while at the same time sending our schools out into the community. New technologies and understanding of the New Digital Landscape can help us perform both. The online world creates virtual highways and hallways to both local and global communities. Whether educators are ready for it or not, we are already seeing this happen. Kids are on TikTok, SnapChat, and Instagram participating in protests and making their opinions known. They are no longer willing to accept adults filtering their exposure to the outside world. Today's generations are actively participating in the world around them, whether adults choose to acknowledge this or not.

If we hope to unfold the full intellectual and creative genius of all of our children; if we want to prepare them for the new and ever changing world that awaits them beyond school; if we're going to help them make their future, not our past; if we are going to march through the 21st century and maintain our tradition of success; if we want our children to have the relevant 21st century skills, then we need to acknowledge they have already created a bridge between their world and ours. They can develop both street smarts and school smarts necessary to survive and thrive in the culture of the 21st century.

For this to happen, there needs to be a fundamental shift in how teaching and learning take place in schools. We must look for alternatives to the traditional organization of schools. We need to uncover our long-standing and unexamined assumptions about teaching and learning, about what a classroom looks like, where learning takes place, and what resources are necessary to support it.

And we also need to reexamine the use of time—the length of the school day and school year, the school timetable, and the traditional methods used for instructional delivery. And, particularly in the light of the post-COVID-19 world we hope to be living in, we must reconsider the potential of online, web-based, blended, and virtual learning that can be used to augment, extend, and transform the role of the traditional classroom teachers.

In other words, we cannot foster street smarts in school smart learners unless we ask the critical and relevant questions around our assumptions of what schools currently are and what they need to become.

Summarizing the Main Points

- In addition to developing school smarts, many of today's students are developing street smarts independent of the existing school system.

- Street smarts can also be referred to as practical intelligence or the ability to deal with daily tasks in the real world using their acquired knowledge, skills, intuition, and creativity.

- Education must move from demanding the compliance of learners, to progressively shifting the responsibility of learning to students.

- The primary purpose of learning is cultivating the essential long-term skills, dispositions, and habits of mind needed so learners can construct their understanding of the world and how it works rather than continuing to operate in a culture of dependency.

- Five fundamental changes that need to be made to make learning more relevant for the future include acknowledging the New Digital Landscape, facilitating and guiding student learning, changing mindsets, assessing holistically, and developing the whole learner.

Questions to Consider

- What is the game called "school"?

- How can educators help learners simultaneously cultivate both school smarts and street smarts?

- What are the implications for learners of progressive withdrawal helping to prepare them for their post-school lives?

- What are some changes schools can embrace to avoid producing highly educated useless people?

- What are some of the long-standing assumptions about teaching and learning that you would like to challenge?

2 Education in the Age of Disruption

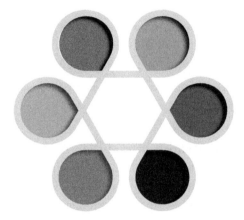

"Learning and innovation go hand in hand. The arrogance of success is to think that what you did yesterday will be sufficient for tomorrow."

—William Pollard

Disruptive Innovation

In his seminal book *Disrupting Class: How Disruptive Innovation will Change the Way the World Learns* (2008), the late Harvard professor Clayton Christensen introduced readers to a concept called disruptive innovation. Disruptive innovation is a change that fundamentally transforms traditional ways of doing things. Disruptive innovations create new markets, products, and services. In doing so, they eventually disrupt existing markets, products, and services.

Today, there is a great deal of discussion about emerging innovations such as digital technology, cloud computing, big data, genetics, smart materials, mobile commerce, social media, biotechnology,

3D printing, nanotechnology, artificial intelligence, robotics, and neuroscience. These are just a few of the big disruptors in our world. They continue to fundamentally transform the way we work, the way we play, how we communicate, how we view our fellow citizens, and how we live in the world around us.

The primary driving force behind disruptive innovation is the incredible technological development occurring in our world today. That's because these disruptions allow us to do things that would have been unimaginable, even a few short years ago.

Let's take a closer look at how disruption happens. Disruptive innovation typically starts with the introduction of a new product but eventually becomes much more because the innovation results in a radical change in human behavior.

The iPhone as a Disruptor

As just one of many examples, let's examine the development of the iPhone and iPad. Apple introduced the iPhone in 2007. In retrospect, it's hard to believe that the iPhone was launched only 13 years ago. The iPhone was a fantastic new idea for a smartphone because it wasn't just a phone. It also had many other features built-in, including a new operating system that allowed users to communicate with the device using voice and natural hand gestures. The iPhone was cool and fun to use. However, at the outset, it would have been difficult to believe that this phone would change the world. Was it a disruptive innovation?

In the beginning, it was hard to see the connections between this device and how it would affect our lives. Many people thought all the talk about the iPhone was just hype. However, once people began using the iPhone, they discovered new ways of doing old things, as well as entirely new things they could do. For example, since people carried their phones with them all the time, they started using the iPhone to listen to music. Being able to store music on their phone meant people no longer needed to carry a Sony Walkman, Discman, MP3 player, iPod, or similar portable music players (Bilyeu, 2017).

As a result, sales of these other devices quickly declined. Formerly dominant products quickly disappeared from the market. As more people bought digital music, the iPhone, Apple Music, then Pandora and Spotify brought dramatic changes to the music industry. People didn't need to buy records, tapes, or CDs; they could purchase or stream individual songs and create personalized playlists and albums (FitzGerald, 2018).

Disruptions allow us to do things that would have been unimaginable, even a few short years ago.

People then shifted to playing digital games on their iPhones. As a result, sales of portable game devices dropped precipitously (Diver, 2017). And since people always carried their smartphones, they used it to take photos, which immediately and significantly cut the sales of point-and-shoot digital cameras (FitzGerald, 2018). Then people started using Netflix to watch videos on their iPhones. It was no coincidence that video stores like Blockbuster began to go out of business and live movie attendance started to drop substantially (Satell, 2014). People not only watched videos on their iPhones but also created videos and uploaded them to YouTube, which started a whole new era of global video sharing and viewing.

Meanwhile, as all this was happening, the banking industry was hit hard by the change in people's behavior as consumers shifted to doing banking online using their iPhones (McArthur, 2016). Simultaneous to this shift in behavior, shoppers started using smartphones to buy and sell products and services online rather than heading to the mall (Danzinger, 2018). The iPhone soon spawned a whole new smartphone industry built around touchable phones with glass faces. Meanwhile, telephone booths and landlines started to disappear (Kieler, 2016).

Three years later, in 2010, Apple extended the design of the iPhone by introducing the iPad. Its introduction created an entirely new digital tablet industry. Amongst many other things, the appearance of smartphones and digital tablets caused a fundamental shift in the way people received news and information (Walker, 2019).

The use of Facebook, Twitter, Snapchat, Instagram, and several other social media tools became hugely popular. At the same time, media companies were compelled to radically change the way newspapers, magazines, and other print media were delivered to ensure they attracted eyeballs and earned advertising revenue (Martin, 2018). Today, almost all media companies have online editions, as well as a social media presence, and many media companies have stopped or limited publishing printed versions (Forbes Communications Council, 2018).

Many more changes came from this one development—far too many for us to mention. But there is one more significant development we want to highlight. We are talking about a change so dramatic and substantial that no one could ever have guessed how one innovation could have repercussions and cause changes so monumental.

Within a few years of its introduction, the iPhone severely damaged the economy of an entire country. When the iPhone was first released in 2007, Nokia, a Finnish company, was the world leader in cellphone design and sales. With the introduction of the iPhone, Nokia's sales started to decline steadily. Microsoft bought Nokia a few years back and almost immediately laid off more than 62,000 employees (Monaghan, 2013). Do you know anyone who has recently purchased a Nokia phone? Probably not!

At that time, other than Nokia, the logging and paper industries were two of Finland's other big employers. They employed tens of thousands of workers. When Apple introduced the iPad, everything started to change quickly. Sales of newspapers and magazines around the world began to plummet. The Finnish paper industry was hit hard by the abrupt decline in sales. Dozens of paper mills around the country closed, resulting in tens of thousands of Finnish forestry workers losing their jobs (Hodgkins, 2014). How could changes of this magnitude happen in just over a decade? That's the power of disruptive innovation!

Disruption Is Everywhere

The point is that the development of the iPhone and iPad is just one of the thousands of similar stories that are happening right before our very eyes. Disruptive innovation is continuously turning our world upside down.

For example, today, Uber, which has become the world's largest taxi company, owns no cars. Airbnb, which is the world's largest accommodation provider, owns no real estate. Alibaba, which is the world's most valuable retailer, owns no inventory. Facebook, the world's largest manager of information, creates no content. Amazon, the online retailer, until recently had no stores. Netflix, the world's largest movie house, has no theatres. And Spotify, which streams over 750,000 tracks and 40,000 hours of music every minute worldwide, owns no music (Goodwin, 2015).

We must emphasize that these examples are the proverbial tip of the iceberg. Yet all these changes occurred in just the past 13 years. If things have happened so quickly, what does the future hold for all of us? The point is, if disruptive innovation can disrupt successful businesses, which it has; if disruptive innovation can disrupt entire industries, which it has; if disruptive innovation can disrupt entire economies, which it has; and if disruptive innovation can disrupt an entire nation, which it has; we can't just assume the same thing can't or won't impact education.

As the former CEO of General Electric, Jack Welch, once commented, "When the rate of change outside an organization is greater than the rate of change inside an organization, the end is in sight" (Whitefield,

disruptive innovation can cause the need to restructure.

2013, p.16). Traditional businesses are not the only ones being replaced by disruptive innovation. Newspaper publishing, manufacturing, music, retail, banking, and postal services were all thriving industries 20 years ago. Today, these same industries have vanished, are struggling, are quickly declining, or are undertaking massive restructuring. That's disruptive innovation!

As parents, citizens, and educators, we must appreciate that if the digital world outside of education has been transformed because of disruptive innovation and constant global change, education will not be immune to the effects of these same dramatic changes. The problem is that some educators believe that change is something that happens somewhere else to someone else, like farmers, steelworkers, factory workers, customer service agents, or car park attendants. They assume that somehow education and educators won't be affected by these disruptive forces.

Based on current trends, it's easy to predict that over the next decade the education system both here and around the world will experience the very same kind of profound disruption and ongoing reconfiguration that Apple, Amazon, Spotify, Google, Facebook, and Twitter have already brought to our lives.

With disruption, there is always a ripple effect. Just like throwing a pebble into a pond, the ripples get bigger and bigger over time. And as these ripples grow in size, so does the disruption that happens in our lives. We see this clearly in the aftermath of the deadly combination of COVID-19; growing social, cultural, and racial upheaval; and increasing financial uncertainty in today's world.

What Is Exponential?

In the book *Living on the Future Edge*, the authors (McCain, Jukes, & Crockett, 2010) identified several global exponential trends occurring in our world today that we believe we absolutely could not ignore. *Exponential* is a word that we are encountering more frequently as we move further through the 21st century.

The big question is, what is exponential? And more important, what does it mean when we say that we are experiencing exponential change? What does exponential change look like? What does it feel like? How will exponential change affect our lives, our families, our communities, our schools, and our nations?

Figure 2.1   Linear Growth Pattern

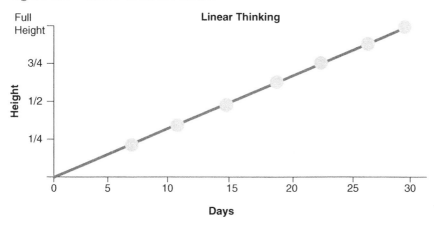

To illustrate exponential growth, let's use the example of the growth pattern of a plant. Suppose you wanted to buy a plant to fill a bay window in your home. So you go to the local nursery, and you buy a plant the clerk tells you will grow to a height that will cover the entire window in 30 days. This plant follows a linear growth pattern. What does this kind of pattern look like?

Figure 2.1 is a graph of the growth of a plant that follows a linear growth pattern—a pattern that sees the plant grow to its full height, covering the window in 30 days.

In a linear growth pattern, after 10 days, you would see 1/3 of the mature plant. After 15 days, you would see 1/2. Finally, after 30 days of growth, the plant would have fully grown, filling the entire window. This type of growth would be very predictable. It's important to note that throughout much of human history, we have dealt with this kind of linear change—steady and predictable.

But what if instead, the person at the garden center sold you a plant that will grow to fill the entire window following an exponential growth pattern? A pattern where the plant doubles in size every day. What would this kind of growth look like, and how would it differ from linear growth?

Figure 2.2 shows what you'd see on Day 1. It's not very dramatic. There's absolutely nothing to see.

Figure 2.2   Day 1

On Day 2, there would still be nothing to see. Days 5–10 (Figure 2.3), still nothing to see here!

Figure 2.3   Day 10

Since nothing appears to be happening, let's jump ahead to Day 20. But before we do let's pause to consider if this was a linear growth pattern instead of an exponential growth pattern, how much of the plant would we see on Day 20? According to our calculations, we should see about 67% of the plant. Figure 2.4 is what we see on Day 20.

Figure 2.4   Day 20

Not very impressive, even though the plant is doubling in size every day. Following an exponential growth pattern, we still see very little, just a couple of green leaves. If you are doing the math, on Day 20, only 1/64th of the plant is visible. So let's jump ahead to Day 25 (Figure 2.5).

Figure 2.5   Day 25

If this plant was following a linear growth pattern on Day 25 we would see almost 85% of the plant. But even though we are experiencing exponential growth—even though the plant is doubling in size every day, the plant is barely over the rim of the pot—and there are only 5 days left in our 30-day growth cycle. So let's take a look at Day 26 (Figure 2.6).

Figure 2.6   Day 26

Something must be wrong—26 days in and all we have so far is stunted growth—and there are only 4 days to go. Let's move on to Day 27 (Figure 2.7).

Figure 2.7   Day 27

The nursery must have given us the wrong plant; it is never going to fill the entire bay window. How could it cover the window in just 3 days? Oh well, onward to Day 28 (Figure 2.8).

Figure 2.8   Day 28

We have reached Day 28 of a 30-day exponential growth pattern, and the plant is only 1/4 of the height of the window. Anyway, let's see what happens on Day 29 (Figure 2.9).

Figure 2.9   Day 29

Okay, something is finally beginning to happen. The problem is that we're almost out of time and only half the window is covered. With only one day left it is incomprehensible that the plant can finish its growth pattern and completely fill the entire window. But here's the critical question to consider. If this plant doubles in size each day, what is going to happen tomorrow on Day 30 (Figure 2.10)?

Figure 2.10   Day 30

Bang—the full plant explodes into view. The entire window is covered, and it seems like all the activity occurred in just 1 day! That's the power of exponential doubling. The interesting point is that by the time people notice something is happening, the exponential growth pattern is about to kick in, and developments explode onto the scene with dramatic effect.

That's the reason the COVID-19 pandemic seemed to come out of nowhere; it was quietly growing, and all of a sudden it was everywhere. For the same reason the internet seemed to explode out of nowhere. The internet had been around for more than 40 years, with only minimal impact on the general public. When exponential growth kicked in, the world was engulfed in a tidal wave of information that seemingly happened almost overnight. That's the power of exponential growth. Once the doubling or tripling starts kicking in, change will occur at breathtaking speeds.

This kind of growth, depicted in Figure 2.11, has been behind most of the disruptive change we have experienced in the latter part of the 20th century and the first part of the 21st century. And this kind of growth will most certainly be behind almost all the disruptive change we experience in the near and distant future.

Figure 2.11 shows the growth of a plant that doubles in size each day. On the right-hand side, it has a telltale shift known as the Knee of the Curve. The Knee of the Curve represents the dramatic upswing that takes place in the last few days. The Knee of the Curve is the pivotal point for exponential change.

Figure 2.11   Exponential Growth Cure

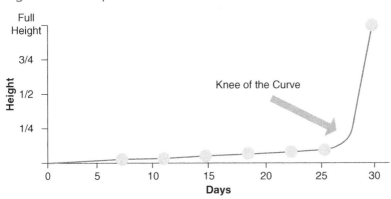

Keep in mind, the Industrial Revolution unfolded over centuries. In today's exponential times, revolutions happen in a matter of years, sometimes months.

We want you to keep the shape of this graph in mind and remember the developmental pattern described in this chapter is behind all the trends we examine.

The doubling of small numbers is deceptive. Take a look. Start doubling .1, .2, .4, .8; at this stage, it all looks pretty much like zero. But after we reach 1, just 30 doublings later, we're at one billion.

That's where things stand at this moment regarding the rate of change. After Day 30, the line goes virtually straight up. The difference between linear change and exponential change is incredible. Inventor and visionary Ray Kurzweil (2010) explained, with 30 linear steps, you get to 30 but with 30 exponential steps, you get to one billion.

The challenge we face is that we are mostly linear thinkers in an increasingly exponential world.

Disruptive technologies are relentlessly transforming products, services, and industries. The only way to deal with this kind of dramatic change is to look continually into the future. We must pay attention to exponential disruptions, new technologies, artificial intelligence, biotechnology, and nanotechnology among many emergent trends. These are just some of the forces that are quickly upending our world.

The challenge we face is that we are mostly linear thinkers in an increasingly exponential world.

We must always be trying to stay ahead of the curve. We must always be trying to plan and act with the future in mind. We must always try to detect new trends and project them out to their logical conclusions. We must start working *now* if we are going to be prepared to anticipate the unique opportunities and challenges that will inevitably confront us because of our fixed mindsets. We call this fixed mindset TTWWADI (That's The Way We've Always Done It) mentality—the inevitable resistance to change we all experience.

As we examine the exponential changes affecting education, and as we project these changes into the future, it's critical that we are continually asking, are we using linear thinking or are we using exponential thinking? It's also important we keep in mind that the world won't stop innovating on Day 30. In a world driven by relentless exponential change, what will our graphs—what will the world—look like on Day 31, or Day 53, or Day 1,777? Once exponential change hits the Knee of the Curve, the effect and the speed at which it happens is almost unimaginable.

HyperInformation

There have been a multitude of disruptive innovations whose ripples of impact have, and are, cascading through our lives. To illustrate our point, let's focus on some of the developments that are impacting what we do in schools today.

Specifically, we want to examine how information in the modern world is changing what educators need to emphasize in their teaching. We want to focus on HyperInformation, which is information structured and connected using hypertext and hyperlinks that can lead to InfoWhelm and information anxiety. This trend affects teachers directly because so much of education involves information. But before we examine this trend, we want to stop and consider this question for a moment. What is the primary skill developed by the vast majority of instruction that takes place in many schools today? *memorization*

Our observation has been that there continues to be a strong emphasis on memorizing course content and procedures. This memorization is often done without students completely understanding what the material means on a deeper level. This approach to instruction has been in place for hundreds of years. The question is, does memorization adequately prepare students for the world that awaits them once they complete school?

To answer this question, let's look at the nature of information in the world today and consider what that tells us about how we should be preparing our students. Let's examine how HyperInformation has impacted the nature of information in the modern world.

Today, there's far more information available than ever before. Also, more than 90% of the scientists who have *ever* lived in all of human history are still alive (Jukes & Schaaf, 2019). The amount of research and innovation conducted has expanded exponentially as a result of all these people doing their work. Add to this the rapid explosion of the internet into our lives and the emergence of powerful new digital technologies.

So now what happens is new research and innovation become instantly available to anyone, anywhere on the planet. Also, global digital networks give people instant access to news and information about everything from natural disasters to politics to sports.

Wikipedia is just one indicator of how big this explosion of up-to-date information is. Wikipedia was created in 2001. Since then, more than 40 million articles in 293 languages have been added to Wikipedia. And more than 800 new articles are posted every day. When you do the calculations, 40 million articles are 1,000 volumes of 1,200 pages each, which represents more than one million pages in total or about 87 yards (80m) of shelf space. In September 2019 alone, there were more than 20 billion page views on Wikipedia. And keep in mind, Wikipedia is just one of many informational sites, including Google, Yahoo, YouTube, and Baidu, to name but a few (Neary, 2014; Wikipedia Statistics, 2019).

The amount of information in the world has quite literally exploded exponentially. To give you a sense of just how much information is now available in the online world, computer giant IBM tried to add up all the ones and zeroes that comprise all the photos, videos, PDF files, email, web pages, instant messages, tweets, phone calls, and other digital data. They determined that by 2012 there were more than 900 exabytes of digital data being generated in the world *every single year* (McCafferty, 2014). Just how much is 900 exabytes of information? Well, if you printed out all that information in standard-sized books and piled them up, there would be so much data in 900 exabytes that, according to our calculations, the stack of books would extend from Earth to that "not really a planet anymore" Pluto. But wait a minute; we're not talking about just *one* stack of books; 900 exabytes of data is equivalent to 23 stacks of books that each reached from Earth to Pluto every year. And this number continues to grow exponentially.

By any measure, that's an overwhelming amount of information. And remember, this is based on projections of the amount of data that were made in 2012. Considering that we live in exponential times, we have to ask, how much data is being generated today? According to a recent

International Data Corporation (IDC) report, 90% of all the data in the world today was created in the past 2 years (SINTEF, 2013). Add exponential development into the picture, and you get an idea of the staggering amount of data that is available now and will be available in the future. As of 2015, only about 0.5% of all data is currently analyzed. That percentage is shrinking, as more data is created and collected (Bansal, 2014).

But we need to know that HyperInformation is about much more than just the *quantity* of available data. It's also crucial that we understand the *quality* of the information now accessible. That's because we are in the midst of a migration of the world's literary works to a digital format. In December 2004, Google announced it would digitize all the books in five major research libraries, including all the books in the library at Stanford University, Harvard University, Oxford University, the University of Michigan, and the entire New York Public Library's collection. Although this undertaking experienced some legal obstacles, the project managed to scan over 25 million books (Howard, 2017). As a result, there's a rapidly growing library of digital books that have been created.

Consequently, you can search for almost any book, by virtually any authors—*like us, for instance*—and instantly get a summary of all the books they have written. And when you search further, you can find the full text of an astonishing number of books. Today, it's not just about downloading content to computers. Disruptive technologies are providing us with amazing new tools for accessing information. Smartphones, tablets, wearables, implantables, as well as a whole range of new digital devices, are capable of displaying multimedia information.

These technologies will continue to transform the way we learn. To put this into perspective, not that many years ago, people read about world events often days after they occurred. Learning what happened was a second hand, after-the-fact experience. Today, people learn about things as they happen in real time, whether it's a hurricane in the Caribbean, a vote in Great Britain, a fire in France, a shooting in Texas, an earthquake in China, or a global pandemic. They can experience events as text, images, video, and sound at the same time.

They can also see historical images, video footage, and archival audio recordings that have been converted to digital formats. This kind of access means that today we can learn about both the current world as well as about history through firsthand experiences. For example, people can see images of Chairman Mao and the Chinese Red Army's Long March in 1934, or images of the rise of Nazism, or hear John

F. Kennedy as he outlines his plans to land a man on the moon, or watch actual video footage that records when astronauts first stood on the moon's surface.

Based on current trends, in the next few years, our students will likely have instantaneous access to virtually any single piece of information. We're talking about any text, photograph, video, painting, TV or radio program, webpage, blog post, tweet, or music produced by anyone around the world.

With the ongoing work of converting information into digital formats, people will likely soon have access to the entire works of humankind, from the beginning of recorded history, in all languages. All this information will be accessible to anyone, almost anywhere on the planet, wirelessly, within a fraction of a second. This vast digital library of multimedia information will be instantly available to anyone using powerful digital search tools.

What has been described here is just a brief overview of what we call HyperInformation. If all this is a reality now and not only in some indeterminate distant future, then we must ask some critical questions about how to best prepare students for the world that awaits them once they complete their schooling.

What does it mean—what will it mean—to be educated in this new world of HyperInformation? Does a predominant focus on memorizing prepare students for a world with anytime, anywhere access to more than one trillion web pages? What is the value of memorizing material when up-to-date data is instantly available through intelligent online searching tools? And if memorization is not *all* that's needed, what other skills do learners need to have to be able to function in a world of HyperInformation?

These are incredibly important issues that we need to think deeply about if we hope to do our job of helping our students prepare themselves for the future. If smartphones can deliver information anytime, anywhere, are there more critical skills needed for students' futures that should be taught rather than simple, easily transmitted, and memorized information?

How will students learn the new information gathering skills enabled by the electronic age? And, are those new skills a priority in our schools and classrooms today?

Where Do We Begin?

We know change is hard. We know change makes us feel uncomfortable. And we recognize it is easy to slip back into traditional assumptions about how the world works. But this is not about you and us and our needs and comfort zones. Too often, we try to make massive changes in a very short period, and inevitably we fail. It's just too much, too quickly. What if instead, we woke up every day and asked ourselves what was the 1% improvement we could make today to better ourselves personally and professionally?

While the 1% strategy may sound counterintuitive, particularly given that we have just devoted an entire chapter to describing the dramatic effects of exponentialism, HyperInformation, InfoWhelm, and information anxiety, breaking things down into small, digestible pieces is one of the only consistently effective strategies you can use to avoid being absolutely overwhelmed by the constant white noise of our digital society.

Summarizing the Main Points

- Disruptive innovation is change that fundamentally transforms traditional ways of doing things, creating new markets, products, and services.

- As parents, citizens, and educators, we must understand that if the digital world outside of education has been radically transformed because of disruptive innovation and constant global change, education will not be immune to the effects of these same dramatic changes.

- HyperInformation is an excess of information potentially leading to InfoWhelm or information overload.

- Information in the modern world is changing what educators need to emphasize in their teaching.

- Today's schools must focus on the new skills needed to utilize digital technologies that make information instantly available to anyone.

Questions to Consider

- Why is change in our personal and professional lives so hard to embrace?

- Can you brainstorm several instances of companies or products that became obsolete due to disruptive innovation that changed a market or the expectations, needs, or wants of citizens?

- What is the significance of exponentialism to learners and educators?

- Why does the existence of HyperInformation require educators to rethink how and what they teach?

- How will students learn the new information-gathering skills enabled by the electronic age? Are these new skills a priority in schools and classrooms today?

3

From Literacy to Fluency: The Starting Point

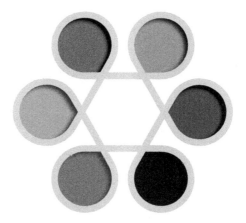

"Student engagement is a product of motivation and active learning. It is a product rather than a sum because it will not occur if either element is missing."

—Elizabeth F. Barkley

In Chapter 1, we characterized many of today's schools as preparing learners who are "highly educated useless people." We also examined how the world has changed outside of school as the result of disruptive innovation and the ever changing modern workforce. Now, let's step into today's schools and examine what is happening inside the "modern" classroom.

A highly revealing study (Poh, Swenson, & Picard, 2010) conducted at Massachusetts Institute of Technology (MIT) on student electrodermal or neural activity at different times of the day supports our experiences and observations related to cognitive engagement. (To access the full study, please visit https://bit.ly/LSBECH#-FLUENCY.) A close look at the study shows that students' brains are far more engaged during activities like social interaction, sleep, labs, and study time than they are during class, where their brains register very little neural activity. The startling reality is that there is more active thinking involved in doing chores and watching TV than there is sitting in a classroom. It turns out that comparatively speaking, sleep generates enormous neural activity. From this evidence, we can extrapolate that if you want to exercise your students' brains, you should let them sleep in class. (Just kidding!)

So the main question is, how do we, as educators, change this reality? In light of this study, how do we promote active, engaged, higher-level thinking in today's and tomorrow's learners? And how do we have it all? How do we address the short-term goals of preparing students for the exams while at the same time addressing the long-term goals of developing engaged, lifelong learners during increasingly disruptive times? How do we address the need for students to simultaneously learn traditional curriculum content as well as the essentials of modern learning? *students brains are more active when they are actively learning

Literacy Is *Still* Not Enough

The first thing that needs to be emphasized is that education's traditional focus on traditional literacies (reading, writing, and arithmetic), while important, is no longer enough. We believe that even if we were to educate all our students to the standards of the 20th century literacies, they wouldn't be literate based on the needs and demands of the modern and future world. Two decades into the 21st century, reading, writing, and arithmetic remain the primary focus of education. A narrow and singular emphasis on traditional literacies means our students will be literate by the standards of the 20th century, but not literate by the standards of the 21st century. A focus on literacy is *still* not enough.

We believe we need to move our thinking, we need to move our teaching, and we need to move learning beyond our current focus on *just* the 20th century literacies, to equipping students with the essential new basics for modern learning. The new basics are mental processes that can be explicitly taught, memorized, learned, practiced, repeated, and, in due course, developed into unconscious habits of mind. The knowledge and skills learned become combined into an intuitive experience.

Noël Burch first theorized in the 1970s four levels of awareness:

1. Being unconsciously unaware (you don't know that you don't know).

2. Being consciously unaware (you know that you don't know).

3. Being consciously aware (you know that you know).

4. Being unconsciously aware (you don't know that you know). (Adams, 2016)

The essential skills for living, working, and learning in the modern world are mental processes that help students learn, practice, develop, and apply so they can, in due course, become unconscious habits of mind. These new mental processes are essential skills that pave the way for success in the modern world. The significant steps in developing modern learning skills involve conscious-to-unconscious application.

We call these modern learning skills the fluencies. The fluencies are the everyday process skills essential for living, working, and lifelong learning in the contemporary world. So let's first try to explain the difference between literacy and fluency.

Think about language. Someone literate in speaking Spanish will have a working knowledge of the language, but if they're only literate, they will have to stop frequently to think about translating their thoughts from English into Spanish. They'll have to think about pronunciation. They'll have to think about the grammatical structure of what they're saying. As a result, while they may be understood, their speech will likely be slow and halting, because they'll have to pause regularly to think about what to say next, and how to say it before they can speak.

Now compare the speech of someone *literate* in Spanish to that of someone *fluent* in Spanish. If they are *fluent*, they can speak fluidly and continuously without having to stop and think about how the language is constructed or having to think through and translate what they need to say next. If they're *fluent*, they have reached a level of *unconscious proficiency* that allows them to think in Spanish without first translating their ideas from English. They don't have to think about pronunciation or the structure of the language or the grammar; they just speak the language. Speaking Spanish has become a fluency. In other words, an unconscious mental process.

literate in a language
vs. fluent in a language

Here's another example: using a pen, or if you don't have a real pen grasp a pretend pen, and write your name using your *dominant* hand. Once you have done that, switch the pen over to your nondominant hand and do the same thing again. You will probably notice that it is a little harder to write with your nondominant hand because you have to consciously think about what you're doing. Writing with your dominant hand is an unconscious act; it's automatic; it's a fluency. Writing with your nondominant hand is a conscious act; it is a literacy; you have to think about it. That's the difference between literacy and fluency.

Fluency transcends merely knowing how to do something. Fluency is about doing things automatically without being conscious of every action. It's like riding a bicycle. Do you remember learning to ride a bike when you were a child? Between then and now, have you gone away from riding a bike for an extended period—like years? So you get on a bike after not riding one for many years; how long does it take you to get comfortable? For most people, it's a matter of minutes, because riding a bike is a fluency. It is an unconscious, learned act. Once you get used to the brakes, the pedals, the gears, the handlebars, and the seat, you don't have to think, you just ride. Instead of focusing on the mechanics of bike riding, you can focus on the destination. Fluency goes one step beyond literacy. Fluencies focus on the metacognitive skills needed to apply literacy skills from one task to another and rapidly make nuanced decisions about how to use them. How is fluency different from literacy? In learning to speak a foreign language, a literate person can speak, listen, and read for comprehension when using the new language. In contrast, a fluent person uses their understanding of the language to create something new, whether it is a story, song, play, poem, or conversation.

[handwritten margin note: ✗fluency means learners can apply skills they are literate in]

[handwritten margin note: good example of use vs. application]

Fluency of ideas refers to the speed, quality, and quantity of responses an individual can use to create answers to questions or quickly make new connections between ideas. A fluent brain quickly sorts through alternatives and identifies the most appropriate solution. Imagine a quarterback standing at the line of scrimmage, getting ready to take the snap as they rapidly scan the entire field. Depending on the situation, the quarterback may choose to throw the ball to exactly where the play was initially planned. At other times, the quarterback may improvise based on what's happening on the field at that very moment. The more experienced and cognitively flexible or fluent the quarterback is, the more likely they will be able to think on the go, and the more options the quarterback has to choose from, the more likely they will be to successfully throw the ball where they want.

fluent thinkers have more options

The same thing is true for any fluency. A writer who chooses between 30 turns of phrase, or 30 examples of how to make a point, has a far greater ability to identify the most appropriate word or phrase to make their point than the individual who can only come up with a single example or use a limited vocabulary. A writer who has 30 ways to describe a "dark and stormy night" will be able to construct better prose and poetry than one who only thinks, "The weather was bad." That's the difference between being literate and being fluent.

Conscious Application of Essential Skills

*this step is needed to get to an unconscious ability

In a conscious application of skills, you develop expertise, but you must think about how to apply the skills. Having to think before doing is an essential and useful stage in skill development. Think back to when you were first learning to drive. In the beginning, you were very conscious of turning the steering wheel, stepping on the brakes, stepping on the gas, using the turn signals, and checking the mirrors, along with a whole bunch of other driving skills. It was hard to do this all at the same time. Simultaneously learning these new skills was a necessary first step in learning how to drive. It is for this very reason that we don't just give student drivers their licenses. They are just not ready to operate a vehicle independently without an experienced driver being there to guide them as they learn the necessary skills.

Since they are new drivers, they must think before applying these skills, and as a result, in the beginning, they often don't operate the car smoothly. They lurch, stall, and stop abruptly. In the beginning, driving is a halting, uneven, uncomfortable experience. To become an independent driver, learners need sufficient practice and experience so they can learn to apply all these skills unconsciously and intuitively.

Experienced drivers can perform these skills at a high level of mastery while still carrying on conversations with their passengers, listening to music, and sipping on their coffee. They can do this because they don't have to think; they just drive. Learners also demonstrate this when they learn a new mathematics skill, grammatical rule, or reading technique. At first, they must consciously think about performing these skills. It is only after practice and repetition that the skills are developed to the point where learners can perform them with little to no thought required.

Unconscious Application of Essential Skills

Experienced drivers have reached a level of unconscious ability. We do not mean they can drive while asleep. In this context, unconscious ability means performing a task instinctively, without realizing or being aware of one's actions. When they attain this level, they can focus on higher-level cognitive functions. They don't just respond; they can also anticipate what other drivers are going to do and take corrective or preventive measures before something happens. This unconscious skill level doesn't just apply to learning to drive; it also applies to reading, writing, arithmetic, research, problem solving, and any other skill needed to develop practical intelligence. Unconscious skills are what conventional notions of multitasking are all about, which is being able to do several things unconsciously and simultaneously. Small and Vorgan (2008) referred to this ability as *continuous partial attention.*

Acquiring the processes of the modern learning fluencies is about developing robust and reliable chains of unconscious procedural practice. When we first learn how to back up a car, it's challenging. We have to consciously and separately think about each step—how to turn the steering wheel, how to use the mirrors, how to step on the accelerator, how to apply the brakes. But once the skills are linked and the process chained, it's easy. It becomes an unconscious process; it becomes automatic; it becomes a fluency. Mastery involves the development of chains of procedural fluency. And once those procedures have been learned and internalized—once they've become chains—they've become an unconscious, structured mental process for life.

Modern Learning Fluencies

We believe that when we're talking about modern learning and the new basics needed to be successful in the fundamentally different and continuously changing world we live in, our goal must be to help our students become fluent, not just literate. Literacy is *still* not enough.

So what are the essential fluencies for modern learning? What are the critical mental processes that *all* learners need to acquire above and beyond an understanding of traditional content areas? What are the new basics, the process skills that are important now and will remain just as essential and relevant 50 years from now when today's learners are retiring from their careers?

These are tough questions. There are any number of essential skills lists circulating out there. One of the most well-known is the list developed by the World Economic Forum that identifies foundational skills, competencies, and character qualities, shown in Figure 3.1.

There's also Tony Wagner and Ted Dintersmith's Essential Modern Skills outlined in their book *Most Likely to Succeed* (2015), The East

Figure 3.1   World Economic Forum 21st-Century Skills

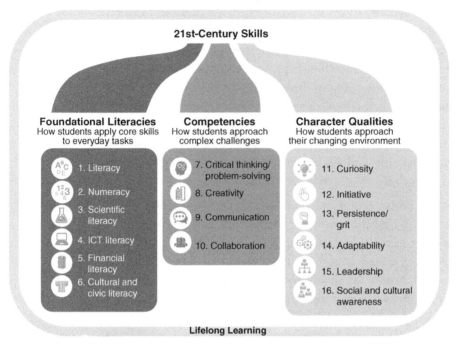

Source: World Economic Forum. (2015). New vision for education: Unlocking the potential of technology. Retrieved from http://www3.weforum.org/docs/WEFUSA_NewVisionforEducation_Report2015.pdf

Asia Society in Partnership with CCSSO (Mansilla & Jackson, 2011), and the Partnership for 21st Century Skills (2009), shown in Figure 3.2.

Nicky and Ian examined, compared, and combined several modern skills lists being promoted or profiled. They discovered there were at least 150 different "essential skills" that have been identified in one or more of these lists. There were far too many skills to teach individually without absolutely overwhelming an already overcrowded curriculum.

Together, we methodically reviewed all these lists and their skills and distilled and categorized them down to a list of six essential fluencies we believe are future-focused and future-proof and that these six fluencies will empower individuals for lifelong personal and professional success. These are six skill sets that can be seamlessly integrated into any subject area at any grade level. We are confident that learning these six fluencies is as relevant and essential today as reading, writing, and arithmetic were for success in the 20th century.

These fluencies include Solution Fluency, Collaboration Fluency, Information Fluency, Creativity Fluency, Communication Fluency, and Global Citizenship.

Figure 3.2   P21 Framework

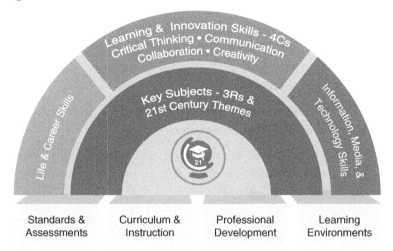

Source: Partnership for 21st Century Skills. (2009). P21 Framework definitions. Retrieved from https://files.eric.ed.gov/fulltext/ED519462.pdf

The Path Forward

Although this chapter provides a thorough analysis of the essential skills of modern learning, there is still so much more to describe, like how we can embed and teach these skills together with existing curriculum content. If learners are to develop the essential, modern-day skills they need to survive and thrive in an ever changing world and economy, then educators must also develop new mindsets and skills to reflect the realities of modern times. Developing these skills is what we examine in the next chapter.

Summarizing the Main Points

- If we were to educate all our students to the standards of the 20th century literacies, they wouldn't be literate based on the needs and demands of the modern and future world.

- Fluencies are the everyday process skills that are essential for living, working, and lifelong learning in the modern world.

- Any mastery involves the development of chains of procedural fluency. Once those procedures have been learned, they form chains and become unconscious, structured mental processes.

- Fluency transcends merely knowing how to do something. Fluency is about doing things automatically without being conscious of every little step.

- The Modern Fluencies are Solution Fluency, Collaboration Fluency, Information Fluency, Creativity Fluency, Communication Fluency, and Global Citizenship.

Questions to Consider

- How do we promote active, engaged, higher-level thinking in today's and tomorrow's learners?
- How do we address the need for our students to learn both traditional curriculum content as well as the essentials of modern learning?
- What are the new process skills that are important now and will remain just as important and relevant 50 years from now when today's learners are retiring from their careers?
- Explain the difference between literacy and fluency.
- Summarize your understanding of what the authors describe as modern-day fluencies.

Modern Learning Pedagogy and the Learning Progression 4

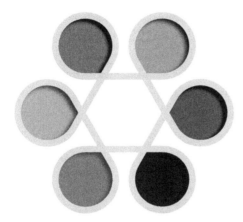

"Knowing is not enough; we must apply. Being willing is not enough; we must do."

—Leonardo Da Vinci

The Modern Fluencies have a proven track record of success. The learning progressions within each fluency have reinvigorated the learning process for thousands of learners and educators spanning dozens of countries over the past decade. As authentic, powerful, and relevant as the fluencies are, it is reassuring to know that each is solidly grounded in learning theory and research.

Educators and educational leaders do not have the time to test unsupported fads or cyclical trends that regularly pop up in education. Educators require strategies and instructional programs that work and are supported by literature and the great thinkers in education. This chapter is an extensive examination of the underpinnings of the steps, progressions, and pedagogical and heutagogical practices associated

method/practice of teaching

self-determined learning

with Solution, Collaboration, Information, Communications, and Creativity Fluencies culminating in Global Citizenship. This chapter outlines the theorists' views on learning and pinpoints their execution within the processes of the fluencies. This review supports the fluencies' application to modern-day learning environments. By the end of the chapter, readers will be able to outline why educators need to integrate the fluencies within their current teaching, learning, and assessment practices.

Learning Theorists and the Modern Fluencies

The history and study of education are expansive. The authors have identified numerous educators, philosophers, and psychologists who are considered groundbreaking and influential with regard to today's teaching, learning, and assessment practices. Figure 4.1 breaks down the theories, contributions, and big ideas shared by 10 highly influential minds in education, and connects their big ideas to the Modern Fluencies.

Figure 4.1   Learning Theorists and the Modern Fluencies

THEORIST/ BACKGROUND	THEORIES, CONTRIBUTIONS, AND "BIG IDEAS"	CONNECTION TO THE FLUENCIES
John Dewey (1859–1952) American Educator & Reformer	• proposed humans learn through a hands-on approach • proposed humans learn through practical application • emphasized student- (or child-) centered learning • combined instructional subjects in an interdisciplinary manner • promoted learning with others (social context of learning) (Dewey, 2011)	The Modern Fluencies explicitly promote hands-on, brains-on learning experiences throughout most or all steps of the learning progression. The fluencies' entire purpose is to promote interdisciplinary learning that is student-centered.
Maria Montessori (1870–1952) Italian Physician & Educator	• focused on students learning through sensory experience • advocated for hands-on learning • believed in cultivating the whole learner (holistic) • focused on developing skills (Hainstock, 1997)	Multiple steps in each fluency encourage learners to use their senses and actions to learn using various materials and interactions. The fundamental nature of the learning progressions in each fluency focus on holistic learning and assessment. Learning does not occur in a vacuum.

Jean Piaget (1896–1980) Swiss Psychologist	• established the theory of cognitive development • theorized that humans gradually come to acquire, construct, and use knowledge • believed people use their prior knowledge and experiences to construct new knowledge (constructivism) (Ojose, 2008)	The fluencies are crafted on a constructivist theoretical platform. Each step requires discovery, reflection, and new knowledge construction. The fluencies require learners to tap into their prior knowledge to solve a problem, create a product, or fulfill a challenge.
Lev Vygotsky (1896–1934) Soviet Psychologist	• advocated for community and culture in learning • developed the theory of the Zone of Proximal Development, which explored the difference between what a child can achieve independently and what a child can achieve with guidance and encouragement from a skilled partner (scaffolding) (Vygotsky, 1978)	The fluencies encourage community-based learning. The teacher becomes a facilitator and can offer support for learners-in-need in a direct manner. Collaboration fluency provides the opportunity for learners to learn from each other in a dynamic and productive team. They can provide support to one another using their prior experiences and leadership and citizenship skills.
Abraham Maslow (1908–1970) American Psychologist	• posited a hierarchy of human needs based on deficiency needs and growth needs • observed that when initial needs are fulfilled, humans can develop cognition, the aesthetic, and fulfillment of their potential (Maslow, 1943)	The fluencies help learners reach their full potential through authentic learning tasks and experiences. The mission of global citizenship is to construct a world that helps meet the needs of all people—the attempt to make a dream into reality.
Paulo Freire (1921–1997) Brazilian Educator & Philosopher	• proposed critical pedagogy • empowered learners and teachers to question systemic oppression in learning • promoted empowerment so learners could become critically conscious (in-depth understanding of the world to improve it) (Freire, 1972) *x must understand the world around you before you can change it*	The fluencies are structured to empower educators and learners. Learners create their own knowledge without an intermediary standing in their way. They must make a substantial number of the decisions involved in the learning progression. Educators are able to create and deliver authentic assessments of student learning and provide valuable feedback and feedforward to learners. The main goal of cultivating global citizenship is to help create a better world.
Seymour Papert (1928–2016) South African born, American Mathematician, Educator, Computer Scientist	• strived to produce and advocate for coercion-free learning environments • launched the Maker Movement • developed the Theory of Constructionism, which promotes the idea that learning should be actively explored through the construction and delivery of a product (Martinez & Stager, 2019)	The fluencies promote the construction of a variety of student solutions and products. However, learners do not just create or produce the product, they must deliver, share, present, or transmit to an authentic audience.

(Continued)

Figure 4.1   (Continued)

THEORIST/ BACKGROUND	THEORIES, CONTRIBUTIONS, AND "BIG IDEAS"	CONNECTION TO THE FLUENCIES
William Glasser (1925–2013) American Psychiatrist	• proposed Choice Theory, which states every part of our behavior—our thoughts, feelings, physiology, and actions—is a choice (Glasser, 1997) • observed that behavior is the attempt to meet basic needs such as survival, longing and belonging, power, freedom, and fun	The fluencies promote numerous opportunities for student choice. Learners practice important skills such as collaboration, problem solving, and creativity, which promote positive behavior.
Benjamin Bloom (1913–1999) American Educational Psychologist	• theorized a cognitive taxonomy predicated on the idea that cognitive operations can be ordered into six increasingly complex levels: knowledge, comprehension, application, analysis, synthesis, and evaluation (Bloom, Englehart, Hill, Furst, & Krathwohl, 1956)	The fluencies promote lower-order thinking (LOTs) and higher-order thinking (HOTs) activities—what we call lots of LOTS and lots of HOTS.

The Modern Fluencies are steeped in learning theory and promote student-centered, discovery learning. The instruction is multidisciplinary and draws heavily on collaboration and communication. The steps of each fluency are rich in questioning, student reflection, and hands-on learning experiences. In the next section, we explore the Progression of Thought and Learning, which provides a visual framework to establish the Modern Fluencies' efficacy.

The Progression of Thought and Learning

Nicky created a progression to illustrate what we have come to know about thinking and learning. She pulled the common threads of learning strategies that work into a Progression of Thought and Learning (POTAL). POTAL (see Figure 4.2) represents the ideas of educational theorists such as Dewey, Montessori, Piaget, Vygotsky, Maslow, Bloom, Papert, and Glasser. This progression is set against the taxonomy of thinking skills created by Benjamin Bloom in 1956. It was Bloom who proposed a hierarchy of thought that runs from relatively straightforward low-level thinking to higher levels of more complex cognitive function.

The POTAL illustrates what these educational thinkers have had to say about the use of different instructional strategies and their effect on learning. According to them, the least effective strategy for teaching is speaking, such as teachers presenting information through spoken

Figure 4.2   Progression of Thought and Learning (POTAL)

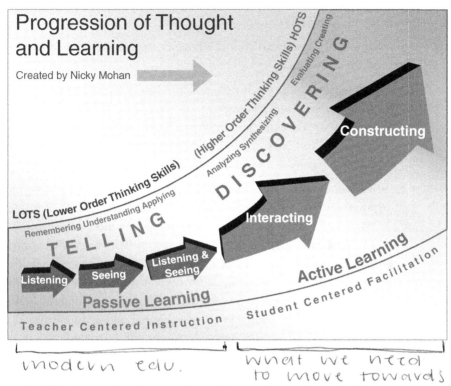

modern edu. | *what we need to move towards*

words. This instructional approach requires students to learn by listening, such as through an audio presentation of instructional content.

A more effective strategy is teaching using text and images together in a visual representation of the material (Rau, 2016). This instructional approach means students learn by seeing. Research shows that visual information is retained in the brain more efficiently (Jukes, Schaaf, & Mohan, 2015), especially for the digital generations who have been raised in the graphical online world. An even better approach is an instructional strategy that combines both audio and visual representations of information. Combining audio and visual representations means students are simultaneously listening to and seeing the instructional material. These activities include watching and listening to a TV program, a video, a cartoon, an animation, or a physical demonstration. All these are examples of primarily passive learning activities, where the learner passively receives information. With passive activities, student engagement is often difficult to evaluate because what might appear at first glance to be engagement may only be temporary entertainment or edutainment.

especially true for newer generations of learners who have grown up w/ the internet

It is important to note that these three instructional strategies encompass the vast majority of teaching that traditionally occurs in schools, especially when students move into high school and beyond. It's also important to note that this kind of instruction fosters only the lower levels of Bloom's Taxonomy.

LOTS

All three of these instructional strategies require very little cognitive work from students.

When sitting and listening, students are generally only at the Remembering, Understanding, and Applying levels of Bloom's Taxonomy of Thought. For more than 100 years, great educational minds have been consistently imploring teachers to move beyond the traditional lecture, demonstration-style of teaching (see Figure 4.1).

What these learning theorists have been saying is that a significant shift in approach is needed to foster higher-level thinking and learning. It starts with a shift towards active learning to a more active role for students. Active learning involves students discussing instructional material with teachers and other students. These types of activities mean students are interacting with others while also interacting with the learning content. In terms of Bloom's Taxonomy of Thinking Skills, students move into higher levels of analyzing and synthesizing. But even this is not the ultimate goal, which is to shift instruction to engage students in real-world activities or simulations of those activities in a multisensory learning environment.

When we do this, students begin constructing their knowledge and learning. And this moves students to the highest levels of thinking and learning, which are evaluating and creating. In other words, teaching strategies that foster the lowest levels of thinking and learning are teacher-centered instructional strategies, where students receive teaching from their teachers, which results in passive learning. In contrast, teaching strategies that promote the highest levels of thinking and learning make the shift to student-centered facilitation that leads to students participating in activities where they take an active role in the learning.

The primary point to take away from this progression is that as we ascend from the lower levels of thinking and learning, toward the higher levels, the instructional approach focuses on facilitation where students are challenged to discover things for themselves. Research consistently shows us that the best environments for learning involve a focus on higher-order thinking skills and active learning in multisensory or real-world situations (Cole, 2008). When we use real-world problems, relevance is quickly evident, so there's no need for students to ask the questions, "Why am I learning this?" or "Where would I use this in the real world?"

We believe we need to make a fundamental shift in the way we approach learning. We do this by first giving students real-world problems, teaching the skills and concepts, then challenging them to identify their own real-world problems and issues to solve. Providing problems first is the most significant change we can make to our teaching. Taking a problems-first, learner-centered approach forces educators to take on a new role. Not to mention, this approach is entirely in sync with the current realities of the world outside of school.

The modern learning formula we recommend consists of engagement, higher-order thinking skills, real-world connections, modern learning skills (fluencies), and authentic assessment.

The fluencies help educators enhance their pedagogical approaches, allowing them to move beyond "teaching as telling, learning as listening" to teaching that facilitates discovery learning.

Providing real-world problems relates to the learner's world outside of school.

Providing problems first is the most significant change we can make to our teaching.

The Role of Technology in the Modern Fluencies

Given that we live in highly disruptive times, we acknowledge that technology plays a vital role in education. We accept that many of our students know more about how to use technology than we do. They are tech-savvy, and many prefer to use digital devices and apps rather than a pen and paper. This growing reliance on technology makes it difficult for learners today to cope when the internet goes down. It has, therefore, become increasingly important for educators to motivate students by emphasizing how they learn rather than what they learn. This approach is both practical and engaging.

The current digital landscape and the demands of the global market leave us with no other option than to consider how to best prepare today's learners as our future citizens and workforce. We believe that this can be accomplished through a careful reorganization of learning to support all our learners so that they are better equipped with the essential skills necessary to help them succeed in an ever changing world.

The ripple effect of empowering students as promoted through the fluencies is that they become good global citizens. Not just in theory, but through their actions. After all, why else do we teach but for learning? And, if we believe that the purpose of teaching is learning, then as educators, we can see that there is an apparent disconnect between traditionally accepted teaching practices and research. We continue to teach in conventional ways despite empirical evidence from the work of

Hattie (2012), Fullan (with Quinn & McEachen, 2018), and the theories of Piaget, Papert, Dewey, Freire, and others. Educators must consider both research and theory to support them when creating learning experiences for their students, experiences that are engaging, relevant, real world, and fun.

Given the complex nature of our ever changing world, the teacher's job is no longer to dispense knowledge. Instead, it is to facilitate learning. Our goal as educators must be to help our learners become fluent and not just literate problem solvers, collaborators, and communicators. The teacher's role is no longer to be the gatekeeper between students and knowledge. Instead, the teacher becomes the architect of the learning environment. We believe that we must help all our students become independent thinkers by teaching them a structured mental process they can use again and again in high-tech, low-tech, and no-tech environments. *Show learners ways of problem solving that are applicable in all environments*

Using Mental Processes

* structured problem solving can increase brain function

The research underpinning the teaching of a structured mental process is outlined in the book *The Overflowing Brain* (2008) by Torkel Klingberg, a Professor of Cognitive Neuroscience at the Karolinska Institute in Stockholm, Sweden. His research demonstrates that if by the time kids are in their mid-teens, they can be taught a structured mental process for solving problems, general intellectual function goes up by more than 15% (and stays up for life) regardless of age, sex, culture, experience, or socioeconomics.

With this in mind, each fluency has been designed as a structured mental process similar to the scientific method, the writing process, the media production process, architectural design, and design thinking. Figure 4.3 provides several examples of processes encountered in everyday life.

Each of the revised Modern Fluency progressions includes nine steps. Although this may seem like a lot of steps, each progression can be adapted based on academic need, grade, or ability level. The fluencies also do not have to be used as a linear progression. Learners may decide to jump ahead or find it necessary to revisit a previous step. Figure 4.4 shows each fluency and its steps vertically to demonstrate the relationship of each step across all the Modern Fluencies. The final column shows multiple research sources supporting why each step is essential in the fluency processes.

Figure 4.3   Examples of Everyday Processes

SOLUTION FLUENCY	SCIENTIFIC METHOD	WRITING PROCESS	MEDIA PRODUCTION	ARCHITECTURAL DESIGN	DESIGN THINKING
Define	Aim	Prewriting	Storyboard	Application Requirement	Understand
Discover	Background/ Introduction	Drafting	Script	Functions	Observe
Determine	Hypothesis	Revising	Location	Autonomic Elements	POV
Dream	Equipment/ Method	Editing	Props/Costumes	Architectural Elements	Ideate
Design	Experiment	Publishing	Risk Assessment	Parameter Selection	Prototype
Deliver	Results	Review	Production Schedule	FE/AE Moder	Test
Diagnose	Conclusion		Shot List	Architectural Optimization	Story Telling
Debrief			Edit List	Evaluation	Pilot
Decide			Filming		Business Model

Heutagogy and the Fluencies

self-directed learning ↗

The fluencies also promote the use of heutagogy as a framework for teaching and learning. Heutagogy is an approach crafted by educators that encourages learners to be highly independent and self-directed. This practice helps prepare individuals who are well-equipped for the complexities of today and tomorrow's world.

This approach supports the core concepts promoted through the fluencies because it is the theory utilized for guiding teaching and learning practices, particularly related to the integration of technology. Like heutagogy, the fluencies create learner-centered environments. The fluencies educate the whole child by creating learning spaces that encourage student engagement. The primary focus of both approaches is on the learning process and how students learn together, share, and reflect (Ashton & Newman, 2006).

Heutagogy applies a holistic approach to developing learner capabilities, with learning as an active and proactive process, and learners serving as "the major agent in their own learning, which occurs as a result of personal experiences" (Hase & Kenyon, 2007, p. 112, as cited in

The fluencies educate the whole child by creating learning spaces that encourage student engagement.

Figure 4.4   Modern Fluency Learning Progressions with Research Support

SOLUTION FLUENCY	COLLABORATION FLUENCY	INFORMATION FLUENCY	COMMUNICATION FLUENCY	CREATIVITY FLUENCY	SUPPORTIVE RESEARCH
Define	Explain	Ask	Pose	Illustrate	Much of the collected literature identifies the importance for students and teachers to ask guiding questions, define instructional tasks, use open-ended challenges, and promote student inquiry. This initial step of the Modern Fluencies asks students to communicate in their own words what the problem, task, or challenge is and how to accomplish their goals (Bartholomew & Strimel, 2018; Cellitti & Wright, 2019; Longo, 2016; Martin & Bollinger, 2018; Patall, 2013; Sato, Hazeyama, & Miyadera, 2016).
Determine	Establish	Audience	Pinpoint	Identify	This step establishes a context for learning and identifies who the intended audiences are for the task, problem, or challenge. Understanding the audience is critical because if the information or solution is not aligned to the needs of the audience, they will not find it relevant. This step also helps better align the entire process and product of the problem, task, or challenge by focusing on the progression and evidence of learning to the intended audience (Dias de Figueiredo, 2005; Madoyan, 2016; Tessmer & Richey, 1997; Westera, 2011).
Discover	Explore	Access	Prepare	Inquire	This step across the fluencies represents the exploration and research phase, during which learners gather information and resources to utilize when solving problems, completing challenges, or accomplishing tasks. The citations below represent literature reviews and studies that underpin this step in the different fluency progressions (Buchanan, Harlan, Bruce, & Edwards, 2016; Chen & Hsieh, 2013; Chen, Chen, & Ma, 2014; O'Neal, Gibson, & Cotten, 2017).

Dream	Envision	Authenticate	Picture	Imagine
Design	Engineer	Assemble	Plan	Initiate
Deliver	Execute	Apply	Produce	Implement

Imagine: Collectively throughout the Modern Fluencies, this step represents the brainstorming, visioning, and ideation phase where learners try to envision the completion of a task, a solution to a problem, or fulfillment of a challenge. Brainstorming, visioning, and imagination are powerful elements in each fluency. The supporting literature underpins the importance of visioning, brainstorming, and ideation during the learning progressions. "Brainstorming is a strategy with which a problem can be attacked—in fact, literally stormed—by dozens of ideas" (Clark, 1958, p. 53; see also Baer, 1993; Cooper, 1995; Costa & Kallick, 2008; Kaplan & Kies, 1995; Malkawi & Smadi, 2018; Mentzer, Farrington, & Tennenhouse, 2015; Ziv, 1983).

Initiate: Learners formulate a step-by-step roadmap or plan that lays out the process and identifies timelines that learners will utilize to solve their problems, accomplish their tasks, and meet their goals. It is a whole-mind process that involves both imagination and logic. The steps help answer the question, "What do I do next?" **Instructional systems design (ISD)** is the practice of systematically designing, developing, and delivering instructional products and experiences, both digital and physical, in a consistent and reliable fashion toward an efficient, effective, appealing, engaging, and inspiring acquisition of knowledge (Merrill, Drake, Lacy, & Pratt, 1996).
The steps present in each of the fluencies represent a progression through a multistep process. This is present in many ISD models such as SCORM, ADDIE, Gagné, and ASSURE (West, 2018).

Implement: At this step across the fluencies, learners develop and share their solutions or products to an authentic audience. There are two components in this step: *Produce* and *Publish*. In modern learning environments, learners create a real-world solution to the problem, but they must also share their solution with the world (Dodge, 1997; Papert & Harel, 1991).

(Continued)

Figure 4.4 (Continued)

SOLUTION FLUENCY	COLLABORATION FLUENCY	INFORMATION FLUENCY	COMMUNICATION FLUENCY	CREATIVITY FLUENCY	SUPPORTIVE RESEARCH
Diagnose	Examine	Assess	Probe	Inspect	This step throughout the many progressions of the fluencies is about assessment and evaluation. It is important during this step to assess both the process and the product. Multiple methods of assessment should be used to engage learners in their personal growth; monitor individual, peer, and class progress; and guide both learners and educators in the steps of the academic journey (Bolat & Karakus, 2017; Darling-Hammond & Snyder, 2000; Heritage, 2008; Litchfield & Dempsey, 2015; Sabtiawan, Yuanita, & Rahayu, 2019; Wiggins, 1998; Wiggins & McTighe, 2005).
Debrief	Evaluate	Analyze	Ponder	Investigate	This step across the fluencies helps learners cultivate personal ownership and responsibility for learning by asking them to revisit each step of the process, reflect on their performance and experiences, and Debrief on both the process, product, or outcome of the learning progression (Bandura, 2001; Dewey, 1910; Grossman, 2009; Leinonen, Keune, Veermans, & Toikkanen, 2016; Quinton & Smallbone, 2010; Reeve & Tseng, 2011; Vaughn, 2014).
Decide	Extend	Action	Pledge	Inspire	During this final step throughout the fluencies, learners internalize their new knowledge and transfer it to new and different situations to determine what future actions might be taken. The transfer of learning is a highly valued outcome of learning. This concept is the application of skills, knowledge, and/or dispositions that were learned in one learning situation to another (Haskell, 2001; Perkins & Salomon, 1988; Perkins & Salomon, 1992; Steiner, 2001).

Blaschke, 2012). When using this approach, the teacher's role shifts from that of an instructor to that of a facilitator. The facilitator's job is to provide guidance and resources that allow students to take responsibility and ownership for their learning. However, we cannot change our practice without teaching our students the learning process.

The fluencies are designed with clearly identified steps to ensure that students know what the next actions are even when they're not sure what to do. Each fluency includes a step where learners are asked to outline their understanding of the expectations for the task to ensure that they are in alignment with the expectations of the teacher.

While heutagogy promotes a student-centric environment, educators must support the learning process while also providing learners with timely feedback and feedforward. This approach supports students becoming lifelong learners as well as fostering student motivation by cultivating learners who "are fully engaged in the topic they are studying because they are making choices that are most relevant or interesting to them" (Kenyon & Hase, 2010, p. 170, as cited in Blaschke, 2012).

feedback & advice for going forward must be provided by the instructor

Educators adopting this approach can concentrate on designing activities to foster skills in high demand, such as problem-solving creativity, innovation, communication, collaboration, and global citizenship. Once learners are familiar with the fluency process, teachers can set the challenges for their students and then get out of the way. The idea of the student being the focus of learning is not a new concept. In 1969, Carl Rogers adapted his client-centered approach to education, identifying it as student-centered learning. Similarly, constructivism and constructionism place the learner at the heart of the educational experience (Bruner, 1960; Dewey, 1938; Freire, 1972; Piaget, 1973; Vygotsky, 1978).

teach the mental process first, then challenge learners

We believe all teachers must become increasingly process focused. The fluencies help guide teachers' emphasis on *how to learn* rather than on only *what to learn*. Teachers also acquire strategies about how to view learning as a process and not just reduce learning to a product. When using this approach, the learning journey becomes more important than the product students create, and against which they are evaluated. We encourage teachers to abandon their preconceived expectations of end products; they believe students need to produce to obtain a good grade. When using a product-focused approach, the learning is reduced to completing an activity or worksheet or making something the teacher or curriculum suggests. Instead, have students follow the steps of the given fluency and use each step as a checkpoint in the learning process, an opportunity to provide feedback and feedforward.

learning is not a product; it's a process

use the steps in the fluency as checkpoints, not worksheets/assignments

As outlined in the POTAL, when learning is only product-focused, we lose student voice and they become passive recipients of content. The ripple effect is disengagement and a lack of motivation. Viewing learning as a process helps educators reimagine and reorganize their teaching so that students become the center of the learning.

Modern Learning Skills

Modern learning skills are the essential process skills we need students to develop. Teachers must be aware of the benefits of including them in their daily practice. However, skills like problem solving, communication, creativity, collaboration, critical thinking, and global citizenship cannot be learned directly from the pages of a textbook. We have found that the most effective way of teaching these skills to learners is by embedding the fluencies into all lessons and making them a relevant part of student learning.

The critical questions are: How do we teach these essential skills, while at the same time helping learners prepare for the mandated tests? Is it possible to do both at the same time? How do we address the short-term goals of preparing students for the prescribed criteria, while at the same time addressing the long-term goals of helping our students develop the modern learning skills needed to thrive in their lives beyond school? What does this kind of learning look like?

The starting point is to shift our instructional approach to a model that parallels what happens in the real world. When interviewing learners, we discovered that, more than any other question, the one students most frequently asked their teachers is, why? Why am I learning this? Followed closely by, where would I ever use what you're teaching me in the real world? *model edu. to real world happennings → eliminate "why?*

Context and Meaning: The Velcro of Learning

The traditional model of instruction is based on something we describe as teaching-as-telling, learning-as-listening. This approach involves telling students what they have to learn because it's the next section in the curriculum or because it might be on the test. However, our experience shows that this approach is not very persuasive or successful. The traditional curriculum is notorious for regularly presenting content without providing a compelling context.

Learning is all about perspective. Context matters! And if educators are not focusing on process and engagement, then many learners won't see the point of what they're being taught and quickly lose interest.

Without a context to add meaning to new content, new information will not be successfully retained in memory.

For example, how many of you can remember the 9-11 attacks on the World Trade Center in New York? Although that happened almost two decades ago, it's still fresh in many of our memories. How many of you can even remember exactly where you were when you first heard about it? That's context! Or how about the birth of your first child? Or the death of someone special like a family member, an entertainer, a sports star, or media personality?

We suspect that for many of these events, you can remember not only *where* you were, but also what you were doing when you heard the news. Why do we remember those details, when we forget so many others? It's because the context of the event provided a cognitive framework to reinforce our memories. Context is the key. Research demonstrates that for information to be remembered, it must be quickly moved from our short-term or working memory to our permanent memory. But for this to happen, new information must connect to something the learner already knows and that already has personal meaning for them. Unless a connection is quickly made, the research tells us that new content only stays in working memory for a few seconds (Medina, 2008).

[handwritten margin note: ✗ the same things will not be meaningful across the board to a group of students; important to let them individually self-direct]

Put another way, if it's not meaningful or interesting or relevant to the learner, new content will quickly be discarded by the brain. That's the difference between rote learning and meaningful learning. If something is not meaningful to the learner, regardless of whether it's meaningful to the teacher, it will quickly be discarded. That's why trying to learn content without context often fails.

Writer Erik Jensen (2005) says we forget 98% of everything that comes into the brain. For example, have you ever been introduced to someone and instantly forgotten their name? Or have you ever given students a test on something, and they do well? But when you administer a follow-up test on the same content a few weeks later, it's as if they've never heard the material before? Here's why—only meaningful learning sticks.

Richard Saul Wurman (1989) explains this phenomenon as follows: "Learning can be seen as the acquisition of information, but before it can take place, there must be interest; interest precedes learning. To acquire and remember new knowledge, it must stimulate your curiosity in some way" (p. 20). *[handwritten: interest precedes learning.]*

Wurman (1989) goes on to say that trying to learn content without any interest or context is like having only one side of a piece of Velcro—it just doesn't stick. Our job as teachers is to create the other side of the

[handwritten top: learning w/o interest is like only having one side of the velcro.]

Velcro by arousing interest in the minds of our learners. Making connections allows information to stick. We believe that creating interest, bar none, is the most critical role educators play.

Modern Fluencies have been cognitively crafted using the major educational theories, contributions, and big ideas of the past and present to help teachers craft the learning experiences of tomorrow. Each of the fluencies is process-driven and consists of nine purposeful steps that create a powerful learning journey for both educators and students. The number of steps in each progression can be modified depending on academic need, grade, or ability level. The fluencies also do not have to occur in a linear progression.

[handwritten left margin: this makes the fluencies usable by all grades & allows educators to start teaching the mental process at a young age.]

Before educators take a deep dive into each of the fluencies, we want to share how modern learning environments can facilitate learning.

Summarizing the Main Points

- Educators and educational thought leaders require strategies and instructional programs that work and are supported by the literature and the leading minds on education.

- The Modern Fluencies are intermixed with learning theory and promote student-centered, discovery learning. The instruction is multidisciplinary and draws heavily on collaboration and communication. The steps of each fluency are rich in questioning, student reflection, and hands-on learning experiences.

- The modern learning formula we recommend consists of engagement, higher-order thinking skills, real-world connections, modern learning skills, and authentic assessment.

- The growing reliance on technology during the learning process may create barriers for learners to cope if there is a lack of access to digital devices or the internet. It has, therefore, become increasingly important for educators to motivate students by emphasizing *how* they learn rather than *what* they learn.

- Each of the Modern Fluency progressions includes nine steps. However, the number of steps in each progression can be modified depending on academic need, grade, or ability level. The fluencies also do not have to occur in a linear progression.

Questions to Consider

- As educators, why is it so crucial to underpin our instructional practices with research and theory?

- Why is it so important for educators to plan multidisciplinary instruction for their students?

- What does the POTAL suggest about teaching, learning, and assessment? How can the POTAL assist in planning instruction using the Modern Fluencies?

- What is your understanding of the concept of "Velcro Learning"?

5 Modern and Future-Ready Learning Environments

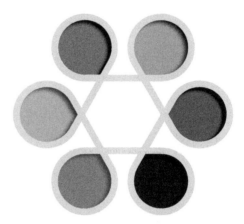

"A student of life considers the world a classroom."

—Harvey Mackay

Today's learning environments must be playgrounds full of questions, ideas, innovative thinking, self-research, tinkering, experimenting, collaboration, empathy, and activity. In this short wish list of future-ready behaviors, state-of-the-art technologies, expensive furniture, and unlimited budgets aren't necessarily part of the equation. Although these resources would be useful to have in abundance, real-world practicality often gets in the way. Education budgets are usually the first thing to be cut when the going gets economically tough. However, modern-day, future-ready learning environments do not require big budgets. A student-centric approach is the most critical component of this type of classroom when it is combined with inspiring teaching and learning. In essence, everything else will eventually find its way into the learning space whether it is face-to-face or virtually. It is not just about tools and resources; it is about heart and mindset.

The learning environments of today and tomorrow will go beyond the traditional brick-and-mortar classrooms of the past. They will involve both digital and real-world experiences that challenge traditional, preexisting mindsets about what a classroom must look like or how it must function. This is, something that was made abundantly clear during the recent pandemic as it forced millions of learners to rapidly transition from face-to-face to virtual learning environments. Even the term *classroom* accesses memories from a time when the world was more predictable and less connected.

Classrooms must be reframed, repackaged, and reimagined into what Mohan (2018) describes as Modern Learning Organizations (MLOs). MLOs are aligned with how today's students learn. They facilitate traditional teaching and learning when needed. However, they also offer flexibility in how classes and groups are structured. MLOs can contain open spaces in the form of breakout spaces, common area spaces, individual or shared spaces, learning hubs, blended learning labs, learning studios, makerspaces, and other multipurpose learning environments. This reconceptualization of the traditional classroom is possible just about anywhere, even online.

This chapter does NOT provide a comprehensive or prescriptive list of the tools and actions essential for modern and future-ready classrooms. Rather, this chapter changes the educational paradigm of the traditional classroom. This chapter is intended to help educators modify any learning space using a list of potential tools, resources, and actions that are useful in developing modern and future-ready classrooms primed to embrace the fluencies. *This chapter is about modifying what is currently available*

Types of Modern Learning Environments

The following section describes a variety of modern-day learning environments that can be used to foster learning experiences using the Modern Fluencies.

Breakout spaces are flexible environments in schools, universities, and libraries. Their purpose is to provide a small space for learners (and educators) to use as an informal area to meet, work, play, study, and discuss. Generally, these spaces are used for individual research, one-on-one interaction, or for small groups to work as a team on a project. Exploring the fluencies promotes the use of these types *breakout rooms in zoom*

Figure 5.1 a-b   Breakout Spaces

Source: Ryan Schaaf

of learning spaces where learners engage in in-depth, hands-on, brains-on learning, both independently and in groups.

Loertscher, Koechlin, and Rosenfeld (2012) define *learning commons* as a shared physical or virtual space designed to propel students beyond informal research, practice, and group work to an ascended level of engagement through exploration, experimentation, and collaboration. A learning commons is more than a room or a website. Developed out of the reimagining of a traditional school library, a learning commons allows individuals to modify, change, or adapt their learning environments to improve their learning journey. Each learning commons is unique and continually evolving. The fluencies encourage small-group and whole-group discussion, sharing, brainstorming, and reflection. A learning commons is a natural environment in which modern-day fluencies can flourish.

A *learning hub* is a technology-rich learning environment with both physical and virtual components that provide both formal and informal opportunities for learners to collaborate with classmates, educators, and other stakeholders during their learning. The purpose of the hub is to create a community of learning and curiosity, where new ideas and innovations are both encouraged and incubated. Technology tools are seen as a means to an end rather than the end itself.

Blended learning describes the process of combining online learning tools and resources with traditional classroom settings and teaching strategies. These environments are about more than simply adding technology. Their purpose is about leveraging the positive characteristics of technology-enriched, student-centered, personalized learning. Applying the modern-day fluencies requires students to work using a variety of digital tools and resources, while simultaneously collaborating with their peers in face-to-face or online venues.

Figure 5.2   Blended Learning Lab

Source: Ryan Schaaf

A *learning studio* is a space where learners define the problems or challenges they wish to face to design their solutions. By leveraging technology and other tools and resources, learners participate in activities, projects, and passions that require them to cultivate skills and approaches such as creativity, researching, design thinking, tinkering, fabrication, and digital and non-digital communications. The Communication, Creativity, and Solution Fluencies are specifically accessed in such an environment in both face-to-face and online environments.

Figure 5.3   Multimedia and Virtual Reality Learning Studio

Source: Ryan Schaaf

STEM labs →

Similar to the Reggio Emilia approach, *makerspaces* are learner-centered environments that encourage participatory, collaborative learning through tinkering and experiential, hands-on learning with digital and non-digital tools or resources that result in the creation of a product. In essence, making becomes a way of learning. Similar to learning studios, makerspaces provide opportunities for educators and learners to focus on all the modern-day fluencies.

Figure 5.4 a-b   Makerspace With Robotics and 3-D Printer Lab

Source: Ryan Schaaf

It's All About Mindsets, Not Materials or Miracles

Learning is all about the BIG A: Attitude. For students and teachers, classrooms cannot feel like intellectual prisons. Today and tomorrow's learning spaces must become incubators of everything excellent about learning. The starting point in this instructional metamorphosis begins with the teacher! Mindsets are one of the most difficult things to change because people traditionally take the path of least resistance and get stuck in their paradigms as if it were day-old oatmeal.

Educators must start with the attitude and spirit of their learners. The excitement and engagement level of all educators must be raised to 110%. After all, engagement, excitement, and curiosity are contagious. Teachers can spread an infectious hunger for knowledge in their students and create an atmosphere of blissful productivity in their learning spaces.

Know Thy Learner: Cultural Competency

For educators, the starting point for creating modern-day, future-ready learning environments is getting to know the learners. Educators must never assume their learners are a homogeneous group. Today's schools serve diverse communities comprised of individuals from different racial, cultural, ethnic, belief, traditional, and value systems. Educators have a real opportunity to incorporate these differences into instruction and leverage their students' cultural identities. Learners thrive when they have a deep sense of ownership of the learning and feel valued.

Any of the following strategies can be used to promote cultural competencies in these learning spaces:

- Provide all learners with opportunities to participate and share.

- Provide opportunities for learners to make choices and voice their opinions and beliefs.

- Cultivate learning spaces that respect everyone's ideas and promote respectful discourse and debate.

- Encourage students to access their culture, beliefs, and values during learning to demonstrate unity, compassion, and acceptance.

- Enrich the curriculum with culturally significant stories, celebrations, and practices.

- Encourage bilingual students to use their language as they learn the dominant language.

- Compare cultures, beliefs, and values to build bridges, celebrate diversity, and promote unity.

- Contextualize learning experiences to scaffold and help learners construct knowledge.

- Be cognitive of personal biases to overcome them.

The Learning Space: Fabricating a Place of Imagination and Endless Potential

Classrooms can no longer be viewed as standardized, cookie-cutter copies of one another. For learning to be engaging and relevant, both educators and learners must possess the spirit, creativity, passion, and commitment needed to create learning communities and spaces to ignite these attributes. Schools must acknowledge the profound impact physical learning environments have on learners. Classroom design directly impacts student engagement.

Essential Attributes of Modern Learning Environments

Flexibility

Flexible learning spaces enable educators to exchange the "front-of-the-room and chained-to-a-desk," lone teacher approach for a collaborative, dispersed, facilitative style of teaching and learning. "In a flexible, open classroom design, student seating is not fixed, and there are no stationary tables or workspaces. These features afforded the classroom space to be adapted to support different instructional strategies" (Rands & Gansemer-Topf, 2017, p. 29). During COVID-19, social distancing is an important factor to consider. Flexible learning spaces allow the room to be reconfigured, reorganized, and adapted to meet any required guidelines.

In a recent case study, participants reported that the flexibility of the classroom design allows both students and educators to move around the environment, enabling social interaction, collaboration, and active learning (Kariippanon, Cliff, Okely, & Parrish, 2019). Physical spaces are not the only characteristic of flexible learning environments. When people think of a classroom, they usually only visualize a physical space. The pandemic has brought home that there is much more to flexible learning environments than just a floor plan or furniture selection. Modern learning environments also address how students are grouped and how time might be used more flexibly. Flexible learning environments

- promote learner movement and discussion;
- encourage collaborative, problem- and project-based learning;
- redefine the role of the teacher as a facilitator;
- decentralize learning, making it more participatory;
- allow the freedom to modify student groups based on any criterion; and
- promote flexibility in the use of class time (short-blocks vs. long-blocks of time).

A lot of this sounds like a montessori style setting

really great for ADHD/ADD learners & educators

Design Thinking For Human Needs

We must first address Maslow's Hierarchy of Needs (Figure 5.5) before we can consider exploring the Modern Fluencies of Learning. Before schools and educators address academic needs, they must first address the essential physiological necessities. These include such things as food, water, warmth, shelter, and rest; safety needs such as safety and security; a sense of belonging based on personal needs such as relationships and friends; and esteem needs such as having a sense of accomplishment and worth. Only after addressing any of the gaps in needs can a student realize their full potential for learning. Educators must collaborate with parents to ensure they meet all the needs of their students.

In the modern classroom, the hierarchy of needs equates to having students who are comfortable and ready to learn. Jensen suggests 70 degrees Fahrenheit, or 21 degrees Celsius, is an optimal temperature for learning spaces. If a room is too hot or cold, a learner's performance will decrease (Jensen, 2008).

Young minds need their sleep because sleep and rest allow the brain to reboot and recover. According to the American Academy of Sleep Medicine, the following guidelines outline the recommended sleep duration for children from infants to teens. It is also important to note that these guidelines are also supported by the American Academy of Pediatrics (2016).

- Children 3 to 5 years of age should sleep 10 to 13 hours per 24 hours (including naps) regularly to promote optimal health.

Figure 5.5   Maslow's Hierarchy of Needs

- Children 6 to 12 years of age should sleep 9 to 12 hours per 24 hours regularly to promote optimal health.

- Teenagers 13 to 18 years of age should sleep 8 to 10 hours per 24 hours regularly to promote optimal health.

Proper nutrition also promotes a healthy brain in its everyday function and development. The body and mind require water rather than sugary sodas or juices high in carbohydrates (Jensen, 2008).

Learners must also eat foods rich in vitamins and minerals, and avoid junk food rich in unhealthy fats, sugars, and carbohydrates (Benton, 2017).

Screen Time

Largely gone are the times where, after school and on weekends, parents sent their children out to play in the backyard, street, or park. For many kids today, fresh air and physical activity have been replaced by hours spent staring at smartphone and tablet screens. A recent study (Walsh et al., 2018) suggests 63% of American children spend more than 2 hours daily engaged in recreational screen time. Other studies suggest the amount of screen time to be even higher than 2 hours. This is in spite of the recommendations from the American Academy of Pediatrics (2016), which indicate children between the ages of 2 and 5 should spend less than 1 hour per day on a screen. For older children, physical activity, sleep, and other healthy habits should take priority over their media habits. Recently, the World Health Organization (2019) published guidelines, recommending that children between the ages of 2 and 4 have no more than 1 hour of screen time per day.

The challenge is that current research on the effects of screen time on infants, adolescents, and teens is extensive and confusing. At one end of the continuum, there is research suggesting any exposure to screens is physically and mentally harmful. At the other end of the spectrum, there is research that suggests the positive, negative, or benign effects of screen time depend on a range of factors related to age, time of day, and type of activity. These concerns have been further amplified by the COVID-19 pandemic and the increased dependence on screens used in support of distance learning. It is essential that both educators and parents diversify learning opportunities during distance education and ensure that both digital and non-digital experiences are included. Parents are the most important advocates and caregivers for their children. Therefore, we urge all stakeholders to use common sense and professional judgment in striking a balance between real and virtual environments to ensure the mental and physical well-being of all our children.

is it fair to the educators to put the needs not being met outside of school hours on them?

how do we rely on parents to ensure these things are happening?

The impact of screen time on children and adolescents is a discussion that goes well beyond the scope of this chapter. We highly recommend reading *The Health Effects of Screen Time on Children: A Research Roundup* (Reichel, 2019).

Finally, the time of day in which kids view digital screens can impact their sleeping habits. Digital screens found on smartphones, tablets, and televisions delay the circadian rhythm (or internal clock) and restrain the release of melatonin, the hormone responsible for sleep. The blue, artificial light of the screens tricks the brain into thinking it is daytime. It is recommended that people refrain from using a screen right before bedtime (University of Haifa, 2017).

Cultivating Optimal Learning Environments

Natural Light

Educators must avoid covering up windows with too many decorations unless there is a problem with glare or outside distractions. Students who are exposed to more natural light in their classrooms outperform peers who get less natural light (Cheryan, Ziegler, Plaut, & Meltzoff, 2014). If you don't have windows, making sure the room is well lit can boost achievement performance (Barrett, Davies, Zhang, & Barrett, 2015).

Bright Colors

Many schools and institutions are replacing mundane paint schemes and traditional school furniture, with bright orange, red, lime green, or blue accent colors. Secondary schools, to mimic a more mature, higher education-like atmosphere, are showing a proclivity toward gray design elements with bold color highlights.

Rooms with a balance of white or light-colored walls, together with the highlighting of a feature wall or organized bright display colors, have the best correlation with learning progress (Barrett et al., 2015). Some additional research-supported suggestions include student displays of work, graphic organizers, mind maps, role model quotes and visuals, and classroom pictures of experiences or events. On the other hand, educators must find a balance in their use of color and displays. Rodrigues and Pandeirada (2018) found that too much clutter or color can have the opposite effect on students. Learning spaces with too many visual stimuli, or what researchers refer to as *high-load visual environments*, reduce learners' cognitive performance.

I see the detachable furniture a lot in elem. schools now, how do we transition that to highschool?

Collaborative Spaces

A recent Harvard study, in conjunction with Beaver Country Day School, found that 95% of students understand topics better when they are learning in collaborative, project-based spaces (Vander Ark, 2019). With an increased focus on learning experiences that involve student collaboration, schools are adopting classroom configurations that allow groups to sit and shift seating quickly. Look for furniture that can detach and be restructured into different groupings relatively quickly. Alternately, educators can contemplate how to optimize existing furniture configurations to promote collaboration or cooperative learning experiences.

Integrated Technology and Learning Materials

As more and more technology enters classrooms, increasingly furniture is being designed to support its use. Trendy high-tech furniture for learning environments includes computer desks and study pods that come with data ports and built-in electrical outlets. As useful as it would be to have such furniture, it is not always practical, possible, or necessary for schools or educators to acquire such expensive classroom solutions. With more and more schools moving toward MLOs and maker spaces, it is imperative to provide as much capacity and storage for various learning tools and materials as possible. Educators must consider how to properly store and display books, journals, laptops and/or tablets, and building materials ranging from glue, paint, and blank paper, to circuits, Legos, and 3D printers in a safe, practical manner.

In a perfect world, modern-day, real-world learning environments would have an abundance of space, plenty of work surfaces, an unlimited amount of resources and funding, powerful digital tools, and easy-to-use storage. However, we live in the reality of the here and now and must always navigate these challenges.

Know Thy Space

School design tends to be quite diverse. Classrooms come in all shapes and sizes. The advice offered in this text will not fulfill the needs and wants of everyone. Instead, start with a mental exercise by answering the following questions:

- What do you want your students to do in this environment?
- What are some of the critical features you want in this area?
- What pedagogical approaches will you utilize as a learning facilitator?
- How can you design, enable, and support your students to ensure that they are at the center of learning?

The main idea of this task was to create your wish list and work within your ability to make it happen. Learning using the Modern Fluencies will challenge students, student groups, and educators to explore a range of projects and experiences using a variety of learning objects, materials, tools, and resources. The spaces hosting these hands-on, brains-on experiences must be flexible and versatile to meet the varying needs of today's learners.

Summarizing the Main Points

- The most critical components of a modern-day classroom are its student-centric approach with the heart and mindset to solve problems, embrace challenges, and flourish.

- Modern Learning Organizations (MLOs) are flexible learning spaces that are configured to assist learners and educators as they explore the Modern Fluencies.

- Before educators can explore higher-order thinking skills with learners, Maslow's Hierarchy of Needs must be addressed.

- Educators and learners must possess the spirit, creativity, passion, and commitment to create learning communities and spaces that ignite the learning process and cultivate the essential fluencies.

- Learning using the Modern Fluencies will challenge students, student groups, and educators to utilize a wide array of project types, experiences, learning objects and materials, tools, and resources. The spaces hosting these hands-on, brains-on experiences must be versatile to meet the needs of the learner and learning.

Questions to Consider

- What learning space configuration would you like to adapt to or use in your classroom?

- As an educator or educational leader, how can you help your learners flourish in different learning spaces?

- Why is it so important for educators to know the cultural background, values, and beliefs embraced by their students and school or learning institution's community?

- What challenges does your current learning space have? How can you overcome or adjust to these challenges?

An Introduction to the Modern Fluencies

Teaching and Learning Using the Modern Fluencies 6

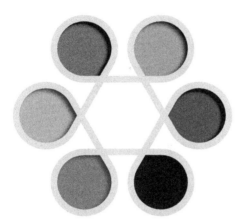

The previous chapters outlined the reasons why we need to teach the Modern Fluencies, the essential skills required by all learners. Disruptive forces are driving a compelling need for substantial change in both what is taught and also how it is taught. The global pandemic has further complicated things; it has caused the world to shift even further away from normal. As a result of all the dramatic changes, no matter what happens from this point forward, we will not be going back to "normal." In these unprecedented times, we are all struggling to balance life.

For these reasons, we believe that there is a growing sense of urgency about the need to foster these essential skills using the Modern Fluencies—skills that learners will find useful now and that will remain just as relevant in the future. This brief chapter describes how to use the fluencies with learners in a wide variety of learning environments, grade levels, and subject areas.

What Are the 6 Modern Fluencies?

The Modern Fluencies include

1. **Solution Fluency**: Real-World Problem Solving—the ability to think creatively to solve problems in real time using the 9Ds process.

2. **Collaboration Fluency**: Global Connections—the ability to collaborate seamlessly in both physical and virtual spaces, with both real and virtual partners, locally and globally.

3. **Information Fluency**: InfoWhelm and HyperInformation— the ability to unconsciously and intuitively access and interpret information in all forms and formats and apply it to solve problems or complete real-world tasks.

4. **Communication Fluency**: Text and Multimedia—the ability to communicate with text and speech in multiple multimedia formats, as well as to communicate visually, through video and imagery, in the absence of text.

5. **Creativity Fluency**: Innovation and Imagination—the ability to generate new and novel solutions to real-world problems.

6. **Global Citizenship**: Citizenship in the Digital Age— becoming a good citizen is a learned process comprising a range of knowledge and skills.

Why There Are Nine Steps to Each Fluency

In almost any instructional design model, there is a sequence of steps. Each fluency has been designed as a structured mental process similar to other structured mental processes such as the scientific method, the writing process, the media production process, architectural design, and design thinking. Chapter 4 explains in detail the theories and research that support the use of a structured process for teaching, learning, and assessment.

The fluencies are designed with clearly identified steps to ensure that students know what the next actions are, even when they're not sure specifically what to do. Each step in each of the fluencies has been deliberately developed to fulfill a particular purpose. Each of the fluencies is comprised of nine steps. While outwardly there are similarities between the steps of each fluency, and, while at first glance, the skills and actions may appear to be the same, creating nine steps was

Figure 6.1   Modern Fluencies and Steps at a Glance

SOLUTION FLUENCY	COLLABORATION FLUENCY	INFORMATION FLUENCY	COMMUNICATION FLUENCY	CREATIVITY FLUENCY	GLOBAL CITIZENSHIP
Define	Explain	Ask	Pose	Illustrate	Global Citizenship does not utilize a learning progression as in the case for the other fluencies. It represents a holistic approach in developing ethical, moral, empathetic, altruistic, and culturally proficient individuals.
Determine	Establish	Audience	Pinpoint	Identify	
Discover	Explore	Access	Prepare	Inquire	
Dream	Envision	Authenticate	Picture	Imagine	
Design	Engineer	Assemble	Plan	Initiate	
Deliver	Execute	Apply	Produce	Implement	
Diagnose	Examine	Assess	Probe	Inspect	
Debrief	Evaluate	Analyze	Ponder	Investigate	
Decide	Extend	Action	Pledge	Inspire	

intentional. We want each fluency to be consistent, having the same look and feel as well as allowing both teachers and learners to gain a sense of consistency for each of the critical skills being introduced. In fact, once the learners become familiar with one learning progression, it helps them learn all the other fluencies because many of the steps and skills overlap and are transferable. We would like to remind teachers that they do not have to teach the fluencies in the same sequence as they appear in the book. In no way is one fluency more important than any other. Rather, they are intended to complement one another. It is important to remember that each fluency is designed to teach a specific essential set of modern skills.

Teachers are free to choose to introduce one, two, or all the fluencies. Teachers may choose to start by teaching Collaboration Fluency if collaboration is the skillset they want to cultivate in their students. Other teachers may want to develop problem solving skills in their students and will use Solution Fluency to teach that skillset. The fluencies promote just-in-time learning, as opposed to just-in-case learning. While the nine steps of each of the fluencies may appear to overlap, they have a different focus depending on the fluency and/or skill being developed. For example, the first step in each fluency requires learners to outline their understanding of what they are being asked to accomplish to complete assigned tasks. To ensure that they are in alignment with the expectations of the teacher, students must produce a written statement that is then used as a checklist. It has been our personal experience and from conversations with many educators that students have been

What would you define the diff. btwn just-in-case vs. just-in-time learning to be?

known to regularly submit work that did not fulfill requirements simply because we did not pause long enough to consider their level of understanding before proceeding to complete a task. While the first step in all the fluencies may seem the same at first glance, a closer look reveals that the focus is completely different, honing in on the specific skills targeted in each fluency.

Another consistent step in each fluency is reflection. Once again each fluency requires students to focus on the specific skills that particular fluency is designed to teach. For example, the reflection for Information Fluency looks at how well students developed the skills of formulating and asking good questions. Whereas collaboration fluency requires learners to reflect on skills and strategies they used both individually and collectively to complete tasks and demonstrate responsibility.

Learners and educators are encouraged to adapt or modify any of the fluencies to best meet the needs, abilities, and skill levels of their learners. We believe that as both teachers and learners become familiar with the fluencies they could choose to reduce, compress, or combine the steps. They may also choose to change the order of the steps.

In Chapters 7–12, you will be introduced to each of the six fluencies. The steps in the respective fluencies will provide you with strategies on how to teach the targeted modern skill.

Solution Fluency: Real-World Problem Solving 7

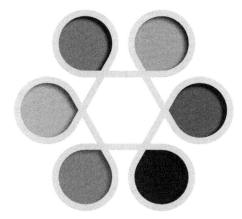

"The best education does not happen at a desk, but rather engaged in everyday living—hands-on, exploring, in active relationship with life."

—Vince Gowmon

The new digital age is upon us, heralding a relentlessly changing future. The children of today will be the builders of tomorrow. If they are to survive and thrive in the modern world, they both need and deserve a skillset that emphasizes critical thinking and develops a mindset for discovering and developing innovative solutions to complex problems.

Learning effective thinking strategies for solving problems equips learners with a robust set of tools for our modern, ever changing world. People with these skills will be sought after because there is a growing demand for problem solvers in the world today. We strongly believe in a *problems-first approach*. Problems come before learning. It is typically problems that spark the motivation to go out and learn something.

Students encounter problems w/o the answer outside of school, we need to teach like that >

Learning effective thinking strategies for solving problems equips learners with a robust set of tools for our modern, ever changing world.

Con to project-based learning: lack of real world connection

We often encounter real-world problems before we know how to solve them. Since this generally is the case in the world outside school, we must adopt the same approach inside school. If we want learners to be independent when they leave school, we must provide them with problems to solve, before they know how to solve them. It is also important to encourage them to find their own problems to solve.

The key to engaging learners is to create problems that lead learners to the material in the curriculum. Educators must become crafters rather than solvers of problems. The problems-first approach encourages independent and collaborative learning. Giving learners problems to solve will lead them to ask questions. Asking questions cultivates interest in the topic. To find answers and solve problems, learners will need to research and discover information.

The ultimate goal of this approach is to help learners become independent thinkers and problem solvers. Problems create a context that provides relevance to learning the content in the curriculum. This approach differs from project-based learning, which requires learners to complete a project to show what they have learned after a unit of study. Although project-based learning is a possible approach to teaching, learning, and assessment, it may lack a real-world connection.

Problem-based learning is different because its goal is to use a problems-first approach and connect the learning to the real world by having learners address authentic problems. This approach includes a problem, essential question(s), and challenges that are at the heart of an authentically crafted real-world scenario.

Problem-based learning provides learners with the opportunity to learn the required content while simultaneously developing essential next-generation skills through inquiry and investigation. Learners are required to conduct research, find relevant information to formulate answers, and improve their conclusions. Problem-based learning also provides learners with the chance to give and receive feedback and share their learning with peers or audiences via presentations, authentic artifacts, as well as the opportunity to work both independently and collaboratively.

This chapter outlines the 9Ds process for real-world problem solving—*Define, Determine, Discover, Dream, Design, Deliver, Diagnose, Debrief,* and *Decide*—and demonstrates how today's "just-in-time" learners can utilize whole-brain thinking to discover and create practical solutions to problems and apply them to the challenges of modern life, business, and education.

Figure 7.1   Solution Fluency: The 9Ds

SOLUTION FLUENCY
Define
Determine
Discover
Dream
Design
Deliver
Diagnose
Debrief
Decide

The 9Ds approach (see Figure 7.1) is about learners becoming analytical thinkers who can compare, contrast, evaluate, synthesize, and apply their analyses to answer difficult questions and solve problems independently in real time without instruction or supervision.

Learners will learn clear steps that can be explained, learned, practiced, applied, internalized, and most important, over time, improved. Learners are active participants at each stage of the learning process where the emphasis is not on the solution, but rather on the learning process that leads to the solution or product.

Step 1: Define

At the *Define* stage, learners first describe and then communicate in their own words the problem, task, or challenge they face. To *Define* the problem is to have the learner provide a written description of their understanding of the problem, and outline what they must accomplish. This step is completed before learners begin to solve the problem.

Learners create a written statement that outlines their understanding of the challenge they face (with younger learners, educators can be the scribe). It sounds obvious, but often learners don't *Define* a problem or at least neglect to *Define* the problem completely.

Define becomes the first checkpoint. It allows educators to provide formative feedback to learners. The written statement becomes the criteria against which learners are assessed and rubrics developed. This written statement can also serve as a contract between learners and educators, as well as used as a checklist for both learners and educators to track their progress. Learners must be made aware that they will be assessed against these criteria during the *Diagnose* step.

The skills and actions in the *Define* phase include restating or rephrasing the problem, the challenges, or tasks in the learners' own words; challenging assumptions; formulating questions, chunking the details (pulling details together or breaking them down into smaller parts); and considering the challenge from multiple perspectives.

Step 2: Determine

Defining the problem prepares learners to *Determine* who the target audiences are. The audiences could include both individuals and organizations. Who needs to know about the problem? Who is experiencing the issue? Who is directly affected by the problem? Who can help solve the problem? Who are the influencers with the ability to help develop a plan that will succeed? What are the desired actions or outcomes for the audience?

The *Determine* step provides a checkpoint for learners to verify the performance criteria outlined in the *Define* step. It also ensures that the appropriate audiences are identified.

Determine skills and actions include identifying the authentic audiences; understanding the cultural, historical, and economic mindsets and backgrounds of the selected audiences; anticipating attitudes and biases of the audiences (What do they think about the topic? What motivates their interest?); connecting with audience members; identifying the purpose of the plan to solve the problem; choosing the goals or preferred outcomes of the presentation (inform, persuade, inspire, entertain); and selecting the appropriate format to deliver the presentation to different audiences (proposal, published content on blogs, wikis, discussion threads, videos, podcasts, etc.).

Step 3: Discover

Discover is the exploration and research phase, during which learners gather information and resources to utilize when solving problems, completing challenges, or accomplishing tasks. Learners are encouraged to ask the following questions: How did we get to this point? What past decisions, actions, events, problems, or challenges brought us here? How have others approached these issues? What strategies could have produced different results? What were some of the successes, failures, or challenges experienced?

The primary purpose of asking these questions is to provide a full context that will help learners better understand the problem, challenge, or task presented. At the *Discover* stage, learners move beyond the *Define* statement to develop a deeper understanding of the issues behind the questions, foster emotional connections, and inspire a passion for creating a solution. *Discover* provides another checkpoint for learners and educators to review before they progress to the *Dream* step.

Skills and actions utilized in the *Discover* step include: tapping into personal knowledge; determining where the sources of reliable information are, skimming, scanning, and scouring that information; filtering relevant information from the inconsequential; note-taking and note-making; journaling, analyzing, authenticating, and organizing materials. Based on what is discovered, and with the understanding that the Solution Fluency process is a flexible, not linear, learners may need to revisit and refine the *Define* statement throughout the process.

Step 4: Dream

At the *Dream* step, learners brainstorm, imagine, and visualize possible solutions for the problem or challenge. *Dream* is a visioning process in which learners not only imagine what is possible but also remain open to what may initially seem impossible. *Dream* is a whole-mind process that allows learners to imagine solutions as they might exist in the future. Learners are encouraged to consider all the possibilities.

It is through extensive visioning that creativity occurs. However, feasibility (time, money, resources, and skills) is a critical factor to consider when identifying possible solutions. With a clear understanding of where learners are (*Define*), who the audiences are (*Determine*), and how they got there (*Discover*), learners are equipped with everything they need to look to the future and *Dream* possible solutions. At this checkpoint, learners must identify their solution before progressing to the *Design* step.

Skills and actions taken during the *Dream* phase include brainstorming, mind-mapping, doodling, daydreaming, whole-group and small group discussions, formulating mental images, performing additional research into potential solutions, lateral thinking, questioning, reframing, thinking in metaphors, pictures, and sounds, decision making, image streaming, and imagining best-case scenarios. Based on *Dream*, and the understanding that Solution Fluency is a flexible process, learners may need to revisit the previous steps before proceeding.

Step 5: Design

At the *Design* step, learners create a written detailed checklist that identifies the steps to solving the problem or challenge, determining roles, and distributing tasks among team members. This step-by-step plan lays out the process learners will utilize to develop the selected solution and, in doing so, transform their *Dream* into reality.

To recap, *Define* tells us where we are now, *Determine* identifies the audiences, *Discover* helps learners understand the background of the problem, *Dream* helps them decide where they want to go, and *Design* is the written checklist that helps learners cross the gap from the problem to a solution. There is much truth in the saying, "A carelessly planned project will take three times longer than the time allotted, but a carefully planned project will only take twice as long" (Kerzner, 2009, p. 247). Learners create their plan to guide them as they work. This plan is a roadmap or strategy that can be checked, discussed, and reevaluated, while at the same time keeping learners on track and helping them avoid wasted effort. It is a process that involves not only logic but also imagination. The steps help answer the question, "What do I do next?"

At the *Design* step, learners build backward from the future to the present, identifying milestones, and creating achievable deadlines for completing the steps of the project.

Skills and actions used in the *Design* phase include being able to take on a role as a leader or follower, goal setting, planning, communications, collaboration, self-management, time management, prototyping, decision making, and writing instructions in small, easy to follow increments that are positive and logical. Based on the understanding that the Solution Fluency process is flexible, not linear, learners may need to revisit and refine the *Define, Determine, Discover*, and *Dream* steps.

Step 6: Deliver

At the *Deliver* step, learners develop and share their solutions to an audience. There are two components to *Deliver*: *Produce* and *Publish*. In modern learning environments, learners create a real-world solution to the problem. The product can be almost anything: perform a play, record a podcast, create a poster, build a sculpture, produce a video, complete an experiment, publish a website, or make a multimedia presentation. The possibilities are endless. This is the *Produce* stage of *Deliver*.

However, *Produce* is only half the task. Learners still have to *Publish* their solutions. Designing a presentation isn't enough; the solutions must be presented. Writing a song isn't enough; it has to be recorded. Developing a script isn't enough; the work has to be performed.

There is an important reason why learners must *Deliver* the goods. Implementing a solution provides learners with the opportunity to pressure test the product. Seeing the product delivered creates a platform for thoughtful feedback. In the same way that scientists first generate a hypothesis and then conduct an experiment, learners must first design and execute their plan and then observe the results. Otherwise, it only remains an untested hypothesis.

Deliver skills and actions include both those related to producing a solution, as well as those needed to publish the solution. These skills include production (both media and multimedia), design (new inventions or innovations), literacy (speaking, listening, reading, writing, visual), and identifying and using the most appropriate format and medium for presenting the information. Based on the *Deliver* step, and understanding that Solution Fluency is a flexible process, learners are encouraged to revisit and refine their *Define, Determine, Discover, Dream*, and *Design* steps.

Step 7: Diagnose

Diagnose is about assessment and evaluation. It is crucial during this step to assess both the process and the product. Multiple methods of assessment should be utilized to engage learners in their personal growth; to monitor individual, peer, and class progress; and to guide both learners and educators in their decision making. These assessments could be summative, formative, formal, informal, written, verbal, recorded, or any combination of different approaches. Evaluations should also involve various assessors, including educators, learners (self), peers, parents, groups, and community members.

The purpose of assessment is to inform teaching and learning facilitated through authentic assessment. An authentic assessment is individualized and provides multiple ways to evaluate learners. By using a variety of methods, educators can assess content as well as process skills such as problem solving, collaboration, communications, citizenship, and creativity applied within real-world contexts.

A practical method of authentic assessment is the use of rubrics as an evaluation tool. Rubrics utilize specific criteria as the basis for evaluating and assessing learner performance. The written statement created during the *Define* step is used as the criteria against which learners are assessed when rubrics are developed. The elements of a rubric include

elements of a rubric:

- a description of the task being evaluated,

- the criteria being evaluated,

- a rating scale that demonstrates different levels of performance, and

- a description of each level of performance for each criterion. (Brookhart, 2013)

Developing assessment rubrics helps determine whether the criteria were met. During the *Diagnose* step, assessors must provide both feedback and feedforward (reactions to a product or person's performance used as a basis for improvement). The constructive feedback and feedforward must be both critical and productive, without being hurtful or biased. By cultivating the necessary academic language associated with assessment, learners can provide constructive feedforward to their peers for future projects, problems, tasks, or challenges. During this step, both educators and learners must revisit the criteria developed and agreed on during the *Define* step. This strategy ensures that expectations are aligned, which provides learners with a roadmap to success.

Diagnose skills and actions include active listening, reporting, rubric development, observation, growth mindset, metacognitive thinking, learning the language of constructive feedback and feedforward, listening, communications, conflict negotiation, lateral thinking, assessment, questioning, risk-taking, open-mindedness, leadership, time management, and collaboration skills.

Step 8: Debrief

In the real world, responsibility for work continues long after the creation of an initial product or solution. However, in education, educators traditionally have done most of the evaluation, which sends a strong message to learners that their work is a linear process that begins with an assignment and ends when learners submit their tasks.

At that point, their work is complete and everything now is the responsibility of the educator. However, the *Debrief* step of Solution Fluency helps cultivate personal ownership and responsibility for learning by asking learners to revisit each of the seven previous steps, reflect on their performance, and *Debrief* on both the process and product.

Debrief involves analyzing how both the process and outcome could be enhanced. If time permits, learners may make adjustments to improve their projects. An understanding of how to improve the product and the process in the future helps learners become better problem solv-ers. The *Debrief* step should also include a group discussion that revis-its the initial assumptions, providing educators and learners with the opportunity to see measurable learning progress and justifies the value of time invested.

Debrief questions to help learners reflect include Was the goal always clear? Were the instructions always clear? What was supposed to hap-pen? What did happen? What went well, and why? What didn't go well, and why? What could have been done differently? Why was there a difference between what was expected to happen and what did happen? What constraints or barriers were faced? How were those barriers over-come? Was there enough time to accomplish all the tasks to make this process a success? Could another approach have been used to reach the goals more efficiently and effectively within the given time frame? Were the criteria for the process and product transparent, understandable, and measurable?

Debrief skills are metacognitive skills involving complex thinking. They include speaking, listening, reevaluating, introspection, self-reflection, critical thinking, practicing wait time, managing impulsivity, question-ing skills, reflective journal writing, and idea incubation. These skills involve revisiting each step of the process and reflecting critically on the pathways followed to get from *Define* to *Deliver*, as well as ask-ing questions about the process being used, acting on those reflections, and internalizing the new learning. These skills help learners relate new learning to existing knowledge, develop strategies for applying new knowledge to complex situations, and transfer this learning to different, similar, or novel settings.

Step 9: Decide

The final step is *Decide*, which involves acting on the reflections of the *Debrief* step. Learners internalize their new knowledge and transfer that learning to new and different situations to determine what future actions might be taken. While taking action may not happen all the time, the opportunity to apply their products or solutions in real-world contexts must be promoted. The action can be big or small, local or global, altruistic or pragmatic, individual or collaborative. The *Decide* step provides learners with an opportunity to make a difference by posi-tively contributing to society and developing good citizenship qualities.

Decide skills and actions include inter and intra-personal skills such as volunteerism, community service, service-learning, role modeling, social activism, ethical behavior, decision making, responsibility, empathy, personal growth, honesty, and integrity.

When using solution fluency, educators must realize the shift in their role. The primary role of the educator is to facilitate learning. The learners are the owners of the learning because they are the problem solvers.

SOLUTION FLUENCY EXEMPLAR: *CRACKED UP*

Title: Cracked Up

Grade: 4

Subject 1: Science

Subject 2: Language Arts

Subject 3: Mathematics

Time: 4–6 hours, plus time for the mail to arrive

Standards

Science

McREL Science—Standard 11.—Level II—2. Knows that good scientific explanations are based on evidence (observations) and scientific knowledge.

McREL Science—Standard 11.—Level II—3. Knows that scientists make the results of their investigations public; they describe these investigations in ways that enable others to repeat the process.

McREL Science—Standard 11.—Level II—5. Understands that models (e.g., physical, conceptual, mathematical models, computer simulations) can be used to represent and predict changes in objects, events, and processes.

McREL Science—Standard 12.—Level II—3. Plans and conducts simple investigations (e.g., formulates a testable question, plans a fair test, makes systematic observations, develops logical conclusions).

McREL Science—Standard 12.—Level II—6. Knows the reasons why similar investigations may not produce similar results (e.g., differences in the things being investigated, methods being used, uncertainty in the observation).

English/Language Arts

CC W.4.2. Write informative/explanatory texts to examine a topic and convey ideas and information clearly.

a) Introduce a topic clearly, and group related information in para-graphs and sections; include formatting (e.g., headings), illustra-tions, and multimedia when useful to aiding comprehension.

b) Develop the topic with facts, definitions, concrete details, quota-tions, or other information and examples related to the subject.

c) Link ideas within categories of information using words and phrases (e.g., another, for example, also, because).

d) Use precise language and domain-specific vocabulary to inform about or explain the topic.

e) Provide a concluding statement or section related to the informa-tion or explanation presented.

CC W.4.7. Conduct short research projects that build knowledge through investigation of different aspects of a topic.

CC W.4.8. Recall relevant information from experiences or gather relevant information from print and digital sources; take notes and categorize information, and provide a list of sources.

Mathematics

CC MD.4.3. Apply the area and perimeter formulas for rectangles in real-world and mathematical problems.

CC 4.NF.4. Apply and extend previous understandings of multiplica-tion to multiply a fraction by a whole number.

CC 4.NF.4b. Understand a multiple of a/b as a multiple of 1/b, and use this understanding to multiply a fraction by a whole number. For example, use a visual fraction model to express $3 \times (2/5)$ as $6 \times (1/5)$, recognizing this product as 6/5. (In general, $n \times (a/b) = (n \times a)/b$.)

CC 4.MD.1. Know relative sizes of measurement units within one sys-tem of units including km, m, cm; kg, g; lb., oz.; l, ml; hr., min., sec. Within a single system of measurement, express measurements in a larger unit in terms of a smaller unit. Record measurement equiva-lents in a two-column table.

Scenario

Everyone loves getting mail. There's something special about getting a package addressed to you and opening it to find out the contents. Between you and whoever sent the package is a complex series of events and machines that brought your package to a sorting facility, transported your package (carefully) to your hometown, sorted the package to the appropriate mail carrier, and delivered the package to a place where you could finally have it in your hands. The package could have traveled in a truck, a train, a plane, or a mail carrier's bag.

It takes careful packing sometimes to make sure that the package arrives without breaking the contents inside. Every year, gifts are sent through the mail in celebration of holidays such as Easter, Diwali, Chanukah, and Christmas. The care and consideration in selecting the perfect gift would result in disappointment if that gift arrived in pieces. Each ounce of extra weight costs money, so the packaging has to be as light as possible. Too much bubble wrap, Styrofoam, or other fancy packaging can also be a frustration for the receiver trying to get to the actual item. The use of these bulky packing materials is also damaging to the environment because many are made from oil, a nonrenewable resource, and are not recyclable. Customs regulations also require that the package be easy to open for random checks. How can you make a package that will protect a fragile object, be inexpensive to ship, easy to open, and use recyclable, compostable, or reusable materials? While working in groups, your challenge will be to first research the stages of your local mail delivery system and the costs associated with shipping packages. You will then create and test four different types of containers that might be used to ship a very delicate item such as a chocolate Kinder Egg. You will need to create a test that will simulate the actual shipping process as closely as possible and test each model so that the lightest and most secure model is chosen. Once you have decided on the lightest and most secure package design, you will use the model to create the actual shipping container. The class set of containers will be shipped from the same mailbox to the school. Inside, a very precious cargo: a Kinder Egg.

Once the package arrives at the school, inspect the egg inside for damage. You will present the results of your study in the form of an informational brochure, which will be used by those attempting to ship small, breakable items through the mail. As a final celebration of your efforts, prepare an informational table with your design ideas, the prototypes, results, final model, and the brochure. Best of luck, and get cracking!

Essential Question

How can we use experiments on models to create the lightest and most secure container to transport very breakable goods through the mail?

Technology Level

High-Tech: Create an informational brochure using presentation software showing how fragile goods need to be shipped.

Low-Tech: Produce a written report showing how fragile goods need to be shipped.

No-Tech: Conduct a classroom expert panel discussion on the results showing how fragile products need to be sent.

Define

Following careful research on the postal system in their area and the dimensions of shipping containers, students will work in small groups to create four models for containers that could be used to ship a hollow, chocolate egg without damaging it.

They will simulate parts of the shipping process to test the models, compare the damage and weight, and decide on the best model to use for shipment. The model will be used to create the actual shipping container containing the egg. The packages must be placed in the mailbox. While waiting for the delivery, the group will create an informational brochure on the mail delivery process and guidelines for shipping containers. Once the package arrives at the school, the group will judge the success of their design and add the result to their brochure. The brochure, prototype, drawings, results, and final model will be presented in a trade show type format as a celebration of their learning.

Student Written Definition

a) Research the stages of mail delivery in their area and costs to ship various containers.
b) Design and test four models of shipping containers.
c) Rank the four containers according to the three criteria: weight, durability, and ease of opening.
d) Use the best design to create an actual shipping container and mail the egg.
e) Assess the final result following delivery.
f) Create an informational brochure discussing the best way to ship small, delicate items.

Discover

The first step in this challenge is to research the route the package will be taking. Where will its journey begin? What are the steps in the mail delivery journey? What's the total distance it will have to travel (don't forget to add in the distance to the sorting center from the mailbox)? What happens at the sorting center? What are the major stresses on the package? Will it be jostled, squished, dropped, or handled? Is there a way to talk to someone with inside information?

Some of the answers to these questions can be found online, others you will have to use more inventive methods. How can we get answers to these questions? Could we take these prepared questions to a local post office to find out the answers? Perhaps we could call the local post office for advice? Is there a *contact us* link on the website? Could we invite a postal worker to visit our classroom to talk about the process? When you design your package, size will be important. How big is the Kinder Egg? How much does it weigh? What is the weight of the foil and exterior chocolate? What is the weight of the plastic container and its contents? How big is the plastic container? What are the permissible package sizes? What restrictions does the postal system have for the package? How much does each type of package cost to ship?

What materials are available to you that are either recyclable or compostable? Can you bring them into class to use for the prototype or the actual model? How much do these materials cost? Students will then sketch out at least three ideas for package designs. How could you wrap, suspend, cushion, and otherwise protect your egg? Are there real-life examples that could be used for inspiration such as parachutes, egg cartons, or boxes used to ship appliances? In their groups, they will explain how each design works to protect the egg. As a group, they select the four designs that they will be using for their prototype. They create a scaled-down diagram showing the top, front, and side view of the package using a standard sheet of graph paper. What scale should you use so that you can show all three views on one sheet of graph paper? What is the size of the egg scaled down? What would be the weight of the egg at this size? How does using a scaled-down model help to conserve resources and time?

Students will construct their prototypes using the scaled-down drawings as a guide. They will also create scaled-down models of the Kinder Egg that are appropriate in size and weight using aluminum foil for the chocolate layer and foil wrapped around a heavier item such as a marble for the inner plastic container. Store the egg models in egg cartons to preserve their shape until they are ready to go into the package. Students need to determine how they will simulate the stresses placed on the packages during transit. What tests will you need to conduct on your model? How will you simulate travel by truck? How will you simulate travel in a mail carrier bag? How will you simulate travel through the sorting facility? How will you make sure each model undergoes the same procedure in the same way?

Determine

Determine the target audience. Who is experiencing the problem? Who is directly affected by the problem? Who can help solve the problem? Who needs to know about the problem? Who can make the project succeed or fail? What is the desired action of the audience? The audiences are

- Local Community
- Postal services/ Post Office
- Recycling Plant Operation-Local Council

Dream

Students fill out the cells on the chart with the cost of the package and rank the packages from one to four with four being the best option (the cheapest in this case) and one being the worst option (the most expensive). They are required to fill out their charts individually at first then compare rankings and create a group chart. Individually, they must decide on a ranking for the environmental cost of the packages and rank the packages from one to four with four being the best option and one being the worst.

How can you determine the environmental cost of the package? Which is better for the environment: using recyclable materials or using compostable materials? What if the materials are reusable? How will you factor in the cost of tape or the environmental cost of the weight? IKEA, the furniture store, claims that in the interest of the environment they only ship items in rectangular boxes. How does the shape of the container have any bearing on the environmental cost?

Students will then conduct their experiment on the sturdiness of the container and how successful each model is at keeping the cargo undamaged. How can you quantify the damage to the aluminum foil egg? How can you make sure that each model is tested fairly? In the ranking system used, which model would get a ranking of four (the best) and which would get a ranking of one (the worst) for *resistance to damage*. How would you rank the packages for ease of opening?

Compare your chart to those of your group members. Are the rankings identical? How will you resolve any differences fairly? Create a group chart that includes any quantitative (number-based) data and the rankings your group decided on. Include any features of the packages that aren't in the chart, but might be nice to know (e.g., having a package that sings when you open it doesn't technically fit under any of the headings, but might be included in a final decision). Decide on the model that you will be making for the actual shipment of the Kinder Egg.

Now it's time to go back to the scale drawings for the model and use the scale to make the shipping container accurately. How do we use multiplication to make a larger version of the model? What happens when the measurement of the scaled-down drawing includes fractions like 1/4 of an inch? How can you double check your calculations? What tools will you need to make it as accurate as possible? What shapes make up your package? What nonstructural design elements could you include to make your package interesting? Where does the address go? What are the requirements for addressing the package? What pictures could you take for the final presentation?

Students will complete the package, insert the egg, seal the package, add the address of the school and a return address (the address of one of the group members), and mail the package.

Design

While they await the delivery of the packages, the students complete a rough draft of the brochure. Have them explore sample brochures, both online and hard copies. What are the common elements of brochures? Which brochures are more interesting than others? How much information is on a brochure? How is this information organized? How long are paragraphs in the brochure?

Open the brochure out flat and look at the layout. When it's flat, where is the front of the brochure? Where is the back of the brochure? Where is most of the information located?

Individually at first, students create a rough copy of their brochure. Include all the following: title, images, sources of information, contact information for the local post office, guidelines and size categories for packages, their design for a secure package, and directions for mailing packages safely.

After sufficient time for initial design, students present their ideas for the brochure. The group must use elements of all four brochures in their final product. How will you decide fairly which parts of each brochure to use?

Deliver—Produce

Students will work together to make their brochure using presentation software. How do the layout tools work? How do you scale the images up or down? What fonts are available? Will you use the same font throughout, or change it to highlight key points? Which images will you use? How can you add a border to the images? How do you change the background color? How much space will you leave for the results of the test on the package? Students will print out a copy of their brochure in draft form and edit it for spelling, layout, and grammar. Once the package arrives, they will photograph the outside of the package then open it and photograph the egg. They will then include the results of the test of the package in the brochure. Using photo-editing software, they will add text to any pictures that they will be using in their table display. They will print out pictures that they intend to use with the models, the actual package, the egg, and the brochure.

Deliver—Publish

Students will set up a table with copies of their brochure, their models, their data chart, and the final package with the egg. How will you compel people to visit your table to learn more? How could you use signage to explain how successful you were? Allow time for groups to visit the display of other groups.

Which package designs were similar? What are the common elements? Did all the packages arrive on the same day? Did the similar packages all get the same results? Why were the results different even though the procedure was the same? What other changes might you make?

Diagnose

Assess and evaluate both the process and product and check whether the objectives described in the *Define* stage were attained. There will be summative, formative, formal, informal, self-, peer, group, and teacher assessment rubrics used to assess both product and process. For ideas on creating and using rubrics for assessing units, refer to Chapter 14.

Debrief

Begin by discussing the task. What were the main hazards in the mail delivery process? How did your testing method attempt to simulate these hazards? How close was the testing to what would happen? How did you make the testing fair or impartial? How did you get quantitative data? How did you come to your final decision? How did design elements like weight, access to the contents, and shape affect the decision? What would you have done differently? As part of the next step, you needed to take the fractional measurements in the scale model and multiply them to make the actual package measurements. What steps did you need to take to multiply a fraction by a whole number? What common mistakes did you have to watch out for? How did you make sure the final parts were the correct size? How did other parts of your package like tape, glue, or string affect the accuracy of the final measurement? How successful was the package you designed? What damage did it sustain? How could you quantify the damage? How did the damage compare to the damage suffered during the prototype testing? How could you change your design if you made another package? What components of the other groups' models would you like to incorporate? What did you learn about the design process?

Decide

Decide involves taking action on the reflections of the *Debrief* stage, internalizing the new learnings, and transferring that knowledge to new and different circumstances to decide what your next actions will be. It's also about applying what has been learned in the real world. This is something that doesn't necessarily happen all the time, but does need to happen occasionally.

Decide is about: What action are we going to take? What are we going to do with our new learning? We are armed with new knowledge, we are aware. So what? Now what? Local or Global?

Figure 7.2 shares a template for the 9Ds process developed by Avalon Public School in Australia. In Figure 7.3, we share an authentic example from Avalon.

Figure 7.2   Solution Fluency Template

Solution Fluency: Real-World Problem Solving

Title:
Grade:
Duration:

Subject/s:
Outcomes:

The Challenge:

Essential Question:
Technology:

DEFINE: What is the problem we face?

Type your text here

Evidence of Learning:

Type your text here

DISCOVER: What's causing the problem, and why and how do we solve it?

Type your text here

Evidence of Learning:

Type your text here

DETERMINE: Who is experiencing the problem, and who will help us solve the problem?

Type your text here

Evidence of Learning:

Type your text here

Dream: What are the possible solutions to the problem?

Type your text here

Evidence of Learning:

Type your text here

DESIGN: How will we create our solution?

Type your text here

Evidence of Learning:

Type your text here

DELIVER: How will we implement our solution?

Type your text here

Evidence of Learning:

Type your text here

DIAGNOSE: How will the learning be assessed?

Type your text here

Evidence of Learning:

Type your text here

DEBRIEF: What are our reflections on both the product and the process?

Type your text here

Evidence of Learning:

Type your text here

DECIDE: What action or actions are we going to take as a result of our learning?

Type your text here

Evidence of Learning:

Type your text here

Courtesy of Avalon Public School & Ashlea Simonetti

Figure 7.3   Sample Solution Fluency Project

The Game Changer: Problem Solving Project

Title: The Game Changer

Grade: 5
Duration: 10 Weeks

Subject/s: History

Geography—mapping; Maths—position, timelines, 2D space, 3D space; Creative Arts—visual art; English—writing.

Outcomes: HT3-1: describes and explains the significance of people, groups, places and events to the development of Australia
HT3-2: describes and explains different experiences of people living in Australia over time
HT3-5: applies a variety of skills of historical inquiry and communication

The Scenario:

As we learned in Year 4, the British Empire expanded to Sydney Cove in 1788 with the arrival of the First Fleet. Over time the colony needed to expand due to a lack of resources (food, fresh water, land for farming, etc.). Many people were involved in contributing to this growth, and through their discoveries, impact and change occurred.

However, there is a lack of creative and engaging resources in our school library to learn about these significant events and people that shaped our history. Avalon School library has asked for our assistance to design board games to help our students learn about the significant people and events that shaped Australian history between 1800 and 1850.

In groups of four, choose a significant person or event from Australian history and design a board game that informs your peers. Once you design your game you will play it with your group to test its effectiveness using the "The Game Changer" Deliver Rubric. Make any necessary adjustments to finalize your game, prior to playing it with your class and other grade members. The best games will be chosen across the grade to be used in our library as a resource to teach others.

Essential Question: What were the significant events and who were the significant people that shaped Australian colonies between 1800 and 1850?

Technology:

Low Tech: Use technology to research and create written material for the board game.

No Tech: Create board game with hands-on materials.

Courtesy of Avalon Public School & Ashlea Simonetti

DEFINE: What is the problem we face?

In this lesson, student groups will research significant events and people that shaped Australian history between 1800 and 1850. Using this information, students will create a classically modeled board game. The play of this board game must explore the issues, themes, and experiences of their assigned events and people. This board game will be played by other groups in the class and grade. Students will identify why these people and events are significant. Student groups have been assigned and given the lesson challenges. They are required to submit a written definition of the challenges before proceeding. As a class, decide on a class definition with all expectations included.

Evidence of Learning:

Students' written definition of the task.

A class definition for students to refer to throughout the project.

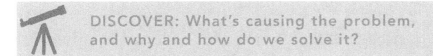

DISCOVER: What's causing the problem, and why and how do we solve it?

Teacher introduces Discover Checklist and Deliver Rubric to the students, with the understanding that their peers will use this to give their friends feedback.

To better understand the time period we will be focusing on, review some of the key events in Australian history that occurred prior to 1800. Students can play The Voyage Game to revise convict journeys to NSW (http://www.anmm.gov.au/learn/voyage-game), view a BTN segment on the First Fleet (http://viewpure.com/MnUNEkMsjfY?start=0&end=0), and read books from our library.

ASK

In small groups, students begin to research their assigned topic. They will need to specifically look at the impact that event or person had on shaping Australia as a colony

Ask students to Q Storm: What is significant? What led to this event? What caused people involved to continually pursue their cause? What obstacles arose? What impact did this event have on the colony? Students must also research classic board games. They must analyze these games to understand how larger concepts are presented in an entertaining and educational way. For example, how does Monopoly explain the financial system of real estate? How do some of the challenges in the game relate to the real-life situation it is teaching?

As a class, create a list of the elements that make a good board game. Students record their information using the questions above.

Courtesy of Avalon Public School & Ashlea Simonetti

Evidence of Learning:

ACCESS & AUTHENTICATE

Students have completed research on their assigned topic using the research scaffold provided. Based on the information gathered by the students through their research, they now possess a basic understanding of the significant person or event. They also have researched classic board games and understand how board games effectively present larger concepts in an entertaining and creative way. This is recorded on a class chart for students to reference.

Students fill out a Discover Checklist to ensure all elements are completed.

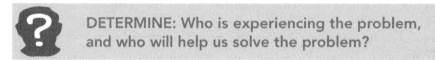

DETERMINE: Who is experiencing the problem, and who will help us solve the problem?

AUDIENCE

The target audience is their peers and future students. The best board games will be stored in the school library to be played by other students.

DREAM: What are the possible solutions to the problem?

Students have a discussion to create a board game that effectively matches the driving factors of their topic.

Using the questions on the research scaffold, how can you creatively incorporate this information into a board game?

What were the main issues of this significant event? Why was it significant? What factors caused this event to occur? When and where did the event take place? Who was involved? What was the immediate outcome of the event? What were the long-term outcomes of the event? Which classic board game resembles the issues of this event? How will we represent the obstacles that this person or event faced? How should game play be structured to enhance the understanding of the event? Students must also begin discussing how they will teach this game to the class (i.e., set of game rules), how many people can play the game, and how engaging will it be.

Evidence of Learning:

Students have explored the options for how they will create the classically modeled board game. They have identified the main issues of the topic, the factors that caused the person or event to sustain itself, and the ways in which they will represent the obstacles of their person or event. They have also discussed how the game should be played. Finally, students have discussed the best way in which to teach their fellow classmates this game.

Courtesy of Avalon Public School & Ashlea Simonetti

DESIGN: How will we create our solution?

ASSEMBLE

Students now begin the creation of their classically modelled board game. During this part of the process, students will finalize the board game they will use to model their new game after. They will identify the ideas, events, and impact of the person or event that will drive their game. They must also outline the rules for game play. Students will assign roles to each group member (board design, game board construction, writer of rules, and game piece construction, etc.). Students also are required to gather all technology for the creation of their board game. They must assign roles to each group member for the presentation of the game (who will introduce the game, who will explain game play, who will demonstrate the game, etc.).

Evidence of Learning:

Students have created an effective outline for their classically modelled board game. They designed game play that will effectively inform the players about the impact of the significant person or event. Students have also gathered all resources required to complete the creation of this board game. After playing the game within their group, students make modifications on The Game Changer Design Checklist and share it with their teacher.

 DELIVER: How will we implement our solution?

APPLY

Students rotate and play each other's board games in their class completing The Game Changer.

Deliver Rubric on each game.

Groups across the grade with the same topics play each other's board games and vote on which game should be submitted to the library.

Evidence of Learning:

Peer evaluations. Completed Deliver Rubric.

 DIAGNOSE: How will the learning be assessed?

ASSESS

The Game Changer Deliver Rubric is used by the teacher to assess and evaluate the board game.

Evidence of Learning:

Board game rubric.

Courtesy of Avalon Public School & Ashlea Simonetti

DEBRIEF: What are our reflections on both
the product and the process?

ANALYZE

Guide students through a discussion about the games they have just played. Allow them to discuss the material and process they used in this unit. Some questions that might inspire conversation are: What were some challenges in creating a board game that represented the ideas of the person or event? Was it easy to incorporate elements of existing board games to fit the ideas presented in their assigned topics? What worked? What would you have done differently? What did you like about other people's board games? Did you include all the important information about your topic so students could develop a deeper understanding? What skills did you need to complete each D?

Evidence of Learning:

Class discussion.

 DECIDE: What action or actions are we going
to take as a result of our learning?

ACTION

Students vote on the best board games in Year 5 to be accessioned by the library.

Courtesy of Avalon Public School and Ashlea Simonetti

Figure 7.4   The Game Changer Deliver Rubric

	BEGINNING	DEVELOPING	CAPABLE	OUTSTANDING
Designed and created an entertaining and challenging board game.				
Created a set of rules that can be easily understood and followed by players.				
Included all the significant information about their person or event.				
Presented an effective way of teaching other students how to play the game.				
The board game is durable and worthy of being selected for the school library.				

Courtesy of Avalon Public School & Ashlea Simonetti

Figure 7.5   The Game Changer Design Checklist

1. Develops a clear and detailed plan to solve the problem with alternative strategies.	2. Generates a timeline and goals.
3. Defines and designates roles for team members.	4. Uses timeline to track progress. Reports on progress according to timeline.

Courtesy of Avalon Public School and Ashlea Simonetti

Summarizing the Main Points

- Educators have a mission to provide learners with a foundation that includes skills and habits of mind that will last a lifetime and will empower them to succeed in their personal lives.

- This chapter is an overview of Solution Fluency or the 9Ds process for real-world problem solving. Solution Fluency consists of *Define, Determine, Discover, Design, Deliver, Diagnose, Debrief,* and *Decide* and demonstrates how today's just-in-time learners can utilize whole-brain thinking to discover and create practical solutions to problems to apply them to the challenges of modern life, business, and education.

- In the *Define* step, learners create a written statement that outlines their understanding of the challenge or task. Learners will often refer back to the *Define* step to stay on target, while educators will use these steps to craft assessment criteria.

- Solution Fluency is a flexible process. Learners are encouraged to revisit any step during the learning process.

- When using Solution Fluency, educators must recognize the shift in their role to that of a facilitator. The learners become the owners of the learning because they are the problem solvers.

Questions to Consider

- How does Solution Fluency help cultivate the critical skill of problem solving?

- Why is *Debrief* crucial to the learning process?
- How does Solution Fluency help transform a teacher's role?
- Why is it crucial for learners to define the problem, task, or challenge before taking action?
- Briefly summarize the nine steps of Solution Fluency.

Collaboration Fluency: Global Connections 8

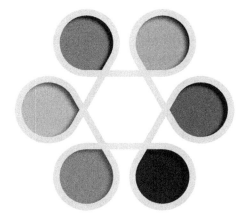

"Children are the Priority. Change is the Reality. Collaboration is the Strategy."

—Judith Billings

Liz Wiseman (2014) stated, "The critical skill of this century is not what you hold in your head, but your ability to tap into and access what other people know." We believe that educators must cultivate in their students the ability to harness collective intelligence, what we call Collaboration Fluency.

Collaboration is not a new concept. Working in teams has been promoted from the time of Socrates (Socratic Circle), who believed that the lecture-style was not an effective teaching and learning strategy. Vygotsky's (1978) *zone of proximal development* is viewed as collaborative learning because it promotes the concept of what a learner can achieve and do with the help and support of peers and teachers. Today, collaboration is deemed an essential modern skill—a skill every person needs to have to be successful in the working world.

For this book, we look at collaboration as the act of working together for a common goal. We developed the 9Es process to help learners master the skills required to become collaboration fluent. Collaboration requires the ability to work effectively with diverse teams and, at the same time, requires the ability to be a helpful team member and make the necessary compromises to achieve common goals.

Through understanding the steps of the 9Es of Collaboration Fluency, we can cultivate an unconscious mental process that can be transferred to similar and different situations. The skills acquired during Collaboration Fluency will enable learners to share ideas with their peers and fellow learners as well as to develop a shared solution, answer collectively, or response, regardless of the diversity within the group.

For the longest time, learning was seen as something that was teacher-directed, done independently in isolation despite being in a classroom full of fellow learners, even to the point of requiring that learners raise their hands with the teacher alone deciding who gets to speak. The shift to a collaborative process of learning is a much-needed disruption to this traditional approach.

Collaboration is a powerful strategy that allows both students and teachers to tap into a wealth of ideas and knowledge. Working in groups has many benefits, given that people have diverse backgrounds, experiences, and strengths that offer an ideal environment for innovation and creativity. While working in groups is beneficial, it also presents challenges. However, these challenges can be overcome by creating environments where learners are equipped with the skills to collaborate on tasks and challenges to achieve shared outcomes.

We recommend that teachers use some fun team-building activities to develop a culture of collaboration within the classroom. The 9Es of Collaboration Fluency help create a climate where cooperation and collaboration are an expectation and every group members' ideas and input are valued and respected. We believe that it is crucial to collectively create a set of group guidelines that can be modified as the need arises.

Collaboration must not be confined only to the classroom. Global digital networks are pervasive in our society, so virtual interaction is now a reality. This development is having an enormous impact on daily life. While we have our students think about local issues, we also want them to develop a global perspective and awareness. Access to technology and the internet is a perfect combination to foster global collaboration.

technology promotes global collab.
→need to create an environment in
the classroom for collab. w/
expectations are there

Today outside of school, children are already playing games and competing against people from other parts of the world. Electronic technology in wired and wireless communications has literally meant the death of distance. There has never been a time where distance has meant less than it does today. Technology has provided us with the tools to be able to collaborate with anyone, anywhere, and anytime at a minimal cost. This trend has tremendous potential for education.

Teachers are encouraged to have their class collaborate with other students from across the globe. There are many advantages to exposing students to different cultures from both their own country and others. First, it arouses curiosity, and once students become curious, they are thirsty to discover and learn. As a result, learner engagement becomes a nonissue. Second, it motivates learners, and they begin to take responsibility for their own learning. Third, they develop excellent communication skills. Students will need to communicate using various modes and mediums to collaborate with fellow learners from different parts of the world. Fourth, they can apply the 9Es process skills in a classroom setting as well as in online environments.

we can connect w/ educators & students across the globe w/ technology

The 9Es also help transform group work into actual collaboration. Students can work in virtual partnerships solving problems and completing challenges with kids from across town or around the world. The skills they develop will help them in the working world, which has been affected by new communication technology. When students enter the world of work, it is with certainty that they will be required to collaborate with fellow workers at some stage in their careers. Therefore, every student must be equipped with the necessary skills to be a valuable contributing member of a team. However, these skills do not come naturally to many students. Collaboration is a learned process. To become fluent requires training and practice.

Collaboration Fluency has nine distinct steps; we call them the 9Es of Collaboration Fluency (see Figure 8.1). Once the 9Es have been learned, they can be combined or modified in any way based on the age, grade, or ability levels of students.

Step 1: Explain

Explain is the step where learners define the purpose of the project; determine shared goals, challenges, or problems; and describe, in their own words, the tasks they are required to complete. It is essential to remind learners that this is a collaborative process and not just group work. They have come together for a specific purpose: to solve a problem, overcome a challenge, or complete a task. They will need to

difference in collaborative process & group work?

Figure 8.1   Collaboration Fluency: The 9Es

COLLABORATION FLUENCY
Explain
Establish
Explore
Envision
Engineer
Execute
Examine
Evaluate
Extend

collectively unpack the problem and view it from different perspectives to ensure all team members have the same collective understanding. Each person is an integral member of the team and, therefore, all input must be considered and treated with respect.

Communication is a critical skill in the collaborative process. Once students have defined, communicated, listened, and clarified the problem with fellow team members, they must develop a shared written understanding of what is expected of them as a team. As students work in teams over extended periods, the ability to work collaboratively and develop creative, innovative, and novel solutions and ideas will improve.

Explain becomes the first checkpoint. It allows educators to provide formative feedback to individual teams. The written statement becomes the criteria against which teams are assessed and rubrics are developed. This statement can also serve as the basis of a contract between groups and educators, as well as used as a checklist for both teams and educators to track progress. Teams must be made aware that they will be assessed against these criteria during a later step.

Explain skills and actions include restating or rephrasing the problem, challenge, or task in the students' own words; challenging assumptions; formulating questions, chunking the details (pulling details together or breaking them down into smaller parts); and considering the challenge from multiple perspectives. Lateral thinking is a crucial skill for teams to utilize to ensure success.

Step 2: Establish

During the *Establish* step, teams identify the target audience or audiences. Questions that students can use to help them determine the different audiences include "Who are the people we can collaborate with to help us solve the problem or accomplish a challenge or task?" "Who will benefit from the end product we create?" and "Who are the people experiencing the problem?"

It is important to remember that learners are working in teams for a common purpose. Working in groups does not imply that all team members learn in the same way as when they are working individually. Teams can also become bogged down when members are not able to agree or come to a consensus. To avoid frustration and the wasting of valuable time, it is important to establish certain norms and shared expectations in advance.

Common goal can = ↓ arguing

Establish skills include identifying authentic audiences; understanding the cultural, historical, and economic mindsets and backgrounds of the different audiences' using appropriate verbal and written communication; understanding body language; developing effective listening skills; asking critical questions; utilizing lateral thinking; developing creative conflict resolution strategies; practicing group divergent and convergent brainstorming; showing passion; demonstrating empathy; and being able to offer constructive feedback.

Step 3: Explore

At the *Explore* step, students work together to gather information and resources to utilize to accomplish tasks and complete challenges. Have students use the strategies acquired during the *Ask* step of Information Fluency to formulate a few good questions that will guide their research and data gathering and help them solve the problem or complete the tasks or challenges. Have learners think about high-, low-, and no-tech resources to utilize when gathering information.

Students can work individually or in subgroups to gather information. The jigsaw strategy is an excellent way to break up a task into smaller bite-size chunks and give individuals, pairs, or small groups an assigned area to research. Students can spend more time on their designated area than if they had to focus on all aspects of the project. Given that they are now the *experts* of their assigned topics when they come together as a team, they can add value and make an informed contribution to the team. Other strategies that could be utilized are buzz groups, fishbowl

* break up the research into chunks & assign them to pairs/individuals. research independentally & come together to share what everyone has learned

discussions, round-robin, and clusters. All these methods promote greater interaction and collaboration in the learning process.

Teams will comprise students with different types of experiences and ability levels. However, these teams need to be allowed to work independently and discover as a group. After all, collaboration is about developing a shared learning experience where students learn from each other, draw on team members' strengths, and support each other to achieve a common objective. Student experts are quickly identified within groups and become group leaders.

As a result, instead of asking the teacher for help, students utilize the expertise within their group. Allow students time to share their knowledge, information, and experiences once the research gathering has been completed. Educators must remind students to listen carefully and be respectful of the information and ideas presented by fellow team members. Remind students to revisit the *Explain* step to ensure that they have the information required to complete the task. They must also discard information they do not require regardless of the individual who contributed the data. During the *Explore* step, students need to ask clarifying and probing questions, as well as learn the language necessary to provide constructive feedback and feedforward to team members.

Explore skills include tapping into personal knowledge, determining where the sources of reliable information are; skimming, scanning, and scouring that information; filtering relevant information from the inconsequential; note-taking and note-making; journaling; analyzing, authenticating, and organizing materials; using appropriate language for feedback and feedforward; demonstrating careful listening; utilizing lateral thinking; and using focused communication.

Step 4: Envision

The *Envision* step is the visioning process. During this step, learners are encouraged to visualize and imagine a variety of possible solutions and outcomes. The *Envision* process is done in two parts: first, individually where learners brainstorm on their own, and then when the team comes together to share their ideas. The brainstorm can also be done as a whole team using a whiteboard, chart paper, or some online tool or app. During the brainstorming and or sharing time, rich interaction by all team members as well as critical inquiry through good questions and clear communication is nonnegotiable. Remind students of the rules for brainstorming, where all ideas are accepted without comment or judgment. Encourage free thinking. Every member is allowed to contribute. The more ideas collected during the brainstorm will help the group when it comes to deciding on the best and most feasible solution.

Teams often start the process feeling highly motivated, energized, unified, and inspired, but there are times when a team member does not play by the rules, personalities clash, or agreements get broken. Teams must learn strategies to help them work through these issues, then regroup and continue with the purpose for which they had come together initially. Conflict is not something that is welcomed, but this is all part of the learning process where students learn how to be nonjudgmental and acquire the skills needed for conflict resolution. It is, therefore, essential to have teams spend time drawing up guidelines, agreements, and protocols that they can refer back to when situations arise. In doing so, they hold each other accountable.

Encourage learners to envision solutions without first placing boundaries. Learners are asked to consider all the possibilities. It is through unlimited visioning that creativity occurs. Once they have generated a list of solutions, have them think about the feasibility (time, money, resources, and skills) as critical factors that must be considered when identifying possible solutions.

le† them think openly first, then have them weed out the list with practicality

Envision skills include individual and group brainstorming, structured brainstorming, rules, mind-mapping, doodling, daydreaming, team discussions, formulating mental images, performing additional research into potential solutions, lateral thinking, questioning, communicating, reflecting, critiquing, reframing, and decision making.

Step 5: Engineer

At the *Engineer* step, learners formulate a step-by-step roadmap or plan that lays out the process and identifies timelines that learners will utilize to accomplish tasks and meet their goals. This plan serves as a guide to ensure learners stay on task. At the *Engineer* step, teams must develop team rules, allocate roles and responsibilities for the team members, assign team and individual tasks, and develop and sign a team performance contract that outlines expectations, rules, and norms. By taking the necessary steps outlined above, each team member is aware of the expectations and the accountability they have to their fellow learners. In this way, when problems arise, they can be sorted within the team by following the guidelines, team protocols, and contracts. Teams also need to revisit these rules regularly. Have individuals and groups ask

This step stops one member from doing all the work or one member not pulling their weight

the following questions: How will I hold myself accountable to meet goals and deadlines? How will we, as a team, hold ourselves responsible for achieving a high quality shared product or solution? How will each team member show responsibility? How will we be held accountable both individually and as a team? How will we ensure that we are meeting our milestones? How will we determine the product created is a result of our shared contributions? How will we assess the overall quality of our shared product?

The roadmap should include several checkpoints. At each checkpoint, have learners spend time doing a team debrief. Creating checkpoints ensures that groups are on track to completing the project in the allotted time. The plan also helps teams evaluate and assess the quality of the product as it goes through the different stages of development.

Engineer skills include time management, scheduling, prioritizing, leadership, goal setting, decision making, reflection, communication (both written and verbal), planning, predicting, forecasting, negotiating, critical thinking, risk management, fostering a culture of belonging, ethics, and morals. Like Solution Fluency, Collaboration Fluency is a flexible, not a linear, process. Learners should be encouraged to revisit and refine the *Explain*, *Establish*, *Explore*, and *Envision* steps as needed.

Step 6: Execute

At this step, the team puts their plan into action by creating a product to solve the problem, task, or challenge. The *Execute* step is the same as the *Deliver* step in Solution Fluency. Since this is Collaboration Fluency, students must be reminded that all team members are included in the process. Every member must play an active part as well as fulfill the roles assigned to them during the *Engineer* step.

At the *Execute* step, learners develop and share their solution to an authentic audience. There are two components to *Execute*: *Produce* and *Publish*. In modern learning environments, students create a real-world solution to the problem. The product is a way for students to document and demonstrate their learning. Therefore, it can be almost anything the learners choose: perform a play, record a podcast, compose a poster, build a sculpture, produce a video, complete an experiment, publish a website, or create a multimedia presentation. The possibilities are endless. This is the *Produce* step.

But *Produce* is only half the task. Learners still have to *Publish* their solutions. Designing a presentation isn't enough; it also has to be presented. Writing a song isn't enough; it has to be recorded. Developing

[Handwritten margin note: X checkpoints make sure the project is on time & quality. Provides buffer so students aren't scrambling at the end.]

a script isn't enough; the work has to be performed. There is an important reason why learners must *Execute* the goods. Implementing their solution provides learners with an opportunity to pressure test the product. Seeing the product executed creates a platform for reflective feedback. In the same way that scientists first create a hypothesis and then conduct an experiment, learners must first design and execute their plan, then observe the results. Otherwise, it only remains an untested hypothesis.

Execute skills and actions include both those related to producing a solution, as well as those needed to publish the solution. These skills include production (both media and multimedia), design (new inventions or innovations), literacy (speaking, listening, reading, writing, visual), and identifying and using the most appropriate format and medium for presenting the information. Based on *Execute* and understanding that Collaboration Fluency is a flexible process, learners are encouraged to revisit and refine any of the previous steps.

Step 7: Examine

Examine is about assessing both the product and the process. Multiple methods of assessment should be utilized to monitor individual, group, and class progress. This assessment can be summative, formative, formal, informal, written, verbal, recorded, or any combination of these different approaches. Various assessors should also be involved in the evaluation process, including self, peers, groups, parents, experts, and community members.

Teachers must both assess and provide feedback on student collabora- *involve the students in the examine stage to further promote the collaboration.* tion as well as team-building skills. We recommend that collaboration skills form a critical component that is evaluated in the *Examine* stage as an essential outcome. Inviting student teams to be part of the assessment process helps reinforce the collaborative culture of a classroom and fosters student agency.

The pinnacle of formative assessment is when peers perform it. The feedback and feedforward provided to other teams are invaluable. There are any number of ways in which peer assessment can be done within the team, by other teams, by other classes, or by students from other schools. The platform for the formative evaluation could be both digital and non-digital. However, both teachers and students must be part of the assessment process throughout the learning journey.

When teachers assess both the product and the process, it sends a message to students that collaboration skills are equally crucial to the

grade the product
& the process to
show the student's
teamwork is just
as important.

end product. The learning process, which is the 9Es, must form part of the assessment criteria.

Assessment must not be viewed as an add-on. Instead, it is a planned ongoing practice that must be integrated within the learning process. Both teachers and students must utilize formative assessment. By taking an active role in the assessment process, learners quickly come to understand that the learning belongs to them and take ownership and responsibility from beginning to end of the process.

Examine skills and actions include active listening, reporting, rubric development, observation skills, interpersonal and intrapersonal skills, learning the language of constructive feedback and feedforward, communications, lateral thinking, assessment terminology, questioning, open-mindedness, leadership, time management, and collaboration strategies and techniques.

Step 8: Evaluate

Evaluate is the step where teams look back at the product and process. Learning is more effective when students reflect not only on the final product but also on their learning journey. It is important for learners to experience both the learning as well as the process. Ask students to review the contract or written statement they completed during the *Explain* step and see whether it was fulfilled. Use this reflection process to provide constructive feedback to team members, as well as other teams within the class.

Reflection is a critical element of learning. Therefore, teachers must ensure that they plan for it and set aside time for a formal debrief. Similar to the *Debrief* step in Solution Fluency, *Evaluate* is the stage where students have the opportunity to articulate their personal and team experiences throughout the process, thereby enriching the learning experience. The *Evaluate* step reinforces collaboration among team members. Start the process by asking students to think and respond to reflection questions such as: How did we function as a group? What did we learn? What worked well? What didn't work as well? What will we do differently the next time? What did we learn individually and as a team? How would you rate the quality of our product/solution? How can we improve as an individual and group member? How can we improve our product?

While the *Establish* step is specifically allocated to the reflection process, we encourage educators to ask their students to reflect on each of the steps of Collaboration Fluency, especially using each step as a checkpoint, and a time for reflection, formative assessment, feedback, and feedforward.

Examine skills and actions include speaking, listening, reevaluating, self-reflection, critical thinking, practicing wait time, managing impulsivity, questioning skills, and reflective journal writing.

Step 9: Extend

Extend is the final stage in the Collaboration Fluency process. During this step, encourage students to take further action. These actions usually come from the solutions or products they designed to solve the given problems, as well as from their reflections during the *Evaluate* stage. While the action must be a collaborative effort, it can be big or small, local or global, altruistic or pragmatic.

extend helps push the global citizen fluency.

This step provides learners with the opportunity to make a difference by positively contributing to society and ultimately develop the qualities of a good global citizen. At the beginning of this chapter, we talked about global collaboration. Encourage students to include global collaboration by extending their local solution or product to students from across the world. The process helps students become more aware of events elsewhere on the planet, as well as create an awareness of different cultures, people, and issues. Remember, Collaboration Fluency is a learned process.

Each of the fluencies is an essential modern skill needed to be successful. Once learned and internalized, the fluencies become powerful tools to utilize both now and in the future. By extending learning to the real world, students come to understand that they can make a difference by contributing through volunteering, creating awareness, developing change projects, campaigning for causes, and raising charitable funds.

Extend skills include inter- and intrapersonal skills such as volunteerism, community service, service-learning, social activism, decision making, responsibility, empathy, personal growth, honesty, and integrity.

Summarizing the Main Points

- Educators must cultivate in their students the ability to harness collective intelligence, what we call Collaboration Fluency.

- Collaboration requires the ability to work effectively with diverse teams and, at the same time, requires the ability to be a helpful team member and make the necessary compromises to achieve common goals.

- Collaboration is a learned process that requires training and practice for it to become a fluency.

- When students enter the world of work, it is with certainty that they will be required to collaborate with fellow workers at some stage in their careers. Therefore, every student must be equipped with the necessary skills to be a valuable contributing member of a team.

- Collaboration Fluency has nine distinct steps called the 9Es: Explain, Establish, Explore, Envision, Engineer, Execute, Examine, Evaluate, and Extend.

Questions to Consider

- What is the difference between working group work and collaboration?

- What activities can educators use to encourage learners to work in teams?

- What is collective intelligence, and why is it so valuable in team-based projects?

- What strategies can you utilize from the ideas outlined in the chapter to use during collaborative projects with your students as well as colleagues?

- Why is it so vital to have students collaborate in both face-to-face and online environments?

Information Fluency: InfoWhelm and HyperInformation

9

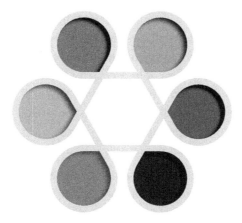

"Learning is not a race for information; it's a walk of discovery."

—Anonymous

Our society has been profoundly affected by a new phenomenon called InfoWhelm. InfoWhelm is the unparalleled access to a wealth of online information. This is access unlike anything that has ever been seen or heard before. As a result, learning has genuinely become a lifelong pursuit, something that can happen anytime, anywhere. As the world moves into a new era of globalization, individuals can conduct their research. The internet has made it possible for people to become "prosumers" (Jukes, Schaaf, & Mohan, 2015), where people produce as well as consume information.

Due to digital access and the internet, we have become increasingly dependent on searching for information online. And because there is so much data readily available at our fingertips, there is not only the danger of information overwhelm, but also the risk of consuming misinformation, mythinformation, and fake news.

With so much information available in both digital and non-digital formats, increasingly, the problem we face is that alongside information that is true, we also find information that is not. Most often, misinformation turns up in places where we least expect. Social media is a go-to place for many people today as a primary source of information. While social media spreads accurate information very quickly, it does the very same with fake and false information.

Before social media burst onto the scene, it was easier to identify misinformation. Now, it is challenging to determine the credibility of news without possessing advanced detective skills. Today, anyone with an internet connection and an ax to grind can create and post whatever content they want regardless of its accuracy. Given this reality, students must be equipped with the necessary skills that will enable them to approach information in all forms and media with a critical eye. As educators, it is our responsibility to help learners acquire the essential skills needed to become savvy prosumers of information.

How do we determine the good from the bad and the right from the wrong? How do we distinguish complete, accurate, and usable data from a sea of irrelevance and digital inundation? The skills needed to effectively understand and utilize the wealth of information at our fingertips are essential to life and success in this century. Information Fluency is the ability to unconsciously and intuitively access and interpret information in all forms and formats, not just in text format, but also multimedia. The steps of Information Fluency help learners consume different types of media to extract the essential knowledge, perceive its meaning and significance, and apply it to solve problems and complete real-world tasks.

This chapter introduces educators to the 9As process of Information Fluency: Ask, Audience, Access, Authenticate, Assemble, Apply, Assess, Analyze, and Action. The 9As allow learners to discover, collect, and explore data to create knowledge. The 9As of Information Fluency can be adapted and embedded into any curriculum for learners at any grade level or age. Students will learn clear steps that can be explained, learned, practiced, applied, internalized, and improved over time. The Information Fluency process gets students to wonder, explore, and learn in different and unique ways. The 9As process has nine steps (see Figure 9.1). At each step, students generate questions that guide their learning as they navigate through various resources looking for information.

Figure 9.1   Information Fluency: The 9As

INFORMATION FLUENCY
Ask
Audience
Access
Authenticate
Assemble
Apply
Assess
Analyze
Action

Step 1: Ask

The starting point is helping our students learn how to ask good, relevant, and meaningful questions. Anyone can find answers, and anyone can ask questions, but not everyone can ask the *right* questions. It's only by asking good, higher-order questions that learners can develop good answers. Learners must be introduced to skills that will enable them to formulate questions that will help them acquire new knowledge. At the *Ask* stage, learners will define the scope of the problems, topics, challenges, and tasks they face.

The critical asking skills our students need to learn include identifying keywords, formulating questions around these keywords, brainstorming, thinking laterally, understanding ethical issues, listening deeply, viewing wisely, speaking critically, and filtering data.

When learners conduct research or navigate resources to gather information, they are faced with two challenges. Either there is too much or too little information. It is critical students first define (*Ask*) the scope of the problems, topics, challenges, and tasks. Similar to Solution Fluency, *Ask* is critical. Having learners take the time to define the scope of the task will be well worth their time and effort. *Ask* is the checkpoint for both learners and educators to determine if they have a clear and shared understanding of the scope of the task ahead. Only when students can ask relevant questions will they be able to unpack the problems, topics, challenges, and tasks presented.

✗need to know the audience for relevancy

Step 2: Audience

The questions students ask in the first stage help identify the target audience. There could be multiple audiences, as was discussed in the *Determine* stage of Solution Fluency. Understanding the *Audience* is critical because if the information is not aligned to the needs of the audience, they will not find it relevant. Understanding the audience requires that we obtain answers to the following questions: Who will have access to the information that is gathered? Who are we answering the question or questions for? Who could help us answer these questions? Who could help us acquire the skills needed to accomplish the task or answer the question? What are the desired actions or outcomes for the audience?

✗helps create targeted & appviate questions

Knowing the audience or audiences helps learners formulate appropriate questions. Remember, the audience is a resource. Therefore, students will need to learn specific skills to complete tasks and challenges. For example, should they need to conduct surveys or interviews, they must learn how to formulate appropriate questions that will allow them to gather the required information.

The essential *Audience* skills include being able to speak and listen effectively, interviewing skills, survey and data collection skills, the ability to be empathetic, and the ability to collaborate with others effectively. It is also important to note that once the audiences have been identified, learners will need to circle back to the *Ask* stage to refine the existing questions and formulate new questions for the different audiences.

Step 3: Access

At the *Access* step, learners gather the most relevant raw, unfiltered data. This step is a challenge because there is an abundance of information that is available on any topic in multiple formats and from multiple sources. The key to wading through overwhelming amounts of information is the questions formulated during the *Ask* step. Good questions enable learners to identify and access the essential raw information from the most appropriate high-tech, low-tech, or no-tech sources.

Access skills include determining where the information is located; prioritizing search strategies; skimming, scanning, and scouring the resources for pertinent data; filtering; cross-referencing; note-taking;

note-making; and most important, knowing when it's necessary to go back to the initial *Ask* and *Audience* stages to generate more questions.

In other words, *Access* is about developing critical information literacy skills, a task that has become more difficult because today, accessing is not just about reading a book or other paper-based materials. Increasingly, the most utilized search tools for students are digital resources like YouTube, Google, Twitter, blogs, Wikipedia, podcasts, and interactive websites and materials that are graphical and audiovisual.

Step 4: Authenticate

One of the scariest things about the internet is that it's an open sewer of untreated, unfiltered information. Having easily accessible information to utilize is wonderful, but at the same time, it is like standing in the face of a tsunami. It's easy to be InfoWhelmed. Only when we know what we are looking for, where it is, and how to get there, can we be successful in our searches. Finding information is just the first step in any research process.

Once students have accessed the appropriate data, they will need to authenticate the raw materials. Authentication is a critical step. Authentication is a skill that must be explicitly taught if we want learners to become savvy consumers of information, something that is increasingly true in times of misinformation, mythinformation, fake news, and truth decay.

Studies show that the average web user will not go past the first five listings on a search engine results page, and 95% of users do not go beyond the first page. Only 5% of users might go on to the remaining search results pages (Kaye, 2013). The key to successful authentication is knowing how to navigate the raw data and being able to determine whether a source is factual. Today, authenticating data is not just about validating paper-based sources. Authenticate is also about validating images, videos, sounds, and other web-based materials. If we want relevant and reliable information, we must encourage students to become skeptics when they are researching. When they are unsure of the accuracy of the information, they must purposefully go back to the *Ask* step.

Essential *Authentication* skills include being able to cross-reference information, determining what is true and what is false, differentiating facts from opinions, assessing the currency of materials, examining data for underlying meaning and bias, identifying where there is incomplete information, and documenting and validating sources through triangulation and formulating good questions.

Step 5: Assemble

At the *Assemble* step, the gathered information is organized into a usable form. *Assemble* is the stage where students combine components or elements of information gathered from multiple sources, which are then summarized and synthesized to form a connected whole. *Assemble* is about organizing and applying the collected data. The critical aspect of *Assemble* is ensuring learners understand the difference between summarizing and synthesizing information. Explicit instruction is required to ensure students learn the essential *Assemble* skills identified below so they can select a strategy best suited to accomplish the task.

Essential *Assemble* skills include using Post-It notes, creating concept maps, categorizing, mind mapping, color coding, discerning patterns, identifying themes, and sorting information into physical or digital folders. The *Assemble* step is similar to the *Design* stage in Solution Fluency. Learners will also need to develop a step-by-step plan of how they will utilize the information to create the product, solve the problem, or complete the task.

Step 6: Apply

✗ use the collected info. to solve real-world tasks & problems

Learners use the information gathered to solve the problem by completing all the tasks and challenges required. Assessing, authenticating, and assembling the information is essential, but information alone is not enough unless we can turn that information into knowledge. Being able to access vast amounts of data means nothing unless that information can be applied to solve problems or complete challenges that have real-world relevance.

Examples of real-world tasks include writing an essay, creating a graph, defending an argument, making a presentation, participating in a debate, completing a science experiment, creating a video, or building a blog or website. There are any number of potential real-world products that students can create.

Essential *Applying* skills include using different forms of learner expression and voice through reports, letters, scripts, magazines, news articles, posters, advertisements, infographics, newsletters, websites, presentations, blog posts, videos, podcasts, speeches, and audio clips, as well as developing speaking and presentation skills.

involve students here to encourage personal ownership/accountability

Step 7: Assess

Assess is precisely the same as the *Diagnose* step in Solution Fluency. However, the focus for the evaluation in the *Assess* step is on assessing the Information Fluency skills. This assessment encompasses all the skills identified at each step of the Information Fluency process. These skills include the ability to formulate questions, access information, authenticate the information, take notes, make notes, synthesize the data, and apply the information to solve the problem or challenge.

The evaluation must also consider whether the questions developed at the *Ask* stage were adequately answered. *Assess* is about the evaluation of the original criteria or objectives. This step could include an assessment of the product, the process, or both. The assessment could be summative, formative, formal, informal, written, verbal, or recorded. Evaluators could be self, peer, group, or teachers.

Learners must be included in the evaluation process. They must be given the opportunity to assess their learning because group assessment, peer assessment, and self-assessment foster personal ownership and accountability.

Assess skills and actions include active listening, reporting, rubric development, observation skills, interpersonal and intrapersonal skills, growth mindset skills, metacognitive skills, learning the language of constructive feedback and feedforward, communication, lateral thinking, and assessment terminology.

Step 8: Analyze

Traditionally, at this point, we allow our learners to quit. We let them sit back and assume their responsibilities and involvement are finished once their product is completed. Traditionally students are excluded from the assessment process, let alone being given the time to reflect. But if we stop here, we have missed a valuable step and an excellent opportunity for improvement and personal growth. *Analyze* is the time for students to reflect. Reflection is a critical step in any learning process. If we do not allow learners to reflect on their learning, then that learning has no relevance and is seen purely as an activity to occupy their time.

Educators must explicitly teach learners how to become critical reflectors through activities like think-pair-share, exit slips, two stars and a wish, and reflective journal writing. Reflection is an active and engaging process. Once students learn how to reflect, they begin to take ownership and responsibility for their learning.

reflection activities: think-pair-share, exit slips, two stars & a wish, reflective journaling xreflect on product AND process

John Hattie's (2008) research of 1,600 studies states that reflection is one of the highest factors impacting student achievement. Hattie further notes that when learners regularly reflect, it allows educators to challenge them to achieve higher standards. During the *Analyze* step, learners must revisit each stage of the process and reflect critically on both the process undertaken and the product created.

Analyze skills include asking reflective questions about both the process and the product: what was learned, how it was learned, and how they could make the product and process better. It is our responsibility as educators to help learners develop the ability to reflect both individually, as well as collaboratively in pairs or groups.

Step 9: Action

Finally, we get to the *Action* stage. Here we ask two questions: So what? Now what? During the eight previous steps of Information Fluency, students have asked good questions, identified the different audiences, accessed data from multiple sources, authenticated the validity of the information, assembled the information through synthesizing, applied that information to solve a problem or challenge, assessed the process and product using different forms of evaluation, and analyzed the product and process through critical reflection. Learners have collected the information and transformed it into knowledge. So what? Now what? What are they going to do with the knowledge they have? Knowledge by itself has no value unless that knowledge is utilized to take action.

This step involves taking action on their reflections. Action is about acting on what was learned at the *Assess* stage, internalizing this learning, and transferring it to new and different circumstances. *Action* is about deciding what your next steps will be, and applying what has been learned in the realworld.

The goal of Information Fluency is to move students beyond the simple consumption of data to be producers of information. The ultimate goal of Information Fluency is to help students use newfound knowledge to solve real-world problems and to take real-world actions as part of being a good global citizen. It is important to reiterate that the nine steps of Information Fluency are only a guide. As educators become familiar with the process, the steps can be combined, adapted, or modified to meet the needs of their students.

Figure 9.2   Sample Information Literacy Project

Endangered Animals: Problem Solving Project

Title: Endangered Animals

Grade: 4

Duration: 10 Weeks (English Unit)

Subject/s: English, Art

Geography—mapping; Maths—position, timelines, 2D space, 3D space; Creative Arts—visual art; English—writing.

Outcomes:

EN2-3A uses effective handwriting and publishes texts using digital technologies

EN2-10C thinks imaginatively, creatively and interpretively about information, ideas and texts when responding to and composing texts

VAS2.1 Represents the qualities of experiences and things that are interesting or beautiful by choosing among aspects of subject matter

The Scenario:

Read the book *The Dream of The Thylasinpe* by Margaret Wild and Ron Brooks.

Essential Question:

How can we educate and persuade people to help save endangered animals?

Technology:

Hi-tech: Documentary/Keynote animation, Book Creator

Low-tech: Drama play/news report

No-tech: Poster

 ASK: What is the problem we face?

From the list of endangered animals from the video you are about to show on the Notebook, ask the students if they think they are endangered or not. Count who does think they are endangered and record the number next to each animal's name.

Show students the video "Do you know your endangered species?" After viewing, ask students what they think the message of the video is. Discuss how people are not aware of the issue of endangered animals or even which animals are endangered. In pairs, ask students to write down what they think the problem is.

Have each pair share with the class their definition of the problem.

Courtesy of Avalon Public School & Ashlea Simonetti

Evidence of Learning:

Students' written definition of the scope of the problems, topics, challenges, and tasks.

A class definition for students to refer to throughout the project.

ACCESS: Research—What's causing the problem, and why and how do we solve it?

Using the Q Focus technique, have students brainstorm on their own as many questions as they can about this topic. Give them 5 minutes to do this on the Q Focus template. Ask them to read their questions and decide if they are Closed or Open questions. You may need to teach them what these questions are. Ask the students to write a C next to their questions that are Closed and an O next to their questions that are Open. Have students look at their Closed questions and try to improve them by using a different beginning. Discuss beginnings that make a question open such as Who, What, Why, Where, When, and How. Finally, ask students to prioritize their questions by choosing their top three questions.

Students could view an episode from The RealNews.com, which discusses how humans have caused the problem of animals becoming endangered.

https://www.youtube.com/watch?v=WBivQG12HAc&ab_channel=TheRealNewsNetwork

Here is another good video to hook students asking what we can do to help:

https://www.youtube.com/watch?v=rigICChwQ6g

Teach the skills of note taking and summarizing.

Using the graphic organizer, have students work on iPads to search information about their chosen topic.

Also ask them to research examples of Notebook as well as presentation ideas and techniques.

Resources: Examples of Excellence Notebook, Endangered Animal Pawerpaint, Red Panda, Orangutan, and African Wild Dog Documentaries (KA videos).

Have students work with their group to decide what topic they want to present and how they would like to present their topic. Refer back to their brainstormed ideas of how they would like to educate their audience.

Evidence of Learning:

Q Focus template, Cornell Notetaking templates, Endangered animal Notetaking template

AUDIENCE: Who is experiencing the problem, and who will help us solve the problem?

Discuss who they think should be their audience. Who should they persuade or educate about this problem? Tell students about the 9D Expo and how this is a perfect opportunity for them to make a difference by educating and persuading their community. In pairs, have students write a solution to the problem. Ask pairs to share their solutions and then brainstorm different ways they can persuade and educate people (e.g., pawerpaint posters, documentaries, sketches, puppet show, role play).

WWF

Evidence of Learning:

Target audience identified: parents and community

AUTHENTICATE: What are the possible solutions to the problem?

Based on information gathered students have a discussion and make decisions regarding the plight of endangered animals. What would they do? How can they spend their money? What programs would they fund and facilitate? How will they encourage people to help protect these species and promote an awareness of why they are endangered? How will they showcase their learning at the 9Ds expo and promote awareness among the parents and community members?

Using questions they generated in the access step to help with their research, students must now carefully look at all the information they collected and decide what to use and what to discard. Guide students in how to check the information they gathered by cross-referencing information, determining what is true and what is false, differentiating facts from opinions, assessing the currency of materials, examining data for underlying meaning and bias, identifying where there is incomplete information, and documenting and validating sources through triangulation and formulating good questions.

Evidence of Learning:

Students' written notes

 ASSEMBLE: How will we create our solution?

Students map out their solution and how they are going to achieve this. On the Assemble Checklist, the group develops a clear and detailed plan to solve the problem by listing the tasks that need completing. Timelines are decided on for all tasks, and progress is tracked using the timeline. Roles and responsibilities are defined and then distributed among the group members for the presentation of the game (who will introduce the game, who will explain game play, who will demonstrate the game, etc.).

Evidence of Learning:

Assemble Checklist

 APPLY: How will we implement our solution?

Students use the information they gathered and produce their presentations.

Students will have various delivery stages of their project.

Courtesy of Avalon Public School & Ashlea Simonetti

First Stage presented to the class: background information of the animal they have chosen and reasons why the animal is endangered.

Second Stage presented to the class: Ways in which they are going to engage their audience and persuade them to help their animal (e.g., create a short movie about their animal that will encourage people to donate to WWF).

Third Stage: When all groups have created their persuasive and informative display they will then present to the class and/or buddy classes.

Fourth Stage: During Term 3's Avalon Learning Expo, Year 4 students will present their endangered animal to parents and friends in the hope that they will donate money to WWF, which will help protect these endangered animals.

Evidence of Learning:

Student work samples

Class observation

Teacher and peer feedback

Book Creator Diaries

 ASSESS: How will the learning be assessed?

The Endangered Species Apply Rubric is used by the teacher and students to assess and evaluate the different stages of delivery.

Some criteria include the following:

Did your image and activities convey a message? Was your intention clear? Did your information include facts about the animal? Why it is endangered, and how we can help?

Evidence of Learning:

Book Creator learning journal

Peer feedback

 ANALYZE: What are our reflections on both the product and the process?

What does it mean to be endangered? How can people help animals that are endangered? How do you think you have helped your chosen animal? Do you feel you have made a difference? Would you do anything differently? Will you continue to encourage people to support your cause?

Evidence of Learning:

Student reflections

Courtesy of Avalon Public School & Ashlea Simonetti

ACTION: What action or actions are we going to take as a result to our learning?

During Term 3's Expo, Year 4 students will present their endangered animal to parents and friends in the hope that they will donate money to WWF, which will help protect these endangered animals. Present money to a representative from WWF.

Evidence of Learning:

Money collected

Courtesy of Avalon Public School & Ashlea Simonetti

Summarizing the Main Points

- InfoWhelm is an overwhelming amount of information combined with unparalleled access to a wealth of online information.

- The internet has made it possible for people to become prosumers, where people can simultaneously produce and consume information.

- Information Fluency is the ability to unconsciously and intuitively access and interpret information in all forms and formats, not just in text format, but also multimedia.

- The 9As process of Information Fluency: *Ask, Audience, Access, Authenticate, Assemble, Apply, Assess, Analyze,* and *Action* will allow learners to discover, collect, and explore data to create knowledge.

- The ultimate goal of Information Fluency is to help students use newfound knowledge to solve real-world problems and to take real-world actions as part of being a good global citizen.

Questions to Consider

- Why is Information Fluency essential in modern times?

- How do people distinguish complete, accurate, and usable data from a sea of irrelevance and digital inundation?

- Why is it important for students to learn how to formulate good questions before embarking on research?

- Why is it critical to determine in advance what audience the newly accessed information will serve?

- Why is reflection such a critical teaching and learning strategy?

10 Communication Fluency: Text and Multimedia

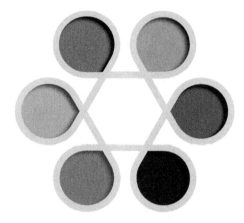

"If you talk to a man in a language he understands, that goes to his head. If you talk to him in his language, that goes to his heart."

—Nelson Mandela

People have been using media for communication since the beginning of recorded history. Thousands of years ago, early humans shared their ideas by painting on the walls of caves or chiseling their language into the surfaces of mighty pyramids, temples, and tombs.

Eventually, paper, whether it was made of linen, cotton, or papyrus, became the next selected medium of choice for widespread communication. New inventions such as the printing press, as well as improvements in the production of paper, meant news and information were no longer transmitted only by word of mouth (Moran, 2010). Books and newspapers became the preferred media of the time, so previous generations were paper-trained.

For generations, graphics were primarily static illustrations, photos, or charts that accompanied the text, which provided further clarification after the fact. If we have a flashback to our youth, many of us can remember reading a paper-based *Encyclopedia Britannica* or a *Webster's Dictionary*. Back then, the primary information was provided by text, and the images were merely intended to complement that text.

But for today's digital learners, the relationship between text and images has been almost completely reversed. Increasingly, the role of text is to provide more detail for something first experienced as an image, video, or sound. The media of our information consumption has completely changed.

In our 2015 book, *Reinventing Learning for the Always-On Generation: Strategies and Apps that Work*, we identified nine core learning attributes of the digital generations. One of the characteristics of learning was that the digital generation's preference was to process pictures, sounds, color, and video *before* they processed text, because members of the always-on generation have grown up in a predominantly visual world—a world captured by the eye and cameras.

images, video, & sound are more import. to learners now. Text is just for context.

As educators, a question we must ask is how do we future-proof our students by equipping them with skills that they will be able to use in a world that is increasingly becoming more autonomous and machine-driven? Today, effective communication is one of the high demand skills that students must learn if they want to compete successfully in an ever changing global economy.

Whether it's holding a conversation with individuals or groups, negotiating a deal, selling an idea or product, or marketing yourself, having effective communication skills is essential. Our task is to help our students develop the necessary skills needed, not only for face-to-face engagement, but also to communicate effectively in the online world. Effective communication requires learners to develop literacy skills beyond reading and writing, to include digital literacy.

Digital literacy skills help learners leverage different media that best suit the message they want to communicate. As Marshall McLuhan (1964) says, "The medium is the message."

The Digital Age has presented us with a vast range of new digital media communication formats that have become as common as traditional text, but far more impactful and thought-provoking.

We often hear politicians, educators, and parents suggest that children today are spending far too much time in front of screens. However, when we were growing up, the screen technology we experienced was

I really like their take on active technology. It's a nice change of pase for it to not be demonized.

primarily television and film. In such environments, we typically sat quietly and passively watched productions. Today's modern technology allows us to do far more than be passive recipients of the information. Individuals and groups can actively watch, engage, and interact while simultaneously viewing a program, playing a game, having a conversation, or creating something.

Some schools view technology as a silver bullet that will magically transform learning and equip all students with essential modern skills. Reorganizing learning spaces, building new schools, introducing new technologies, or changing the organization of a school does not of itself translate to changes in teaching and learning (Elmore, 2009). While some schools see an urgency to digitize classrooms, it has been our observation that digital technology is often primarily used for passive consumption. Today's digital technologies have the potential to enable learners to engage in the learning experience actively.

The world has moved beyond communication using primarily text. Visual communication through graphic design and multimedia has become the new basic. However, today the world has moved even further because kids are growing up in the YouTube, Snapchat, and TikTok era. We have advanced beyond still images to a new video standard. Messages are being constructed using a new audio-visual standard that not only requires an understanding of graphic design but also utilizes video production tools. Ten years ago, these tools were prohibitively expensive, but now they are free or cheap.

These tools have allowed learners to move from being primarily consumers of media to being prosumers. They not only consume but also produce media. The ability to be prosumers is why, in an increasingly visual world, visual communication design must be a regular part of the curriculum at every grade level and in every subject. Students must be able to communicate effectively in text and speech as well as in multimedia formats.

Students have little difficulty finding resources to complete a task or challenge when they are involved in inquiry- or problem-based learning. The problem they face is that there is too much information from too many sources. Not only do they experience InfoWhelm, but they also face the even more significant challenge of presenting their findings and new knowledge to their identified audience. In the Solution Fluency process outlined in Chapter 7, the *Deliver* step is used to promote student voice. Students are provided with the opportunity to become the source of information and thus responsible for conveying their knowledge in the medium of their choosing accurately in the form of a blog post, letter, video, song, podcast, skit, play, poster, artwork, infographic—the possibilities are endless.

However, the crucial skill students need is to select the medium that will best capture the interest of the identified audience while at the same time conveying the intended message. Student voice could include the creation of advertisements, audio recordings, avatars, banners, blogs, board games, book jackets, brochures, bulletin boards, cartoons, choice boards, class books, collages, comic strips, comedies, commercials, costume design, crosswords, dances, debates, demonstrations, digital games, digital mash-ups, discussions, discussion forums, displays (classroom), dioramas, drawings, escape rooms, experiments, fashion shows, flow charts, genius hours, Google Earth tours, graffiti, graphs, graphic organizers, infographics, infomercials, interviews, journals, learning logs, literature circles, magazines, maps, mind maps, mobiles, models, monologues, movie/book reviews, multi-genre projects, murals, news reports, photos, photo galleries, place-based projects, podcasts, poetry, portfolios, posters, public service announcements, puppet shows, rap songs, reenactments, road signs, role-play, scavenger hunts, scrapbooks, sculptures, set designs, show and tell, simulations, sketch notes, slideshows, social media pages, Socratic seminars, solving "crimes," songs, speeches, story maps, tag clouds, Ted Talks, text conversations, theatrical plays, thought bubbles, timelines, Twitter hashtag discussions, videos, webpages, Wikis, word splashes, and word walls.

[handwritten margin note: Student voice examples]

Our aim as educators is to ensure students experience life when they are in school and not wait to experience life once they leave school. To paraphrase John Dewey (1916), who said that "education is not preparation for life; education is life itself," for students to gain experience, they must have agency; they must have a voice; they must have the opportunity to make valuable contributions to the world, no matter how big or small. But for them to be able to share their learning experiences and aptly present the information they have acquired, they must have a different set of skills. We call these skills Communication Fluency.

Using the 9Ps of Communication Fluency—Pose, Pinpoint, Prepare, Picture, Plan, Produce, Probe, Ponder, and Pledge—allows learners to leverage the most appropriate media for communicating. Student engagement and motivation are intangibles in this learning process. The 9Ps empower students to use their authentic voice to design personalized solutions and products.

This chapter provides educators with an overview of the 9Ps process that can be utilized to enable student voice and help learners develop excellent communication skills to use online or offline, oral or written,

Figure 10.1   Communication Fluency: The 9Ps

COMMUNICATION FLUENCY
Pose
Pinpoint
Prepare
Picture
Plan
Produce
Probe
Ponder
Pledge

formal or informal, verbal or nonverbal, and traditional or digital. Learners must also be encouraged to use multimedia and art to express their newfound knowledge.

The 9Ps of Communication Fluency can be embedded into any curriculum or content area (see Figure 10.1). Students will learn clear steps that can be explained, learned, practiced, applied, internalized, and most important, improved on over time.

Step 1: Pose

This first step is critical for learners working individually, with a partner, or in a group to ensure that all are in agreement and have a common understanding of the following: the message to be conveyed, the platform to be used, the medium best suited for the message, and the format of the presentation.

It is also essential for students to clarify whether or not they will use more than one means of communication to convey their message to different audiences. Students must then present their teacher with a written understanding of what (content) needs to be presented, how (format), and the platform (medium) they will utilize to make their product. This step helps the teacher gauge whether students have a clear understanding of what they are required to do to complete the task within the given timeframe.

The failure on the part of some educators is not taking enough time to ask whether students understand what is required of them. This situation may lead some teachers to blame students for not following directions.

The mere fact that students did not understand what was asked of them clearly shows there is incomplete communication. Thus, the authors once again stress that time spent at this step is time well spent.

*make sure students know the expectations

Allow time for communicat. & questions

The *Pose* step provides both teachers and students with the opportunity to clarify things they are unsure about or ask questions to determine whether they have access to the appropriate resources needed to complete the task. Resources include technology, people, time, money, and required knowledge and skills. Once feasibility is clarified, students can revisit and finalize their written statements. This written statement is then viewed as the agreed criteria against which students will be assessed. The statement also serves as a checklist that both teachers and students can use to keep on track.

Critical communication skills include multimodal literacies (making sense of various media, video, images, text, and sound in both digital and non-digital formats). However, unlike other fluencies, where the specific skills students need to acquire at each step are identified, this does not apply with Communication Fluency because many of the skills need to be learned just-in-time. For example, if students choose to use Keynote or PowerPoint as their medium to convey their message, they will need to learn how to use presentation software. The same approach applies if they are required to write a report. Students will need to learn report writing skills and techniques.

Other *Pose* skills and actions include being able to restate or rephrase a challenge or task in the learners' own words, understanding media, medium, and message, identifying keywords, formulating good questions, brainstorming, thinking laterally, understanding ethical issues, active listening, and speaking clearly.

have learners break down tasks/challenges in their own words for better understanding

Step 2: Pinpoint

Students must recognize that communication is not just about sending out or broadcasting information. Communication is a two-way process; it involves both a sender and a receiver. At the *Pinpoint* step, students must identify who the audience or audiences are who will be the recipients of their message and/or information.

Once the audiences have been identified, students must ensure that they develop an understanding of the audiences' interests, biases, perspectives, and agendas. Knowing the audience is vital because if the presentation is not aligned to the audiences' needs, they will not find the presentation relevant or interesting. Knowing the audience helps learners decide the most effective forms of communication to use to ensure their message is not only well received but also has an impact on the audience.

Learners may choose any one of several communication approaches: oral or written, formal or informal, verbal or nonverbal, and traditional, digital, or a combination of both. Having a good sense of the audience helps learners tailor their medium and message in a manner that best suits the needs of the audience. Teachers need to stress that students take the time at the *Pinpoint* step to carefully identify and consider the audiences, as this will help them adapt their presentation in ways that will be effective in different situations. Determining the audience in advance will ensure that they never ask, "What were they trying to say?" or "What was that all about?"

Pinpoint skills and actions include identifying the authentic audiences; understanding the cultural, historical, and economic mindsets and backgrounds of the selected audiences; anticipating the attitudes and biases of the audiences (What do they think about the topic? What motivates their interest?); connecting with audience members; identifying the purpose of the presentation; choosing the goals or preferred outcomes of the presentation (inform, persuade, inspire, entertain); and selecting the appropriate format and medium to deliver the product to different audiences (a proposal, published content on blogs, wikis, discussion threads, videos, podcasts, etc.).

Step 3: Prepare

Prepare is the research phase of the process during which learners gather information about their intended audiences. Ask students to revisit the *Pinpoint* step and clarify who the audiences are, because this will guide students as they collect data. At this step, have learners explore the resources they intend to utilize for preparing and delivering their presentations. The primary purpose of the research is to ensure learners have a specific context of the different audiences, which will help them choose the most appropriate presentation style and platform to deliver their message.

Have learners think about high-, low-, and no-tech resources they can utilize for their presentations to convey information, whether it is face-to-face, online, or both. Students can work individually or in groups to gather information about different audiences. Encourage students to use some of the strategies used during the Collaboration Fluency process. For example, the jigsaw strategy allows tasks to be broken up into smaller bite-size chunks and assigned to individuals, pairs, or small groups, who are then allocated an area to research.

At the *Prepare* step, ask students to research and familiarize them-selves with excellent communication skills, including social emotional intelligence, cohesion and clarity, friendliness, confidence, empathy, respect, ability to listen, and open-mindedness.

Prepare skills and actions include tapping into personal knowledge; understanding the cultural, historical, and economic mindsets and backgrounds of the selected audiences; and acquiring specific skills tar-geted at various formats to deliver the presentation to different audi-ences (a proposal, published content on blogs, wikis, discussion threads, videos, podcasts, etc.). Students must familiarize themselves with effec-tive presentation and communication skills. These include empathy, body language, tone, eye contact, respect, listening, speaking, and inter-personal skills.

Step 4: Picture

At the *Picture* step, learners brainstorm, imagine, and visualize possible modes and media to convey their message to the various audiences identified at the *Pinpoint* step. The *Picture* stage is the visioning process during which learners are encouraged to visualize and imagine a variety of possible solutions and outcomes. Remind students of the rules for brainstorming, where all ideas are accepted without comment or judgment. The more ideas that are collected during brainstorming help students in deciding the best and most feasible options. Ask learners to think about the feasibility factors (time, money, resources, and skills) that must be considered when identifying both the media and format they will use.

The nine steps of Information Fluency equip students with valuable skills about how to gather, analyze, synthesize, and apply data within a given context. However, it is critical that students also learn the skills of communication so they can leverage the power of different media and presentation formats to share information.

At the *Picture* step of Communication Fluency, students are encouraged to think of creative and unique ways in which to present information to a specific audience so that it is exciting while at the same time informative and easy to understand. Living in an age of InfoWhelm, anyone and everyone can easily find information. But that information has little or no value if there is no context or perspective.

Learners must think carefully about how to manage information by summarizing and identifying the core message they want to deliver to the intended audiences. The way the information is presented is critical.

Choosing the most appropriate option of mode and media will not only add value to the content but also help the audiences better understand and make sense of the intended message.

Picture skills and actions include brainstorming; mind-mapping; whole and small group discussions; formulating mental images; performing additional research into potential options for mode and media to be used; lateral thinking; questioning; reframing; thinking in metaphors, pictures, and sounds; decision making; imagining; viewing different options; open-mindedness; creativity; innovation; and focused communication.

Step 5: Plan

Having a good solid plan makes it easier to perform and complete tasks or challenges. Careful planning involves putting together the different parts that are required to complete a task. Just like a puzzle, a plan is made up of many tiny pieces that are only complete once they are all brought together to form a whole picture. In the same way, students must consider many different components when designing and delivering a presentation.

A plan helps us make sense of what is required to complete a product, task, or challenge by breaking it up into manageable chunks. Learners create a plan to guide them through the project. It is a roadmap or strategy that can be checked, discussed, and reevaluated, while at the same time keeping learners on track and helping them avoid wasted effort. At the *Plan* step, learners build backward from the future to the present, identifying milestones and creating achievable deadlines to complete their presentations.

Failing to plan is planning to fail. Having a plan is critical. The plan is an essential form of communication and, therefore, must be clear and concise. The plan must also be designed in a manner that is simple and unambiguous. Everyone must understand what is required and when and how learners are going to achieve set goals and within what timeframes. A carefully constructed plan helps convey information and instructions efficiently and effectively. Remind students to revisit the *Pose* step to ensure that their plan includes measures to achieve the agreed criteria.

When creating a roadmap, students could use SMART goals to help in the planning process. Specific: clearly state their goals or outcomes. Measurable: How will they track progress? Achievable: Is the goal(s) achievable? Realistic: Are these goals or aims practical? Timely: What are the deadlines for each milestone?

Plan skills and actions include being able to take on a role as a leader or follower, goal setting, planning, communications, collaboration, self-management, time management, prototyping, decision making, budgeting, flexibility, resource management, prioritizing, record keeping, multitasking, and writing instructions in small, easy-to-follow, positive, and logical increments.

Step 6: Produce

At this step, the students put their plan into action by creating their presentation and delivering it to a predetermined audience. Effective communication involves relaying, disseminating, and providing information clearly and concisely. Effective communication is also the ability to convey complex topics in a simplified and easy to understand manner to different audiences.

Communication goes beyond just the written and spoken words. And it is more than just the imparting of information. Communication is also the ability to deliver a compelling and convincing message to your audience with ease. The purpose of creating and delivering an effective presentation is to ensure people understand your message and can form a connection with you through your delivery. Therefore, remind students that they will need to present differently to the different audiences identified at the *Pinpoint* step.

Students will need explicit instruction and time to learn and practice the following for both the design and delivery of their presentation: tone of voice, body language, eye contact, hand gestures, facial expression as well as all the nonverbal signals, active listening, speaking clearly and concisely, showing empathy, conveying respect, being open-minded, and displaying confidence.

use this time to teach learners good presentation skills

Teachers are encouraged to use explicit instruction through activities that help students develop their speaking skills. These include role-playing, discussions, storytelling, interviews, and simulation games. Also, teachers are encouraged to use explicit instructions and media for presenting the information.

Step 7: Probe

Probe is about assessment and evaluation. The focus of the assessment must include the content of the presentation, the delivery of that presentation, and a review of the entire learning process. This evaluation must be aligned to the original criteria, objectives, and outcomes outlined in the *Pose* step. Evaluations could be summative, formative, formal,

*If students help create rubrics, they'll better understand what is expected of them

informal, written, verbal, recorded, self-, peer, group, or teacher-driven. Students must be given the opportunity to assess their learning because group assessment, peer assessment, and self-assessment foster personal ownership and accountability.

The purpose of assessment is to inform teaching and learning as facilitated through authentic means. Teachers are encouraged to use a variety of assessment methods to evaluate content as well as process skills such as problem solving, collaboration, communication, citizenship, and creativity applied within real-world contexts. Rubrics are one method for authentic assessment and help determine whether the criteria were met. The authors encourage teachers to include students in the development of these rubrics.

Rubrics must be created to evaluate both the presentation and the delivery. Students should be clear about how they will be evaluated before they begin creating their presentations. For every rubric, ensure that there are listed criteria on specific aspects. Rubrics used to assess student presentations must be simple and easy to read and understand. Ensure that students are made aware of their role as a listener when other groups or individuals are presenting.

During the *Probe* step, assessors must provide both feedback and feedforward on presentations (product) as well as the delivery of the presentation. Giving and receiving feedback and feedforward are essential communication skills. Educators must cultivate in students the necessary academic language associated with an assessment so that they can provide constructive feedback and feedforward to their peers for future projects, problems, tasks, or challenges. Constructive feedback and feedforward must be both critical and productive without being hurtful or biased. Ask students to listen carefully to the feedback and feedforward, and encourage them to communicate how they would act positively in moving forward. During this step, both educators and learners must revisit the criteria developed and agreed on during the *Pose* step.

Probe skills and actions include active listening, reporting, rubric development, observation, metacognitive thinking, learning the language of constructive feedback and feedforward, listening, communications, lateral thinking, assessment, questioning, open-mindedness, leadership, and collaboration skills.

Step 8: Ponder

We must emulate what happens in the real world if this is where we are preparing our students to operate. Reflection is a critical element in the learning journey. Teachers must ensure they plan for adequate time to reflect and provide the opportunity for a formal debrief. Reflection is a time where students have the chance to articulate their personal and team experiences throughout the process, thereby enriching their learning. While the *Ponder* step is a specifically allocated time for reflection, we encourage educators to have their students reflect throughout the entire Communication Fluency process, explicitly using each step as a checkpoint and a time for reflection, formative assessment, feedback, and feedforward.

It is important to remember that the skill of reflection is not learned automatically, but has to be explicitly taught and deliberately practiced. Reflection is a conscious process where students use their own experiences to learn something. Reflection helps students make meaning of their learning. If we aim to help students become both consumers as well as producers of knowledge, then we must teach them strategies and skills on how to reflect.

Because teachers are busy meeting mandated demands, it is easy to skip the reflection step and move on to the next unit of work. But when we do this, we miss a critical opportunity to enhance student learning. The *Ponder* step of Communication Fluency helps cultivate personal ownership and responsibility for learning. It asks learners to revisit each of the seven previous steps, reflect on their performance, as well as all the other aspects of this learning journey. At this step, there should be a particular focus on the learning process, presentation creation, and delivery. Reflection can be written or oral and can be done through interviews, questions, discussions, blogs, or journals, as well as individually, in pairs, and small or large groups.

Ponder skills include asking reflection questions about the process, the product, and delivery: what was learned, how it was learned, and how they could make the product as well as the process better the next time.

Step 9: Pledge

The final step of Communication Fluency is *Pledge,* which involves learners taking targeted action. While taking action may not happen all the time, the opportunity for students to apply their products or solutions to real-world contexts must be promoted. The action taken can be big or small, local or global, altruistic or pragmatic, individual or collaborative. The *Pledge* step provides learners with an opportunity to make a difference by positively contributing to society and developing good citizenship qualities.

Communication is complicated because there are many components and skills involved. However, these skills can be learned, and Communication Fluency is a start. The nine-step process enables students to take a leading role in their learning. They are encouraged and guided to share their knowledge and expertise through various creative modes and media to authentic audiences. At the *Pledge* step, learners are encouraged to take their knowledge to a new level. Educators must promote student voice and agency so that learners become independent, contributing global citizens.

Pledge skills and actions include inter- and intrapersonal skills such as volunteerism, community service, service-learning, social activism, decision making, responsibility, empathy, personal growth, honesty, integrity, student voice, and student agency.

The goal of Communication Fluency is to move learners beyond the reality of simply consuming information. The ultimate goal of Communication Fluency is to help students develop into prosumers, both consumers and producers of knowledge to solve real-world problems and to take real-world actions as part of being a good global citizen.

Summarizing the Main Points

- To prepare learners for their futures, educators must provide them with diverse instructional experiences and the ability to express themselves using real-world and relevant mediums.

- Today, some educators continue to use traditional methods for teaching their lessons. Many learners are expected to communicate their new knowledge using antiquated or overused means. Today's learners are different; they want to express themselves in a wide variety of new ways. Moreover, they want their work to be relevant, engaging, and fun.

- We live in an increasingly interactive and participatory world. This is a world where it is essential to be able to create and communicate original digital and non-digital products.

- The 9Ps process of Communication Fluency—*Pose, Pinpoint, Prepare, Picture, Plan, Produce, Probe, Ponder,* and *Pledge*—allow learners to communicate knowledge in new, exciting, and engaging ways.

- Learners need Communication Fluency to understand how to effectively use digital and non-digital tools to solve problems and create real-life products that communicate, inspire, and entertain.

Questions to Consider

- What is a prosumer? And why must the digital generations develop into prosumers?

- Revisit the list of different ways learners can express themselves. Are there additional methods not included?

- What is student voice and agency? Why is it so crucial for the future?

- What is the new role for images and video in communication for the digital generations?

- Using Communication Fluency, how could you promote student voice and agency?

11 Creativity Fluency: Innovation and Imagination

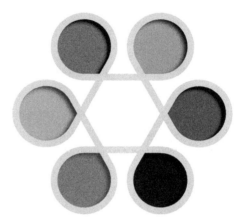

"The principle goal of education is to create men and women who are capable of doing new things, not simply of repeating what other generations have done—men and women who are creative, inventive, and discoverers . . . who have minds which can be critical, can verify, and not accept everything they are offered."

—Jean Piaget

It is relatively easy to identify creative people or ideas. It is much more difficult to define or explain creativity accurately. Dr. E. Paul Torrance, the creator of the Torrance Tests of Creative Thinking (TTCT), describes creativity as

> a process of becoming sensitive to problems, deficiencies, gaps in knowledge, missing elements, disharmonies, and so on; identifying the difficulty; searching for solutions, making guesses, or formulating hypotheses about the deficiencies;

testing and retesting these hypotheses and possibly modifying and retesting them, and finally communicating the results. (p. 6)

Sir Ken Robinson similarly described creativity as a process of having original, authentic ideas that have value. He went on to describe creativity as putting imagination to work. In essence, creativity is applied imagination (Robinson & Aronica, 2015).

When discussing creativity, there are two related concepts to keep in mind: imagination and innovation. Imagination is the root of creativity, the ability to bring to mind things that aren't present to our senses, while innovation is putting these new ideas into practice (Amabile & Pratt 2016; OECD/Eurostat, 2018).

IQ versus CQ

IQ tests are standardized tools for measuring intelligence or intelligence quotient. With intelligence tests, there is a phenomenon called the *Flynn effect* named after Dr. James Flynn, a New Zealand professor who discovered that every decade, IQ scores go up by about 3 points (Trahan, Stuebing, Fletcher, & Hiscock, 2014).

For example, if the average IQ score was 100 in 1932, by 2020, the average score should be about 129. The IQ scale has to be regularly renormed so that 100 remains the median score. A simple explanation for the Flynn effect is that increasingly enriched learning environments are making kids smarter.

Like intelligence, a creativity quotient (or CQ) can be measured using a tool known as the Torrance Test, which has been in use for more than 50 years. Like IQ tests, the Torrance Tests also have to be regularly renormed because they too show the Flynn effect, with scores around the world going up about 3.2 points every 10 years (Bronson & Merryman, 2010).

However, a July 10, 2010, article in *Newsweek* highlighted there is one critical difference between IQ and CQ scores (Bronson & Merryman, 2010). IQ scores consistently show the Flynn effect. IQ scores keep increasing. But with creativity and the Torrance test, Kyung Hee Kim, a researcher at the College of William & Mary in Virginia, identified a startling reverse trend. Three hundred thousand Torrance scores that children and adults have taken over 50 years were reassessed (Kim, 2011). Kim's findings showed that until 1990, creativity scores like IQ scores had been steadily rising. However, since then, all the components and subscales that make up the CQ of creativity scores have consistently inched downward. The decrease in CQ scores has been more in

[handwritten margin note: # are CQ scores declining b/c younger kids are using technology too passively? ie: TV, video games, phones?]

[handwritten margin note: this is POWERFUL. why aren't we empowering students & how do we make that shift? Does this need to come from the top down or individual educators?]

recent years than in earlier years, and this decline is very significant. In addition, it's the scores of younger children, from kindergarten through sixth grade, for whom the decline is most acute.

It is too early to determine conclusively why creativity scores are declining while IQ scores around the world continue to show the Flynn effect. One possible culprit is the number of hours kids now spend in front of the TV, playing video games, or staring at their smartphones rather than engaging in creative activities.

Dan Pink talks about this decline in his book *A Whole New Mind* (2005). He tells the story of a professor who went into a kindergarten class one day and asked students to raise their hands if they could dance. Of course, the kids all put their hands up. Draw? Sing? Again, they all raised their hands. Then he went into a college class and asked the very same questions of students there, and of course, no one raised their hands. He concluded that education is the process of teaching us what we can't do rather than what we can do.

This decline is further amplified in the book *Breakpoint and Beyond: Mastering the Future Today* (1998) by George Land and Beth Jarman. They showed the results of a longitudinal study on the Percentage of Genius in the general population:

Genius Level Creative Capacity by Age

Kindergarten level student = 98%

Children (ages 8–10) = 32%

Adolescents (ages 13–15) = 10%

Adults (ages 25 and up) = 2%

A creativity study, conducted by George Land and Beth Jarman, measured the creativity ability of the same subjects beginning in kindergarten and ending when they were adults. The study found 98% scored at genius level in kindergarten, 32% at age 10, 10% at age 15, and only 2% when they were adults (Rivero, 2012).

It is apparent that somewhere along the line, we unconsciously start comparing ourselves and our work to others, and our internal voice tells us we just aren't creative. We convince ourselves that we are not talented, and we carry this perception for the remainder of our lives.

This decline is an absolute recipe for disaster. The necessity of human ingenuity has never been greater. All around us are matters of local, regional, national, and international importance that are crying out for creative solutions. Whether it's overcoming the effects of a global pandemic; or stopping an out-of-control nuclear power plant from suffering a core meltdown; or overcoming the effects of global warming, overpopulation, and famine; or figuring out how to reduce plastic and microplastic pollution in our oceans; or dealing with terrorism and militancy; or bringing peace and tolerance to all people, we want people who can innovate their way through the challenges with which they are confronted. Everywhere we turn, there is a desperate need for people who can, while under enormous pressure, think outside the box and create unique and captivating solutions that can transform our world.

Creativity is a much sought after skill, especially in today's highly competitive global market. This chapter introduces educators to the 9Is process of Creativity Fluency. Creativity Fluency encourages innovation and imagination and is designed to help learners generate innovative thinking that leads to original ideas for creating and improving both products and processes. The 9Is—Illustrate, Identify, Inquire, Imagine, Initiate, Implement, Inspect, Investigate, and Inspire—is one strategy for teachers to use that will help unleash the creativity in all our learners. Creativity Fluency encourages students to wonder, imagine, explore, and share their knowledge in unique and powerful ways.

Creativity Fluency helps learners through a step-by-step process to turn ideas into solutions, including the creation of products. The process guides learners to generate new and novel solutions to real-world problems. While Creativity Fluency can be taught in isolation, the authors strongly recommend that teachers use the 9Is to help students with the *Dream* step in Solution Fluency. The *Dream* step is about having students brainstorm possible solutions for the problem or challenge with which they are faced. The process of Creativity Fluency also empowers learners to find creative ways to communicate their ideas and products. Once again, the authors recommend that Creativity Fluency be utilized during the *Picture* step in Communication Fluency, where learners are asked to brainstorm creative ways of presenting their solutions, ideas, and thoughts to authentic audiences.

Creativity is about form and function. Imagination is about the form of something. Innovation deals with its function. Creativity includes both innovation and imagination. Innovation is about developing new ideas. Imagination is about adding value to existing ideas. Thus, while innovation makes things better (function), imagination helps enhance its beauty (form). Learners will be able to utilize the 9Is to convey meaning and add value to something beyond its function.

For learners to create new and novel solutions to problems, we must provide them with ample opportunity to take risks by exploring, experimenting, questioning, creating, imagining, challenging, and discovering. Albert Einstein perfectly illustrated the power of creativity and the limitation of knowledge when he wrote, "We cannot solve our problems with the same thinking we used when we created them." And, "Imagination is more important than knowledge. Knowledge is limited. Imagination encircles the world."

The 9Is process will allow learners to turn imaginative ideas into new innovations. The 9Is of Creativity Fluency can be adapted and integrated into any curriculum for learners at any grade level or age. Learners will explore concise steps that can be explained, learned, practiced, applied, internalized, and improved over time.

The Creativity Fluency process encourages students to wonder, imagine, explore, and share their knowledge in unique and powerful ways. During each step, students develop questions that guide their learning as they generate and communicate their understanding. Figure 11.1 is an outline of the Creativity Fluency process.

Figure 11.1   Creativity Fluency: The 9Is

CREATIVITY FLUENCY
Illustrate
Identify
Inquire
Imagine
Initiate
Implement
Inspect
Investigate
Inspire

Step 1: Illustrate

As with all the other fluencies, Creativity Fluency also requires that educators assume the role as a facilitator of the learning. When students undertake a task where they are asked to be creative, it seems evident that we expect them to be imaginative and innovative. We also assume that their creativity will be reflected in the work they present for assessment. However, setting students up for success to be creative and imaginative requires more than merely assigning them with tasks or projects to complete. To stimulate creativity in our students requires training combined with innovative learning approaches where students are encouraged to utilize technology, social media, and any other available resources.

Therefore, before students go off to complete a task, it is critical that at this first step, they define the scope of the topic as well as their understanding of the challenges and tasks they are expected to complete. Learners must also clearly articulate in their own words how their solution or product will illustrate creativity and innovation. The *Illustrate* step requires that students present the teacher with a written description of their understanding of what they are expected to accomplish.

letting them rewrite things in their own words increases the likelihood they will retain & understand.

This written statement must identify the problem they are solving, the solution or product they will create, the mode and media for the presentation, and how they will demonstrate creativity and innovation in both the design and presentation of the solution to their respective audiences.

This step helps the teacher gauge whether students have a clear understanding of what they are required to do within the given timeframe provided to complete all required tasks.

Illustrate skills and actions include restating or rephrasing the challenge or task in the learners' own words; understanding media, medium, and message; identifying keywords; identifying the problem and gathering facts and materials that are needed to find new solutions; formulating good questions; thinking laterally; understanding ethical issues; active listening; and speaking clearly. Further skills are all the creative competencies, which include imagination, resilience, motivation, brainstorming, collaboration fluency, information fluency, solution fluency, communication fluency, and global citizenship.

Step 2: Identify

During the *Identify* step, students are asked to determine their target audiences, which could be individuals or organizations. Students must realize that solving a real-world problem impacts real people. Encourage students to take the time to identify the different audiences. These include those for whom they are solving the problem, those they will present and/or market their solution or product to, those who can help them achieve their goals in solving the problem, and those who will benefit from the solution or product.

*identify:
- who are you solving the problem for?
- who are you presenting to?
- who can help solve the problem
- who will be effected?

= b/c each group needs something different.*

Students must ensure they develop an understanding of the different needs of the various audiences. Having this knowledge is crucial because it helps learners decide on the most appropriate solutions and/or products as well as the best forms of communication to use.

Identify skills and actions include identifying the authentic audiences; understanding the cultural, historical, and economic mindsets and backgrounds of the selected audiences; anticipating the attitudes and biases of the audiences (What do they think about the topic? What motivates their interest?); connecting with audience members; identifying the purpose of the plan to solve the problem; choosing the goals or preferred outcomes of the presentation (inform, persuade, inspire, entertain); and selecting the appropriate format to deliver the presentation to different audiences (proposals, published content on blogs, wikis, discussion threads, videos, podcasts, etc.).

Step 3: Inquire

The *Inquire* step is where learners access a whole range of resources to gather information to help them complete tasks, find a solution, or create a product for the problem with which they are faced. They must also collect information to help them identify the specific mode and media they will use to communicate their message. However, students must be reminded that while the *Inquire* step is about research, it is not merely about knowledge acquisition. The research must focus on creativity.

Instead of teaching or showing students that there is only one correct solution to a problem, it is our job as educators to encourage them to utilize divergent thinking. Using divergent thinking will help nudge learners to consider different ways to approach problems. Creativity is a much sought after currency in the 21st century. Therefore, we need to ensure that all students are given every opportunity to be innovative and creative. Remind students that every time they are faced with a problem, task, or challenge, it is an opportunity for them to be creative.

It is essential that during the *Inquire* step, learners focus not only on the solution or product but also on how to make it original in the form of a new concept, idea, or improvement on an existing product or design. They must also look at the specific vocabulary to use when conveying or presenting their ideas and products to their respective audiences.

Encourage learners to utilize the skills learned during the *Ask* step of Information Fluency. Remind students to formulate some compelling question starters that will help them during this research phase. Question starters could include why, how, what if, could we, how would, why do, might it; in other words, have them ask probing questions. Ask students to share their thinking with others as well as respond to their peers' thoughts and ideas. While students are encouraged to think independently, they must also be able to challenge their own and others' assumptions and the conventional ways of doing things.

Inquire skills and actions include drawing on their skills learned from Information Fluency, having students use the new research information, and making connections to previous knowledge. Have learners reinterpret the information gathered so that the information can be used in creative and innovative ways for their chosen solution or product. Once again, remind learners to think about novel ways to communicate their message simultaneously. Have students revisit the steps in Communication Fluency to guide them through this process.

Step 4: Imagine

Imagine is the brainstorm step. Students must be encouraged to develop as many different ideas as possible for their solution. It is through unlimited visioning that creativity occurs. However, feasibility (time, money, resources, and skills) is always a critical factor that must be considered when identifying possible solutions. Remind learners of the rules for brainstorming: Focus on the topic, generate as many ideas as possible, accept all ideas, offer no judgment, be visual, write down everything, and build on ideas. Also, remind students that when generating ideas during brainstorming sessions, they must focus on creativity and innovation. The *Imagine* step is a fun way to ask students to imagine how they would invent, design, and create a solution, product, and presentation.

Explain to students that the *Imagine* step is an opportunity for them to explore ideas in creative ways to solve a real-world problem that will benefit their community or the world. Learners should feel free to voice their thoughts and opinions. The *Imagine* step is a time for students to feel safe so that they can take risks. Remind them that not all ideas will work and that not all suggestions will be practical, but that generating many ideas is an essential part of the creative process. This step provides them with the opportunity to imagine and see things in their mind's eye without fear, a time for students to visualize any number of alternatives to their chosen solutions and products. Imagination allows students to look at things from multiple points of view and to envision possible solutions and products.

Imagine skills and actions include brainstorming, mind-mapping, doodling, daydreaming, whole group and small group discussions, formulating mental images, performing additional research into potential solutions, lateral thinking, questioning, reframing, thinking in metaphors, pictures, and sounds, decision making, image streaming, and imagining best-case scenarios. Remember, Creativity Fluency is a flexible process, so learners may revisit previous steps before proceeding.

Step 5: Initiate

The *Initiate* step is about visioning and planning to achieve goals as laid out in the *Illustrate* step. A plan helps us succeed in fulfilling all the criteria identified in the initial step. A good plan helps us make sense of what is required to complete a task, challenge, or create a product by breaking it up into manageable chunks. Predicting the future is difficult; therefore, having a plan and dividing up tasks and responsibilities among team members facilitates the process of creating a solution or product. A plan helps the team work together to achieve solutions to solve real problems.

The *Initiate* step is neither a linear nor prescriptive process but instead serves as a guideline. It provides learners with a step-by-step process and identifies milestones in creating achievable deadlines to complete required tasks. At this step, students are expected to plan and design first before executing that plan.

To develop solutions that are creative and innovative, students must draw on the skill, experience, and knowledge of all team members. However, orchestrating a team of diverse individuals requires proper planning. Therefore, at the *Initiate* step, it is crucial to ensure the plan includes guidelines for team members to work together to meet common goals. The plan also serves as a personal and team guide that is used to track progress and ensure that everyone is on target to achieve the required goals.

Remind students that while the plan they develop lays out a step-by-step guide, it is flexible. They are encouraged to revisit any previous step as needed. For example, as learners design their product, they may need additional information, which may require them to go back to the *Inquire* step. Planning is vital; therefore, spending time planning is time well spent. Planning will help students manage both time and resources and keep them focused on what needs to be done to achieve the desired outcomes.

Initiate skills and actions include being able to take on a role as a leader or follower, goal setting, planning, communications, collaboration, self-management, time management, prototyping, decision making, budgeting, flexibility, resource management, prioritizing, record keeping, multitasking, and writing instructions in small, easy-to-follow increments that are positive and logical.

Step 6: Implement

Coming up with ideas is often considered to be a relatively easy task. The challenge comes when the designs must be executed. The *Implement* step is about following through with the plan. Given that the focus is on creativity remind students to keep an open mind, be flexible in their thinking, and be prepared to adapt or modify their original ideas. When creating their solution or product, encourage students to try new and different ideas. Also, ask them to look at their initial ideas from alternative perspectives. However, remind students that when experimenting and tinkering with the creation of a product, they must be mindful of time and budget. In other words, students must be conscious of the importance of completing the tasks within an allotted time frame with the available resources.

There are two components to the *Implement* step: *Produce* and *Publish*. The authors believe that creativity is about having good ideas and having the skills to turn those ideas into reality. First, students must create their product; this is the Produce part of the *Implement* step. Remembering that the product can be almost anything—perform a play, record a podcast, compose a poster, build a sculpture, produce a video, complete an experiment, publish a website, or make a multimedia presentation—the possibilities are endless.

Students then need to present their solution and/or product to their respective authentic audiences, which is the Publish component of the *Implement* step.

It is essential that students first identify creative solutions and determine whether their ideas are new or an improvement on an existing one (Produce). And second, identify a creative way of presenting their ideas, solution, or product (Publish).

Implement skills and actions include both those related to producing a solution, as well as those needed to publish their solutions. These skills include production (both media and multimedia), design (new inventions or innovations), literacy (speaking, listening, reading, writing, visual), and identifying and using the most appropriate format and medium for presenting the information.

Step 7: Inspect

Creativity has been identified as one of the critical skills for the 21st century. Many countries have included creativity as a part of their curriculum. Given that we live in a highly competitive global economy, people with creative skills are in high demand. Schools are increasingly expected to develop this essential skill in students. To ensure that creativity is valued and taught in all schools, we need to evaluate these skills through some form of authentic assessment. Rubrics are an effective strategy to assess creative competencies.

For this to happen, creativity must be given the same status as the traditional 3Rs and other core subjects. Before the Torrance tests, creativity was thought to be a natural ability that some people were born with. However, using the step-by-step process of Creativity Fluency, creativity skills can be taught through explicit instruction.

At the *Inspect* stage, students are asked to ensure all the criteria identified at the *Illustrate* step have been completed. Learners need to revisit their written statements and use them as a checklist. The *Inspect* step is the stage when students' work is assessed. The assessment could be summative, formative, formal, informal, written, verbal, or recorded. Assessors could include teachers, peers, individuals, community, experts in the field, and so on. Identifying the assessment type and assessors at the *Illustrate* step is a way for both students and teachers to agree in advance.

Another essential component of the assessment is feedback and feedforward. Teachers are encouraged to use feedback as a method of formative assessment. The authors recommend that teachers use each step of Creativity Fluency as a checkpoint where they can provide feedback as well as feedforward to students. At each of these checkpoints, students also have the opportunity for self-, peer-, or group assessment. In this way, feedback is relevant, personal, and timely. Just-in-time feedback enables learners to review, revise, and improve their work before moving forward. Students must be included not only in the assessment process but also provide their peers with feedforward (Hattie, 2012).

To model creativity, the authors ask that teachers use creative means and modes to assess and provide feedback to students. We encourage the use of audio, visual, written, oral, and action-oriented feedback. Some examples include a mobile phone, Snagit, Screencast-O-Matic, Screencastify, VoiceThread, Google Docs, Peergrade, Explain Everything, Vocaroo, FlipGrid, the Review tools like Track Changes and Commenting in Microsoft Office apps, and other various screencasting tools.

Inspect skills and actions include active listening, reporting, rubric development, observation skills, interpersonal and intrapersonal skills, growth mindset skills, metacognitive skills, learning the language of constructive feedback and feedforward, listening, communications,

[handwritten margin note: revolutionary along the way allowing teachers to give just-in-time feedback & feedforward, allowing the students to have checking & make adjustments as needed before something is due, or the final feedback.]

conflict negotiation skills, lateral thinking, defining assessment terminology, risk taking, being open-minded, leadership, time management, and collaboration.

Step 8: Investigate

Becoming a life-long learner requires transferable skills. Reflection is one of those essential skills that we need all our students to develop. We believe that students must look back to move forward. The *Investigate* step is as important as all the other steps in Creativity Fluency. This step allows educators to stop and provides time for reflection. This step is frequently omitted in the learning process. Too often, the focus is on moving forward without deliberately taking the time to have students look back. This activity can be done individually, in pairs, groups, silently, orally, verbally, or written.

The *Investigate* step is an opportunity for students to reflect critically on both the product and process of their learning, as well as on their ideas, actions, and outcomes. The *Investigate* step allows for reviewing progress, inviting and incorporating feedback, providing constructive feedforward, and asking reflective questions.

Was the goal always clear? Were the instructions always clear? What was supposed to happen? What did happen? What went well, and why? What didn't go well, and why? What could be done differently? Why was there a difference between what was expected to happen and what did happen? What constraints or barriers were faced? How were those barriers overcome? Was there enough time to accomplish all the tasks to make this process a success? Could another approach have been used to reach the goals more efficiently and effectively within the given time frame? Were the criteria for the process and product transparent, understandable, and measurable? What have I/we learned? How have I/we learned? Will this new learning help me/us? Why is it important to know this?

Reflection is an effective teaching and learning strategy. The *Investigate* step ensures that value is given to the reflection process. Reflection provides students with the opportunity to learn by making meaning from past experiences and casts insight into future learning. Reflection also helps us think about how we can apply our knowledge to new, different, or similar situations.

At the *Investigate* step, students are encouraged to develop their reflective skills. The starting point is to set some expectations for the reflection process. Ensure all students are held accountable. Remind them to be kind, helpful, and specific. Educators could utilize the six thinking hats (de BONO; https://www.edwddebono.com/). The hats promote lateral thinking, and when used during the reflection process, it helps students focus on different aspects without being judgmental.

The *Investigate* step is the same as the *Debrief* (Solution Fluency), *Ponder* (Communication Fluency), *Analyze* (Information Fluency), and *Evaluate* (Collaboration Fluency) steps. The respective steps allow students to analyze their learning experience or journey freely. It is through the reflective process that students have the opportunity to make meaning of their learning and express their understandings and misunderstandings.

The authors recommend that teachers use a guided process to help students develop practical reflection skills. Some strategies teachers could use to facilitate the reflection include discussions, questions, logs, and journals.

Investigate skills are metacognitive skills involving complex thinking. They include speaking, listening, reevaluating, introspection, self-reflection, critical thinking, practicing wait time, managing impulsivity, questioning skills, reflective journal writing, and idea incubation. These skills involve revisiting each step of the process and reflecting critically on the pathways followed to get from *Illustrate* to *Implement*, as well as asking questions about the process being used, acting on those reflections, and internalizing the new learning. These skills help learners relate new learning to existing knowledge, develop strategies for applying new knowledge to complex situations, and transferring this learning to different, similar, or novel settings.

Step 9: Inspire

Creative thinking is divergent. *Solution* Fluency recommends a problems-first approach. Students are presented with a problem, preferably real world. Using Creativity Fluency in conjunction with Solution Fluency guides learners in solving the problem while at the same time helping them cultivate creativity.

Creative thinking opens up possibilities and gets students reimaging existing or conventional solutions. Cultivating creative thinking encourages students to think differently or take an alternate approach. Everyone is creative; they just need the opportunity to exercise their creativity. All students can learn to be creative using the structured mental process of Creativity Fluency. Learners use a step-by-step approach to help them come up with original ideas by connecting their learning to their own life experiences in different ways.

The *Inspire* step extends learning into the real world. Learners are allowed to apply their learning beyond the school to their local or global community. Learners find creative and innovative ways to use their new knowledge and, in doing so, make a real difference. The *Inspire* step helps prepare students for life. Given that we live in disruptive times, we must prepare our students for jobs that do not exist and have not yet been created. We, therefore, must foster creativity by providing them an environment in which they can explore their ideas in creative ways and finally be able to use them to take action to meet the needs of their respective audiences.

Rather than being passive recipients of information, students construct their own knowledge through the actions they take and the contributions they make to the world. Remember, creativity doesn't involve students creating and handing in a project or task that's visually attractive. Creativity can be an idea, concept, or approach. In other words, discovering or creating something that did not exist before. Creativity Fluency enables educators to move beyond bubble tests to approaching teaching, learning, and assessment in innovative and creative ways.

Inspire skills and actions include inter- and intrapersonal skills such as volunteerism, community service, service learning, social activism, decision making, personal responsibility, empathy, personal growth, honesty, and integrity.

Summarizing the Main Points

- Torrance defines creativity as a process of becoming sensitive to problems, deficiencies, gaps in knowledge, missing elements, disharmonies, and so on; identifying the difficulty; searching for solutions, making guesses, or formulating hypotheses about the deficiencies; testing and retesting these hypotheses and possibly modifying and retesting them; and finally communicating the results.

- Creativity includes both innovation and imagination. Innovation is about developing new ideas. Imagination is about adding value to existing ideas. Thus, while innovation makes things better (function), imagination helps enhance its beauty (form).

- The 9Is process of Creativity Fluency includes: *Illustrate, Identify, Inquire, Imagine, Initiate, Implement, Inspect, Investigate,* and *Inspire.* Creativity Fluency allows learners to turn imaginative ideas into new innovations.

- Creativity Fluency doesn't end with a single cycle of the 9Is. As children move through the process, they generate new ideas and continue to the next iteration of this creative spiral, with another cycle of imagining, creating, playing, sharing, and reflecting.

Questions to Consider

- Why do you think creativity decreases as children age and continue through their academic careers?

- What is the difference between imagination and innovation?

- Is your classroom, school, or organization innovative? How do you nourish creativity?

- Why is creativity such an important skill to focus on for the future of learning?

Global Citizenship: Citizenship in the Digital Age 12

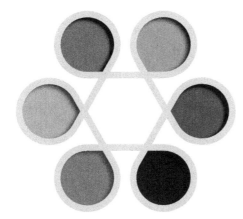

"Don't ever forget that you're a citizen of this world, and there are things you can do to lift the human spirit, things that are easy, things that are free, things that you can do every day: civility, respect, kindness, character."

—Aaron Sorkin

One of the many critical responsibilities educators have is to help learners become good global citizens. This chapter provides ideas and strategies that support educators to help their learners apply the elements of good citizenship to the situations, problems, circumstances, and challenges encountered daily in the real world.

As educators and parents, we all want what's best for our children. We want them to do well in school, and be successful in their working and personal lives. It is also our desire that they become contributing members of society at both the local and global levels. Given that the world is changing at warp speed, we need to equip them with skills that will last a lifetime. The fluencies described in the previous chapters are those essential skills. That's because the fluencies never become outdated. They have no expiry date and are transferable to a wide variety of different situations. The authors believe that the overarching fluency is Global Citizenship. We are failing our children if we do not mentor, guide, and support them in becoming good, ethical, contributing members of society. Becoming a good citizen is a learned process comprising a variety of knowledge and skills. Once acquired, learners must be given every opportunity to apply these skills not only in school but also to situations encountered as part of everyday lives.

The last step in each of the fluencies outlined in previous chapters has been a strategic move to encourage and enable student agency and empowerment. At this step, students have the opportunity to take action and make a difference through their contributions, no matter how big or small those contributions might be. From an early age, students learn that their actions can make a difference. The fluencies provide students with learning experiences that allow them to make a difference in their personal lives as well as in the lives of others. Through the use of the fluencies, students not only learn to solve real, authentic problems and make decisions, but also develop critical skills that help them leverage personal agency, voice, and power as responsible citizens.

Cultivating Good Citizens Online and Offline

While we live in an increasingly digital age, we recommend that educators not get bogged down with the buzzword *digital citizenship* because they believe that being a good citizen, whether offline or online, comprises essentially the same behaviors and characteristics—being kind, being respectful, being honest, and being responsible—in other words, just doing the right thing.

Being a good citizen is no different than being a good global or digital citizen because the characteristics traditionally identified for good citizenship traits apply equally well to the modern world. Citizenship today is no longer limited to the community, town, city, or country in which we live. Today we are experiencing the death of distance; physical boundaries are disappearing. Digital technologies seamlessly facilitate communication and collaboration equally well whether it's across town or around the globe, making world events only a click away. People are now able to connect with anyone, anywhere, anytime. No longer do we live in isolation from the rest of the world. We have all become global citizens!

At the same time, digital technologies and ready access also present many challenges, with privacy concerns, cybercrime, and digital addiction

[handwritten margin note: interesting take that good citizenship in the traditional sense is now no different than global or digital citizenship b/c technology has bridged that gap & we've all global now]

to name but a few. Educators are increasingly being called on to add digital citizenship to an already overloaded curriculum (Lapus, 2018). A singular focus on digital citizenship overlooks the fact that many of the traits of a good citizen (such as empathy, altruism, responsibility, respect, kindness, honesty, ethics, etc.) apply equally well whether they are local, global, offline, or online.

When preparing students for success in our interconnected world, it is important to ensure learners understand that global citizenship comes with responsibilities. It is essential that all citizens develop awareness about the various issues related to religions, cultures, traditions, values, perspectives, beliefs, and situations faced daily by our fellow global citizens. Tolerance, understanding, acceptance, and sensitivity are all essential core values that need to be developed by all citizens.

Increasingly, we have a global workforce where teams comprise people who work collaboratively on projects while physically located in different locations around the globe (Future of Work Institute, 2012). As a result, countries can no longer exist in isolation. Instead, they need to become more interconnected and interdependent. What happens in one country may have an impact on the rest of the world directly or indirectly. The global pandemic, COVID-19, has dramatically and emphatically demonstrated this. That is why it is critical we ensure our students understand their place in this world. As global citizens, they must accept their responsibilities and work together to ensure that our Earth continues to be a livable place.

Good citizens are lateral thinkers and have the ability to manage their thoughts, feelings, attitudes, and actions to achieve collective goals. By cultivating empathy and interpersonal awareness, students learn to shift the focus from themselves to community, national, international, and world issues. Communities become more inclusive when everyone is given a voice (Gurchiek, 2018). After all, being successful in life takes more than just performing well at school. One of our jobs as educators is to ensure our students develop moral characteristics and agency that will help them build relationships and understand how their actions impact both themselves and the world. It is for these reasons that the fluencies have been strategically designed in a manner that requires us to make a shift from a focus on outcomes to a focus on the process of learning.

Thinking Globally, Acting Locally

Educators must seize the opportunity to help students cultivate personal responsibility. We believe that schools need to collectively develop

[Handwritten margin note: Devils advocate here: if we are pushing learners to always be thinking of others at such a large scale, are we raising a generation of people pleasers & couldn't that potentially cause a lot of anxiety?]

and implement a program that clearly defines appropriate behavior in different situations and circumstances. It is essential that this program includes not just a simple list of rules, but rather takes the form of a citizenship contract that also incorporates an acceptable use policy for the internet. It is imperative that this contract, as well as accountability measures, be created collaboratively with students.

Having students involved in the entire process is an effective teaching and learning strategy, one that fosters independence as well as a personal and collective responsibility. We recommend that this contract be reviewed, revised, and signed on a yearly basis. The contract must include principles collectively identified and agreed to by all stakeholders. The number of principles included depends on the emphasis the organization wishes to focus on. For example, they may choose five principles such as respect, responsibility, kindness, honesty, and ethics. It is essential educators work closely with students to ensure that there is a shared understanding of what each of the principles entails. For example, respect includes respecting oneself and others, as well as respecting personal property, the property of others, and intellectual property. These principles apply regardless of whether students are offline or online.

Further to the drawing up and signing of a contract, it is critical that disciplinary actions also be discussed and identified with students and other stakeholders. Students must understand that, as in the real world, actions have consequences. Because the fluencies immerse students in real-world situations, they must be prepared to accept responsibility for their choices. This contract will help guide students in determining whether their actions are aligned to the principles they committed to in the contract.

If we want to help our students prepare for success in a dynamic, interconnected, rapidly changing world, Global Citizenship education cannot be an option. Thus, Global Citizenship skills must be taught to every child in all schools and at every grade level. The authors believe that Global Citizenship should not just be considered an add-on to the curriculum, but rather must be deeply embedded in every subject area.

Today our children are growing up in a diverse and unpredictable world. While they may have only local experiences and exposure to their local culture, it is our mandate as educators to expose them to the global world by bringing that world to them either directly or through sites such as Skype Classroom, Mystery Skype, ePals, PenPalSchools, Exploring By the Seat of Your Pants, and Google Classroom.

*have U-HErs help create an annual contract for member expectations & display it at all meetings

make sure that everyone is on the same page in terms of meaning of each principle.

Local community members are also a powerful resource that can provide a rich learning experience for students. For example, a local store may carry exotic overseas products, a local ski resort might attract foreign tourists, a local entrepreneur might have extensive international travel expertise, or a town might be known for a particular product or service.

Bringing local experts into the classroom gives students the opportunity to hear other people's experiences and perspectives and ask questions. This is an effective strategy that allows students to make connections with their local community experiences as well as those of the global world. It is critical for students to not only develop an awareness of global events, but also be provided with opportunities to participate in international events such as World Peace Day, International Woman's Day, or World Teacher's Day (https://en.unesco.org/commemorations/international-days). This experience also encourages students to produce authentic artifacts such as interviews, videos, podcasts, or other creative products.

Global Citizenship Passport

The process skills developed through exposure to each of the fluencies not only help students become good global citizens but also develop citizens who are globally aware and competent.

Solution Fluency involves learning processes related to solving real-time, real-world problems, a skill that helps learners compete in an increasingly global job market.

Information Fluency equips students with process skills that can be utilized to wade through the vast seas of information so readily available in the age of InfoWhelm. The steps of Information Fluency help learners identify, gather, and analyze different types of media to extract the essential knowledge, perceive its meaning and significance, and apply that knowledge to solve problems or complete real-world tasks. By using the Information Fluency process, students become aware of related issues experienced by other global communities, allowing them to connect local to global matters.

Communication Fluency equips learners with process skills that allow them to leverage the most appropriate digital and non-digital means to effectively communicate with diverse audiences. Helping students become good global citizens requires they have a voice and use that voice to share their perspectives and views on matters of local and global significance, while simultaneously being sensitive to and accepting of other cultures and beliefs.

Creativity Fluency is about teaching students processes that help learners generate innovative thinking to develop original ideas for creating and improving both products and processes. Creativity Fluency empowers learners to find creative ways to communicate their ideas and products, enabling them to be successful in an increasingly competitive global market.

Collaboration Fluency is about forging global connections in a world that is becoming increasingly interdependent. There is an urgent need for learners to develop skills that will allow them to work and interact with both real and virtual partners. They can also learn to effectively collaborate with people from diverse cultures and backgrounds, while collectively working toward common goals. In applying the fluencies, students quickly realize we are all citizens of the greater world and that our individual actions can affect the world both positively and negatively.

Taking action is the culminating step in each of the fluencies. At this point, there are two simple but powerful questions educators must ask students to ensure they are adequately prepared to be good citizens. These questions are: "So what?" and "Now what?"

This is how these questions work:

So what? Information by itself is of little value until that information has been transformed into knowledge. At this point when students have only information, we ask the question "So what?"

The knowledge is developed through the *application* of the skills learned by students via the steps of each of the fluencies. This application must demonstrate that learners are utilizing their newly acquired skills and knowledge for relevant and authentic purposes. However, understanding content, while important, is only part of the learning journey. Now is the time to ask the question Now what? Now that you have this knowledge and the fluencies have armed you with the skills needed to do something with this knowledge, what are you going to do to make a difference in the world? At this point, students can choose to take action either individually or collectively. Regardless of how they choose to take action, they must be prepared to take responsibility for their decisions and actions and accept the consequences these actions have on the world.

Citizenship education must be the central goal of our schools. Our purpose as educators is to help learners prepare themselves for their future, while at the same time being good contributing citizens. To be clear, citizenship is a complex topic. There is no single consensus on what it means to be a good citizen; schools, together with students and other stakeholders, and guided by the *Define* step of Solution Fluency, must collectively develop an agreed definition and set of values to define what it means to be a good citizen. This definition must then be used to create a performance contract to which all members of the school are committed.

While it is important to know the values related to being a good citizen, as well as to sign a performance contract agreeing to them, it is also essential that individuals demonstrate their understanding, belief, and commitment through their actions. The authors recommend that, as is the case with all the other fluencies, students be authentically assessed against these citizenship goals. If we truly want to prepare students to be good citizens, we must go beyond just the superficial identification of a list of values. We must dig deeper. We must focus on teaching knowledge and skills as well as providing learners with opportunities to apply this knowledge and skills by taking action, no matter how big or small they might be.

Authentic assessment is a true assessment of intellectual achievement and ability because it requires students to demonstrate their deeper understanding, higher-order thinking, and complex problem solving through the completion of real-world challenges and standards of performance people might experience in their later life or the modern workforce. Actions, skills, and the observable evidence of learner dispositions can be assessed and evaluated. What cannot be authentically assessed are the elements of learning that cannot be easily observed and measured. For example, you cannot assess what someone thinks, you can only assess the evidence of their thinking.

Teachers are reminded to use the process outlined in the *Define* step of Solution Fluency to draw up these citizen contracts. The *Define* stage ensures that students and teachers reach a common understanding about the tasks that need to be completed. This consensus becomes the basis of a contract between teachers and students in which both agree what students need to accomplish to demonstrate that they are developing good citizenship skills.

The authors suggest that, like with Solution Fluency, teachers use a scenario based on their unique school contexts to help students acquire the skills, knowledge, and dispositions needed to be positive global citizens. See the next example for a suggestion to create a scenario.

Sample Essential Question: How can we help create or foster a positive school climate at Avalon?

From the scenario below, students will develop a written definition.

Scenario: Both younger and older students have complained about being bullied by their peers. Teachers have also commented that some children are being excluded from games and that some students occasionally do not share equipment with others. Recently, several students reported damage to their personal property. The librarian has observed that books from the library have been scribbled on. Some staff have reported incidents where iPads and computers have been mishandled, and student monitors have reported missing cords and chargers.

The principal wants our help in resolving these issues. He wants the school to be a positive place where all students and their property are treated respectfully. He also asks for student help in ensuring that everyone at Avalon is a good, responsible, contributing member of the school community. He thinks that a good way to begin is to get everyone to agree to the following:

Students' Written Definition/Contract Items

- Embrace and celebrate diversity
- Demonstrate empathy and tolerance to one another
- Participate and engage actively in school life
- Cooperate and collaborate
- Show respect to self, people, and property
- Fulfill commitments
- Contribute positively
- Follow mutually accepted social norms
- Pledge allegiance to _____ (school, community, etc.)
- Take responsibility both personally and collectively
- Offer altruistic service
- Provide environmental stewardship

By developing a challenge using a familiar context (such as a school scenario) the hope is to generate a teaching and learning experience that goes well beyond students simply learning the attributes of being good citizens. Students must be provided with opportunities to apply this learning to the interconnected world and in doing so, demonstrate they are good global citizens. If we want our children to be life-long learners, learning cannot just be confined to the classroom.

Life-long learners must also be able to adapt and apply their knowledge and skills to new and different situations and circumstances outside the school. They must also utilize these skills to solve problems and over-come challenges, while at the same time, making a positive contribu-tion as good global citizens in a constantly changing world.

How do we make this transition w/ older students w/o over whelming them?

Preparing students to be good global citizens is no easy task. As is the case with all the other fluencies, the role of the teacher is that of a facilita-tor. To be clear, facilitators are not expected to know everything. Rather, our job is to guide our learners and help them discover, inquire, solve problems, make decisions, and take action. Global citizenship cultivates the essential modern skills we are all familiar with: critical thinking, problem solving, creativity, collaboration, and communication. These skills are not accidentally learned, but rather deliberately taught in every school, embedded in all subject areas, and learned at all grade levels.

While learning the attributes of good citizenship, students must also be aware of the diversity of the multiple cultures, religions, ethnicities, and races that exist in our world (Yilmaz & Boyan, 2016). Students should learn how to be sensitive to global issues such as inequalities (resources, technol-ogy, and power), conflict, and environmental problems (pollution, nonre-newable resources depletion). We believe that a global citizen is one who identifies themselves as belonging to both a local and a global community.

The fluencies are the path to attaining a global citizenship passport. The fluencies not only teach students processes and skills, but also how to exercise flexibility, adapt to different contexts, become culturally com-petent, and continuously contribute positively to society. A global citi-zen is one who works together with other members of their community to improve the world.

If we hope to sustain our planet and prevent it from being devastated, then helping students earn their global citizenship passport is key. Students quickly learn that being a good contributing global citizen comes with both benefits and responsibilities. Once they have their global passport, they are no longer restricted to just the local commu-nity. Learners are now free to share their voice and work toward solu-tions to the many problems and challenges experienced in our world today. By teaching global citizenship skills to our students as a critical part of the curriculum we are empowering them for the future.

Summarizing the Main Points

- One of the many critical responsibilities educators have is to help learners become good global citizens.

- Educators must mentor, guide, and support learners in becoming good, ethical, contributing members of society.

- Using the Modern Fluencies not only allows students to solve real, authentic problems as well as make decisions, but they also develop critical skills that help them leverage personal agency, voice, and power as responsible citizens.

- Being a good citizen is no different than being a good global or digital citizen because the characteristics traditionally identified for good citizenship traits apply equally well to the modern world

- If we hope to sustain our planet and prevent it from being devastated, then helping students earn their global citizenship passport is key. Students quickly learn that being a good contributing global citizen comes with both benefits and responsibilities.

Questions to Consider

- What shared beliefs and values does your school have?

- How can educators think and act locally to help cultivate global citizenship skills in learners?

- What are some strategies you will use to promote good citizenship qualities?

- What does it mean to be a good global citizen?

- Why is it crucial to include learners in the development of a global citizenship contract?

Authentic Assessment: Techniques and Strategies

13

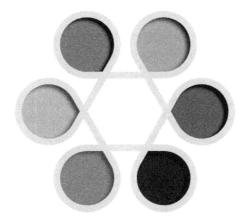

"Learners need endless feedback more than they need endless teaching."

—Grant Wiggins

The future is here! The idea that change is happening is old news. We need to acknowledge that using 20th century teaching, learning, and assessment models and approaches will not be enough to resolve 21st century problems. Trying to improve traditional pedagogy will not allow us to equip learners with problem-solving, innovation, critical thinking, communication, collaboration, and creative thinking skills needed to operate in an increasingly changing world. Both the future of education and the future of our children depend on what we can do now to ensure that students are ready to meet the future head-on. We need to teach today for tomorrow and beyond.

This chapter articulates the differences between formative and summative assessments, explains authentic assessment, and provides strategies for creating useful rubrics to assess authentic learning tasks. It also highlights the importance of reflective practices and articulates how educators can provide constructive feedback and feedforward to promote a growth mindset in learners. Readers will be introduced to a wide range of authentic assessment strategies, as well as how these processes can be designed to leverage learner results. This data allows educators to make informed instructional decisions that they can use to integrate the modern fluencies.

Traditional educational systems place too much emphasis on standardized testing; testing that only focuses on one particular type of intelligence. Psychologist and Cornell University professor Robert Sternberg created his triarchic theory of intelligence, "which identifies three kinds of smarts: the analytic type reflected in IQ scores; practical intelligence, which is more relevant for real-life problem solving; and creativity" (Sternberg, 1985, 1997; Wallis, 2017).

Most standardized tests strictly measure analytical intelligence and completely ignore practical and creativity-based intelligences. The mission of education must be to prepare learners for their futures—futures that require them to develop the other two types of intelligences. The authors and many practitioners recommend using the Modern Fluencies for teaching, learning, and assessment because the fluencies promote learners becoming competent in all three types of these intelligences.

Figure 13.1   Sternberg's Triarchic Theory of Intelligence

ANALYTICAL INTELLIGENCE	PRACTICAL INTELLIGENCE	CREATIVITY INTELLIGENCE
This intelligence is associated with analyzing and evaluating ideas, solving problems, and making decisions.	This intelligence is associated with individuals applying their knowledge into real-world contexts.	This intelligence is associated with using existing knowledge and skills to deal with new problems or situations.

Images from Tumisu from Pixabay; rollymaiquez from Pixabay; Hebi B. from Pixabay.

Summative and Formative Assessments

Summative assessments (such as standardized tests) occur at the end of the instructional process. Although summative assessments have their uses as instruments to provide performance data about each learner and the school's academic program, this only represents one data point in the assessment profile of both. To use an analogy, it is like assuming that a party was fun by seeing one random picture from the event. However, if you have multiple photos of a party taken from different perspectives, there is more evidence to go by to inform your conclusions. As educators, we cannot determine the success and potential of our learners using a single high-stakes test.

Formative assessment is ongoing and can be used by both teachers and students to evaluate and make adjustments throughout the learning experience. Formative assessment is a crucial way for educators to gauge students' understanding, and then use the information to guide future instruction. Unlike the linear design of summative assessment, where learners participate in a learning progression and finish with a test, formative assessment is a nonlinear cycle. Educators continuously guide students to access their prior knowledge, engage them in learning activities to build on their knowledge base, help demonstrate their instructional gains (through a variety of assessment methods), and reflect on the process, product, and outcome of the learning cycle.

Authentic Assessment

Authentic assessment involves a more practical approach, requiring more hands-on involvement than traditional assessment types. According to the late educational leader Grant Wiggins (1989), authentic assessment

Figure 13.2 Formative Assessment Versus Summative Assessment

FORMATIVE ASSESSMENT	SUMMATIVE ASSESSMENT
Occurs in a flexible progression	Occurs in a linear progression
Occurs throughout a learning activity or unit	Occurs at the end of a learning activity or unit
Occurs frequently (daily, a few times per unit, etc.)	Occurs sporadically throughout the academic year
The purpose is to monitor student learning and understanding	The purpose is to measure and evaluate student learning
Takes the form of various types of activities, questions, or tasks	Uses limited types of question formats
Provides student feedback or feedforward	Results in a score or grade

is "a true test" of intellectual achievement or ability because it requires students to demonstrate their deep understanding, higher-order thinking, and complex problem solving through the performance of exemplary tasks. Authentic tasks replicate real-world challenges and standards of performance that experts or professionals (mathematicians, scientists, writers, doctors, teachers, or designers) typically face in the field.

Future-focused learning must utilize authentic assessment approaches that evaluate both the processes and products of learning. These types of evaluation are carefully crafted to provide students, teachers, parents, and other stakeholders with performance data that informs decision making and supports student success both inside and outside the classroom.

Using the fluencies for modern-day teaching and learning is a natural fit for authentic assessment. Since the learning progressions present in each of the fluencies require real-world problems to be solved, challenges to be mastered, or tasks to be completed, educators must use authentic assessment to measure learner performance. Assessments of this nature are ideal for supporting learning experiences in the design and facilitation of units or lessons utilizing the fluencies.

Rubrics

A rubric is a scoring tool that definitively communicates the required performance expectations for a learning task, assignment, or project (Brookhart, 2013). A rubric dissects the assigned work into different components called *criteria*. A rubric must provide clear descriptions of the characteristics of the work associated with each criterion at varying levels of performance. Rubrics help take away the subjectivity sometimes unconsciously practiced during the assessment process by providing a clear roadmap to success in an instructional activity. Popham (1997) adds that rubrics should have a scoring strategy if they are used to evaluate students' work for a traditional grade or performance score.

A well-constructed rubric can be used to assess an array of learning assignments: projects, research papers, creative writing, roleplays, oral presentations, artistic performances, group projects, podcasts, videos, and simulations to name but a few.

Figure 13.3 provides a visual to identify the components of a rubric crafted to assess the development, publication, and analysis of a podcast created by a team of fourth-grade learners. Once their podcasts have been published, each student is provided with another team's podcast to analyze its message. The educator (facilitator) then assesses the

Figure 13.3   Podcast Rubric

a. Common Core State Standards ELA Grade 4 Writing 1. Conduct short research projects that build knowledge through investigation of different aspects of a topic.

b. Common Core State Standards ELA Grade 4 Reading Informational Texts 9. Integrate information from two texts on the same topic in order to write or speak about the subject knowledgeably.

c. Common Core State Standards ELA Grade 4 Writing 1. Write opinion pieces on topics or texts, supporting a point of view with reasons and information. a. Introduce a topic or text clearly, state an opinion, and create an organizational structure in which related ideas are grouped to support the writer's purpose. b. Provide reasons that are supported by facts and details. c. Link opinion and reasons using words and phrases (e.g., for instance, in order to, in addition). d. Provide a concluding statement or section related to the opinion presented.

d. Common Core State Standards ELA Grade 4 Writing 7. Participate in shared research and writing projects (e.g., explore a number of "how-to" books on a given topic and use them to write a sequence of instructions).

e. Common Core State Standards ELA Grade 4 Speaking and Listening 3. Identify the reasons and evidence a speaker provides to support particular points.

PODCAST RUBRIC EXAMPLE WITH LABELS		PERFORMANCE LEVELS (FOR THIS RUBRIC A 4-POINT SCALE IS USED TO DIFFERENTIATE STUDENT PERFORMANCE)			
		(4) EXEMPLARY	(3) PROFICIENT	(2) DEVELOPING	(1) UNACCEPTABLE
Criteria (aligned to a CCSS; each is observable and measurable)	Research topic for a podcast (a)	All relevant information is obtained and sources are valid.	Most information is obtained from numerous sources.	Some information is obtained from different unverified sources.	Little or no information is found. Sources not provided.
	Integrate information from multiple sources (b)	Information was obtained from more than three verified and authenticated sources for the podcast script.	Information was obtained from two verified sources for the podcast script.	Information was obtained from one verified source for the podcast script.	Information was obtained from no verified source for the podcast script.
	Construct a podcast script (c)	The script included a compelling - opening introducing the topic and organizational	The script included a mostly compelling - opening introducing the topic and	The script included a somewhat compelling - opening introducing the topic and	The script included an uncompelling - opening introducing the topic and organizational

(Continued)

Figure 13.3   (Continued)

		structure for the podcast - set of at least three complete details, reasons, or opinions supporting the topic - conclusion summarizing the topic and the podcast's content	organizational structure for the podcast - set of three complete details, reasons, or opinions supporting the topic - conclusion summarizing the topic and the podcast's content	organizational structure of the podcast - set of complete details, reasons, or opinions supporting the topic - conclusion summarizing the topic and the podcast's content	structure of the podcast - set of three complete details, reasons, or opinions supporting the topic - conclusion summarizing the topic and the podcast's content
	Collaborate with a team to produce and perform the Podcast (d)	Each member of the team demonstrated a captivating performance by: - assuming the role of a leader open to the team's input and ideas - supporting the leader and team by performing required tasks - completing all required podcast tasks - providing feedback and suggestions to aid their team members	Each member of the team demonstrated a mostly captivating performance by: - assuming the role of a leader open to the team's input and ideas - supporting the leader and team by performing required tasks - completing all required podcast tasks - providing feedback and suggestions to aid their team members	Each member of the team demonstrated a somewhat captivating level of performance by: - assuming the role of a leader open to the team's input and ideas - supporting the leader and team by performing required tasks - completing all required podcast tasks - providing feedback and suggestions to aid their team members	Each member of the team did not demonstrate a captivating level of performance by: - assuming the role of a leader open to the team's input and ideas - supporting the leader and team by performing required tasks - completing all required podcast tasks - providing feedback and suggestions to aid their team members
	Analysis of a podcast's message (e)	Learners analyze with 100% accuracy the message of another team's podcast to determine its purpose	Learners analyze with 80% accuracy the message of another team's podcast to determine its purpose	Learners analyze with 60% accuracy the message of another team's podcast to determine its purpose	Learners analyze with less than 50% accuracy the message of another team's podcast to determine its purpose
		Descriptors for Performance Levels			

Source: National Governors Association Center for Best Practices & Council of Chief State School Officers. (2010). Common Core State Standards for English language arts and literacy in history/social studies, science, and technical subjects. Washington, DC: Authors.

steps of the podcast creation (the process) as well as the finished podcast (the product).

For the rubric shown in Figure 13.3, you will observe that several Common Core State Standards (CCSS) that align with a persuasive podcast project for a fourth-grade student have been selected.

The language and instructional actions defined in each of the selected academic standards have been infused into the rubric's criteria and descriptors for each performance level. Each criterion and rubric descriptor must be observable and measurable. A flawed criterion will often try to measure something that cannot be measured, such as student thinking or their understanding of a topic. The secret to overcoming this mispractice is to assess ways learners demonstrate or reflect their thinking and understanding of content.

Rubric Organization: What counts in a student's work?

- Content. Does the rubric cover everything of importance? Does it leave out unimportant content?
    - Does the content of the rubric represent a demonstration of competency of the skills, process, and product being evaluated?
    - Does the content directly align with the academic standards or learning goals it is intended to assess?
    - Does the rubric measure what it is intended to? Is it what you look for when you evaluate the quality of a student product or the learning process?
- Criteria Organization. Is the rubric divided into understandable criteria as needed?
    - Is the number of criteria appropriate for the complexity of the learning goals or product?
    - Are the descriptors for each criterion clear, understandable, observable, and measurable?
    - Does the relative emphasis among criteria represent their importance?
    - Is each criterion clear and unique with no overlap?
- Appropriate Number of Performance Levels. Is the number of performance levels appropriate for the intended learning goal?
    - Can learners distinguish among each performance level?
- Clarity. Does everyone have the same understanding of terminology?

- Levels Defined Well. Is each level of the rubric clearly defined?

  o Do definitions include descriptive words and phrases rather than nonspecific terms such as exemplary and detailed, or counting the number or frequency of something? (Both quantitative and qualitative descriptions)

  o Would two separate raters give the same rating to the same product or performance?

  o Are the descriptors non-evaluative?

  o Performance Level Parallel. Are the levels of the rubric parallel in content?

  o If an element is mentioned at one level, is it also said at all other levels?

(Adapted from Arter & Chappius, 2006)

Types of Rubrics

There are many variations and design choices present in rubrics. For this book, we examine three rubrics: holistic, analytic, and single-point. Educators should choose the type of rubric most appropriate for tracking or measuring student performance; and the data they wish to collect and use to inform teaching and learning. Educators are encouraged to use single-point rubrics to provide students with feedback and feedforward throughout the learning process. Holistic and analytic rubrics should be used when assessing multiple performance areas across different levels.

A **holistic rubric** maps out the project, challenge, or task by listing all the criteria at the same time. The rubric facilitates an overall judgment of the quality of student work as the assessor evaluates across several different performance levels. An **analytic rubric** splits the description into individual criterion and requires assessors to assess each separately. A **single-point rubric** is constructed with only a single dimension for measuring the quality of student work by focusing on a single performance level.

The single-point rubric contains two additional columns for extensive educator or peer feedback. The first column represents a place for educators to explain how student performance must grow and improve. This feedback and feedforward must be constructive, personalized, non-subjective, and actionable for students. The second column is a space articulating how student performance exceeds the expectations for the solution, challenge, or task; and is a performance level above the proficient standard. (Consult Figures 13.4, 13.5, and 13.6 for rubric examples.)

A positive teaching and learning practice is for educators to review a rubric before the task begins. As mentioned previously, the first step across Solution Fluency, Collaboration Fluency, Information Fluency, Communication Fluency, and Creativity Fluency involves learners (or learners in conjunction with their teacher) describing and then communicating in their own words the problem, task, or challenge they face. They then create a written statement that outlines their understanding of the challenge encountered. In doing so, the learners have generated many of the elements that will be infused into the rubric for their fluency unit.

Figure 13.4   Example Holistic Rubric Based on a Fluency Activity

Exemplary (4): Student groups thoroughly examined air pressure, its effects on weather, and weather safety procedures. The group recorded or calculated the estimated and air pressure measurements with 100% accuracy. They constructed accurate weather maps with labels, cities, and weather data. The team created a weather report script that included all the following: an introduction to air pressure and how it's measured, the 5 days of barometric pressure readings on the map, weather predictions based on the data observations, and weather safety tips. Learners performed the weather report for the viewers at home or in the studio audience and delivered a segment on preparing for extreme weather in a compelling manner.

Proficient (3): Student groups mostly examined air pressure, its effects on weather, and weather safety procedures. The group recorded or calculated the estimated and accurate air pressure measurements with at least 80% accuracy. They constructed mostly accurate weather maps with labels, cities, and weather data. The team created a weather report script that included most of the following: an introduction to air pressure and how it's measured, the 5 days of barometric pressure readings on the map, weather predictions based on the data observations, and weather safety tips. Learners performed the weather report for the viewers at home or in the studio audience and delivered a segment on preparing for extreme weather in a most compelling manner.

Developing (2): Student groups performed a limited examination of air pressure, its effects on the weather, and weather safety procedures. The group recorded or calculated the estimated and accurate air pressure measurements with at least 60% accuracy. They constructed somewhat accurate weather maps with labels, cities, and weather data. The team created a weather report script that included some of the following: an introduction to air pressure and how it's measured, the 5 days of barometric pressure readings on the map, weather predictions based on the data observations, and weather safety tips. Learners

(Continued)

Figure 13.4   (Continued)

performed the weather report for the viewers at home or in the studio audience and delivered a segment on preparing for extreme weather in a somewhat compelling manner.

Emerging (1): Students performed little or no examination on air pressure, its effects on weather, and weather safety procedures. The group recorded or calculated the estimated and accurate air pressure measurements with less than 60% accuracy. They constructed inaccurate weather maps with labels, cities, and weather data. The team created a weather report script which included a few of the following: utilized an introduction to air pressure and how it's measured, the 5 days of barometric pressure readings on the map, weather predictions based on the data observations, and weather safety tips. Learners performed the weather report for the viewers at home or in the studio audience and delivered a segment on preparing for extreme weather in an uncompelling manner.

Creating Assessments and Rubrics Aligned to the Modern Fluencies

Creating rubrics aligned to the fluencies is made easier because the very first step in each of the learning progressions requires learners to brainstorm the criteria for their learning journey. This action provides a clear understanding and transparency for the learner as to what the expectations are for the problem, task, or challenge since they are codesigning the rubric with the educator. Here is an example of a science, mathematics, and geography fluency unit called *Full of Hot Air*. What follows is a brief overview of a real-world scenario along with a holistic, analytic, and a single-point rubric that an educator could use to assess student work.

The Overview of the Unit: Full of Hot Air

A weather team is required to prepare a weather report based on the air pressure readings in specific parts of the country for the next 5 days. The readings will help the audience determine what the weather might be according to the air pressure reports. Using the collaborative team's knowledge of decimals, they must record the millibars or inches of mercury (exact and rounded to the nearest whole number) in various locations throughout the country and observe air pressure and weather changes over the next 5 days to report to the local (and global) audience.

The Importance of Peer and Self-Assessment

There is little focus on peer and self-assessment. Both peer and self-assessments are powerful teaching and learning strategies.

Figure 13.5   Example Analytic Rubric Based on the Fluency Activity

CRITERIA	(4) EXEMPLARY	(3) PROFICIENT	(2) DEVELOPING	(1) EMERGING
Conducting Air Pressure Research	Student groups thoroughly examined air pressure and its effects on the weather.	Student groups mostly examined air pressure and its effects on the weather.	Student groups performed a limited examination on air pressure and its effects on weather.	Students performed little or no examination on air pressure and its effects on the weather.
Calculating Air Pressure	The group recorded or calculated the estimated and accurate air pressure measurements with 100% accuracy.	The group recorded or calculated the estimated and accurate air pressure measurements with at least 80% accuracy.	The group recorded or calculated the estimated and accurate air pressure measurements with at least 60% accuracy.	The group recorded or calculated the estimated and accurate air pressure measurements with less than 60% accuracy.
Constructing Weather Maps	They constructed accurate weather maps with labels, cities, and weather data.	They constructed mostly accurate weather maps with labels, cities, and weather data.	They constructed somewhat accurate weather maps with labels, cities, and weather data.	They constructed inaccurate weather maps with labels, cities, and weather data.
Creating a Weather Report Script	The team created a weather report script which included all the following: an introduction to air pressure and how it's measured, the 5 days of barometric pressure readings on the map, weather predictions based on the data observations, and weather safety tips.	The team created a weather report script which included most of the following: an introduction to air pressure and how it's measured, the 5 days of barometric pressure readings on the map, weather predictions based on the data observations, and weather safety tips.	The team created a weather report script which included some of the following: an introduction to air pressure and how it's measured, the 5 days of barometric pressure readings on the map, weather predictions based on the data observations, and weather safety tips.	The team created a weather report script which included few of the following: utilized an introduction to air pressure and how it's measured, the 5 days of barometric pressure readings on the map, weather predictions based on the data observations, and weather safety tips.
Performing a Weather Report	Performed the weather report for the viewers at home or in the studio audience and delivered a segment on preparing for extreme weather in a compelling manner.	Performed the weather report for the viewers at home or in the studio audience and delivered a segment on preparing for extreme weather in a mostly compelling manner.	Performed the weather report for the viewers at home or in the studio audience and delivered a segment on preparing for extreme weather in a somewhat compelling manner.	Performed the weather report for the viewers at home or in the studio audience and delivered a segment on preparing for extreme weather in an uncompelling and unfocused manner.

Figure 13.6   Example Single-Point Rubric Based on the Fluency Activity

AREAS TO FURTHER DEVELOP	PROFICIENT	AREAS THAT ARE EXEMPLARY
	Conducting Air Pressure Research Student groups examined air pressure and its effects on the weather.	
	Calculating Air Pressure The group recorded or calculated the estimated and accurate air pressure measurements with at least 80% accuracy.	
	Constructing Weather Maps They constructed mostly accurate weather maps with labels, cities, and weather data.	
	Creating a Weather Report Script The team created a weather report script which included most of the following: an introduction to air pressure and how it's measured, the 5 days of barometric pressure readings on the map, weather predictions based on the data observations, and weather safety tips.	
	Performing a Weather Report Performed the weather report for the viewers at home or in the studio audience and delivered a segment on preparing for extreme weather in a mostly compelling manner.	

Peer assessment is a collaborative learning strategy in which learners evaluate their peers' work, and in turn, have their work evaluated using an agreed list of criteria or directions.

There are numerous advantages to using peer assessment in the classroom:

- Encourages students to reflect on their thinking and roles as a contributor and evaluator of the task.

- Focuses on developing students' critical analysis skills.

- Involves students in the instructional and assessment processes, so they can be empowered and have a voice in how they are evaluated.

- Provides an opportunity for multiple assessors, not just the teacher. (Adapted from the University of Exeter, 2019)

Self-assessment is a process of critical evaluation of one's performance, in which explicit criteria are used to evaluate and scrutinize work against a set of agreed benchmarks (Tillema, 2010). Tillema also goes on to cite that learners engaged in self-assessment are found to be more engaged in their work and better able to interpret why and what they are doing. Self-assessment goes beyond learners, providing themselves with a grade. It involves self-reflection and self-analysis of both the product and process.

The fluencies are deliberately constructed to offer numerous opportunities for students to participate in both peer and self-assessments. The fluencies promote collaboration to solve problems and complete tasks or challenges. Collaboration provides opportunities for formal and informal peer assessment throughout the learning process.

Feedback and Feedforward

A study by Hattie and Timperley (2007) found that students who engage in strong feedback loops show a remarkable 29% gain in student achievement. Using a range of assessment strategies to create constructive feedback and feedforward loops promote growth mindsets in both learners and educators.

Educators spend a great deal of time, providing students with feedback, suggestions, advice, guidance, gentle reminders, and coaching. Feedback is built into a teacher's DNA! However, the feedback loop should not end with the teacher providing feedback to students without students having the opportunity to respond. In this kind of setting, the feedback is a lost opportunity for student growth.

The fluencies provide opportunities for both peer and self-assessments, as well as allocated time for teachers to give feedback to students. Each fluency comprises nine steps. The authors recommend that the end of each step be used as a checkpoint or time for formative assessment. Both teachers and students must take the time to review and reflect on the previous steps and give and receive feedback and feedforward before progressing to the next step. The fluencies support continuous and timely feedback and feedforward. Feedback and feedforward allow educators to support learners who may be struggling or require additional scaffolding. It is essential that the feedback provided by educators not rate or demean students' work. Feedforward is the practice of helping learners develop and grow for the future. Instead of rating and judging a person's performance in the past, feedforward represents actionable suggestions and guidance meant to perpetuate a growth mindset in learners. While positive feedback is good, it may only verify what the learner already knows. When educators provide feedforward instead of simple feedback, they are helping their learners see what the possible next steps are.

Reflection

John Dewey (1910), regarded as one of the most influential and prominent American scholars, stated, "We don't learn from experience. We learn from reflecting on experience" (p. 3). When students develop reflective skills and practices, they empower their capacity to learn. Metacognition is thinking about one's thinking. When learners develop and utilize reflection, they can adapt their learning to new contexts and tasks, identify their strengths and weaknesses, make connections to prior experiences, plan next steps, and assess their knowledge (Chick, n.d.).

Using reflection during the fluencies is a powerful strategy for teaching and learning. Zohar & Ben David (2009) found that metacognition is most effective when adapted to reflect the distinct learning contexts of a specific topic, course, or discipline. Hence reflection is an essential component of all the fluencies. The eighth step in each fluency is specifically designated as a time for reflection on the product, process, and experience of the learning journey.

Tools for Formative Assessment and Rubrics

Below, we have collected several different tools and suggestions for formative assessment and rubric development.

Rubric Development

Rubric Maker (www.rubric-maker.com/) is a creation tool that allows educators to create rubrics online for free. Add a title and select an academic level such as primary, elementary, middle, and high, and the tool provides performance areas and descriptor spaces to fill in. Once the educator or learner has created the rubric, they can download it as a PDF file.

Get Started with Rubrics (creativeeducator.tech4learning.com/2015/articles/Get-Started-with-Rubrics). Published by Melinda Kolk at Creative Educator, this article provides readers with the benefits of using rubrics during project-based learning and walks users through the steps of creating one from scratch.

iRubric (https://www.rcampus.com/indexrubric.cfm) is a rubric development, assessment, and sharing tool that supports a variety of applications in an easy-to-navigate package. *iRubric* is free to individual educators and students. Educators can build a rubric in a matter of minutes using the Rubric Studio, which allows easy customization of rubric components in an intuitive environment. Educators can assess their rubrics in seconds. In the spirit of crowd-sourcing and mass sharing, created rubrics can be accessed in the Rubric Gallery.

Formative Assessment Tools and Techniques

Exit Tickets

A versatile yet straightforward assessment strategy, Exit Tickets informs educators what students are thinking and what they have learned at the end of a lesson or activity. The ticket can consist of the essential question of the lesson, a math problem, or some other activity requiring a short-form answer. Once learners have had the opportunity to complete the task, the educator can review the problem with their class, have a student share the answer aloud, or review all the tickets to assess their understanding. Exit tickets allow educators to gauge whether students have "caught what they taught quickly." Teachers can use this information to plan for the next lesson.

3,2,1

This strategy provides a structure for learners to demonstrate their understanding and summarize their learning. Learners can also identify areas they still do not understand, as well as areas of extreme interest. At the end of the lesson, have learners record three new ideas they learned during the lesson. Next, have them record two elements they found interesting during the lesson and about which they want to learn more. Finally, have learners share one idea or concept about which they still have questions. This activity can be done orally and written form.

Kahoot

Kahoot (https://kahoot.com/) is a gamified learning platform used in schools and other educational institutions. Kahoots are multiple-choice quizzes that allow user-generation and can be accessed via a web browser or the Kahoot app. The Kahoot collects student performance data during lesson closure or test review. Kahoot is a fun and engaging method for formative assessment.

Padlet

Imagine a digital canvas where users can pin notes, pictures, files, and weblinks. Padlet (https://padlet.com/) is an easy and intuitive tool with many different possibilities for classroom application: exit tickets, group brainstorming, group note-taking, group projects, and collaborative workspaces are just a few of the learning and assessment applications possible with this free resource. Select a template or start with a blank slate, share with collaborators who will help you develop the space, post content, and share with anyone.

Summarizing the Main Points

- Most standardized tests (a form of summative assessment) measure strictly analytical intelligence and ignore practical and creativity intelligences.

- Formative assessment is a crucial way for educators to check students' understanding, and use the information to guide future instruction. Unlike the linear design of summative assessment, formative assessment is more cyclical.

- Authentic assessment is an accurate measure of intellectual achievement or ability because it requires students to demonstrate deep understanding, higher-order thinking, and complex problem solving through the performance of exemplary tasks. The fluencies help educators craft these types of exemplary tasks.

- A rubric is a tool that communicates the expectations for a task by listing criteria and describing different levels of quality for each criterion. A rubric provides a clear roadmap that takes away the subjectivity, which sometimes occurs during the assessment process.

- Reflection is a critical component of the learning process. The eighth step in each fluency is specifically designated as a time for reflection on the product, process, and experience of the learning journey.

Questions to Consider

- Why is it important to use both summative and formative assessments in learning programs?

- Describe the three types of intelligence: practical, analytical, and creativity.

- What are the crucial elements to consider when designing a rubric for assessment?

- Why is it of paramount importance to share the criteria of a rubric before beginning the instructional task?

- What is the difference between feedback and feedforward?

Moving Forward

The Future of Education Is Now: Are You Ready?

14

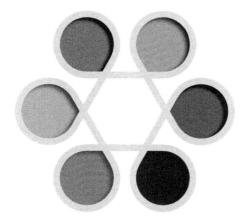

"Great teachers engineer learning experiences that put students in the driver's seat. Then, they get out of the way."

—Ben Johnson

If educators want to tap into the full intellectual and creative potential of every learner, if they want to ensure that learners are prepared for the world that awaits them once they leave school and not just the world of yesterday, If they want learners to develop the essential next-generation skills needed to survive in the New Digital Landscape, then education must build a bridge between traditional and progressive learning. Education must move beyond perpetuating pedagogies of control to facilitating learning experiences that empower the generations of today and tomorrow, going beyond 20th century literacies, to cultivating the modern-day fluencies.

The strategies identified in this book may sound exciting, but the challenge is that when many educators are asked to reconsider how they teach and think about education, they lose their excitement and unconsciously build mental barriers that cause resistance to change.

After all, in being asked to change their daily practice, educators are not being asked to change a few behaviors or habits like saving money, stopping smoking, or losing weight. It's REALLY hard to change an entrenched habit, even a small one. What we are doing is asking educators to reconsider some of the most fundamental parts of their life experiences and habits of mind. Educators can't do this by throwing out everything they have ever done or believed in as a student or teacher. That's not practical and certainly not what the authors are advocating here. Former British Prime Minister David Lloyd George once wrote, "There is no greater mistake than to try to leap an abyss in two jumps." You either jump across on the first bound, or you're going down.

Inevitably, people try to do too much, too quickly. They try to lose 30 pounds on a crash diet or break a habit that has been years in the making, and inevitably they fail and quickly revert to their previous lifestyle choices.

Embracing the fluencies is not about abandoning the long-time practices of an educator, and it is certainly not about creating some far-out vision for learning in the future. At the same time, this call to action is not about fixating on the teaching practices of yesterday. Instead, it is about understanding that the world has changed; students have changed and, therefore, schools *must* change. On the one hand, the successful tradition of schools must be honored. However, the mentality of "That's The Way We've Always Done It" will not sustain education. Systematic change is urgently needed for the learners of today and tomorrow.

In this chapter, we are asking educators to consider what they have read in this book, and then ponder how they can change one activity in a lesson, one lesson in a unit, one unit in a term—in other words, to take baby steps toward making meaningful change.

This book is designed to provide educators with guidelines for lesson and unit development utilizing the fluencies to help them cultivate the essential modern learning skills required by all students to be successful in life. Included in the book are a few samples of units to help readers see what these units look like when they are fully developed using the nine steps of any of the fluencies.

The lessons and units we strive to create must be crafted to invoke a sense of challenge and in doing so we bring adventure and curiosity back into learning. We are excited to share our ideas with you on how you can use the fluencies as a strategy for teaching, learning, and assessment in modern times. We hope that you find the lesson writing process engaging and rewarding for both yourself and your students. The fluencies is an approach to teaching and learning that places a vital emphasis on the new skills students will need when they leave our schools to begin building their unique part of the future. Even when students are no longer in the classroom, their learning journey will continue.

It is for these reasons that the lesson plans embedding the fluencies enable teachers to help students develop the essential skills needed to be effective problem solvers, collaborators, communicators, researchers, and creators. These skills will allow learners to be successful as they make their way into the New Digital Landscape, and our modern collaborative and entrepreneurial world.

An Overview of the Fluencies

The goal of your lesson development is to help students thrive in a world that changes and challenges us daily. With these modern skills embedded within each of the fluencies, and through a step-by-step approach, students will be better prepared to face the challenge of change head-on. They will be able to recognize and utilize the many opportunities for learning that these skills will bring them both today and tomorrow. We believe the fluencies are the very essence of the critical must-have skills. What follows is a brief review of the fluencies.

Solution Fluency: Real-World Problem Solving is the ability to think creatively to solve problems in real time using the 9Ds process. The steps are: **Define** clearly the problem that needs to be solved; **Determine** the target audiences, those experiencing the problem and those who can help solve the problem; **Discover** the information that gives the problem context; **Dream** a creative and appropriate solution; **Design** the process in measurable, achievable steps; **Deliver** the solution by both producing and publishing; **Diagnose** through the assessment and evaluation of both the process and the product using a variety of methods of assessment and utilizing multiple assessors; **Debrief** both the process and product, identifying potential improvements and reflecting on what has been learned and achieved; and **Decide** on next steps on how to make a difference locally and globally.

Collaboration Fluency: Global Connections is the ability to collaborate seamlessly in both physical and virtual spaces, with real and virtual partners, locally and globally. **Explain**—groups collectively unpack the problem and describe, in their words, what tasks they are required to complete; **Establish**—students identify the target audiences and establish group expectations, rules, and norms; **Explore**—gather information and resources. **Envision**—visualize and imagine a variety of possible solutions; **Engineer**—a step-by-step plan laying out the process and timelines to accomplish tasks; **Execute**—learners create a product (Produce) and then deliver their solution to a determined audience (Publish); **Examine**—assessing both the product and process; **Evaluate**—reflecting on the product and process; **Extend**—acting on their reflections.

Information Fluency: InfoWhelm and HyperInformation is the ability to unconsciously and intuitively access and interpret information in all forms and formats, extract the essential knowledge, perceive its meaning and significance, and apply it to solve problems or complete real-world tasks. The steps are: **Ask**—learners define the scope of the task; **Audience**—identify the target audience; **Access**—the most relevant data utilizing good questions; **Authenticate**—validating all sources; **Assemble**—summarize and synthesize the information; **Apply**—use the data to solve the problem; **Assess** is precisely the same as the *Diagnose* step in Solution Fluency with a focus on assessing the information fluency skills; **Analyze**—explicitly teach learners to become critical reflectors through various activities and allow learners to reflect, **Action**—utilize new knowledge to take real-world actions as part of being a good global citizen.

Communication Fluency: Text and Multimedia is the ability to communicate with text and speech in multiple multimedia formats, as well as to communicate visually, through video and imagery, in the absence of text. The 9Ps of Communication Fluency are: **Pose**—learners come to an agreement and develop a shared understanding of the message to be conveyed, the platform to be used, the medium best suited for the message, and the format of the presentation; **Pinpoint**—students identify the audience or audiences that will be the recipients of their message and/or information; **Prepare** is the research phase of the process during which learners gather information about their intended audiences; **Picture** is the visioning process where learners brainstorm, imagine, and visualize possible modes and media to convey their message to the various audiences identified in the *Pinpoint* step; **Plan**—students develop a simple roadmap designed to help everyone understand what is required, when and how learners are going to achieve set goals and identify timeframes; **Produce**—students put their plan into action by creating their presentation and delivering it to a predetermined audience; **Probe** is the assessment and evaluation step with a focus on the content of the presentation, the delivery of that presentation, and the entire learning process; *Ponder*—specifically allocated time for reflection (reflection is a conscious process where students use their own experiences to learn something); *Pledge* involves learners taking targeted action. The *Pledge* step provides learners with an opportunity to make a difference by positively contributing to society and developing good citizenship qualities.

Creativity Fluency: Innovation and Imagination is the ability to generate new and novel solutions to real-world problems. To think and work creatively in both digital and non-digital environments to develop unique and useful solutions. The steps are: *Illustrate*—students present the teacher with a written description of their understanding of what they are expected to accomplish including how they will demonstrate creativity and innovation in both the design and presentation of the solution to their respective audiences; *Identify*—students determine their target audiences, which could be individuals or organizations; *Inquire*—learners access a whole range of resources to gather information to help them complete tasks, find a solution, or create a product; *Imagine* is the brainstorm step, where students develop as many ideas as possible for their solution with a focus on creativity and innovation; *Initiate* serves as a guideline, and it provides learners with a step-by-step process and identifies milestones in creating achievable deadlines to complete required tasks; *Implement* has two components: *Produce* and *Publish,* where students create their product and/or solution and then present it to their targeted audience; *Inspect*—students' work is assessed, and the assessment could be summative, formative, formal, informal, written, verbal, or recorded; *Investigate*—time to have students look back and reflect individually, in pairs, groups, silently, orally, verbally, or written; *Inspire*—this step extends learning into the real world. Learners apply their learning beyond the school to their local or global community.

Regarding Global Citizenship: Citizenship in the Digital Age, becoming a good citizen is a learned process comprising a range of knowledge and skills. Global citizenship comes with responsibilities. All citizens must develop awareness about the various issues related to religions, cultures, traditions, values, perspectives, beliefs, and situations being faced daily by our fellow global citizens. Tolerance, understanding, acceptance, and sensitivity are all essential core values that need to be developed by all good citizens. Being successful in life takes more than just performing well at school. Our jobs as educators are to ensure that students develop moral characteristics, agency, and voice, which will help them build relationships and understand how their actions impact both themselves and the world.

When and How to Use the Fluencies

Because the fluencies represent all the critical skills learners need, they cannot be taught in isolation. Each fluency represents an important component of a critical skill required by all learners. A single fluency is just like one cog in a machine. Even when one part is missing or neglected, it will lead to inefficient functioning and impact the other components. All the cogs are required for the machine to function properly. Robert Swartz and colleagues' (2010) Parts-Whole Thinking framework shows that all components must be considered to create the best opportunities for success in a modern learning organization (MLO). While we may only focus on one fluency at a time, it is important to recognize that we cannot ignore the others (Graue, Hatch, Rao, & Oen, 2007).

We recommend beginning with Solution Fluency. We view Solution Fluency as the biggest cog in the machine. Once students are familiar with the steps of Solution Fluency, teachers can then introduce other fluencies. However, we would like to stress that while the other fluencies are stand-alone, they have been designed to support the different steps within Solution Fluency. What follows is a brief overview of where and how each fluency can be used within Solution Fluency.

Information Fluency is a plugin for the *Discovery* step in Solution Fluency. Teachers are guided by the steps in Information Fluency to explicitly teach students information literacy skills.

Collaboration Fluency is a step-by-step guide to support teachers in getting students to acquire skills that will help them not just work effectively in groups but also learn how to collaborate when solving problems (Solution Fluency).

Communication Fluency supports the *Deliver* step in Solution Fluency. Students are explicitly taught how to communicate their solutions to different audiences.

Creativity Fluency enables students to think and work creatively in both digital and non-digital environments to develop unique and useful solutions. Creativity Fluency can be used to support both the *Dream* and *Design* steps in Solution Fluency.

Global Citizenship is the overarching umbrella inside of which the fluencies are learned. It is our desire that all children become contributing members of society both locally and globally. As parents and educators, it is our job to mentor, guide, and support our children so that they become good citizens. Becoming a good citizen is a learned process comprising various elements and skills. The fluencies provide students with learning experiences that allow them to make a difference in their personal lives or the lives of others. In learning the fluencies, students not only discover how to solve real problems and make decisions, but also develop critical skills that will help them leverage personal agency, voice, and power as a responsible citizen.

Today's Learners Are Different

Schools are changing, but the world is changing many times faster. The challenge is that learners are digital, and many educational institutions are analog. In this changing world, the role of a teacher is not just to stand up in front of a class and show the learners how smart the teacher is. The mandate of teachers is to prepare students to learn independently. However, to be an effective 21st century teacher, we must first possess the very same 21st century fluencies our learners need to develop.

Collectively, Nicky, Ian, and Ryan have spent many years teaching in the classroom. We believe that the secret to success in the classroom has very little to do with being a good disciplinarian and classroom manager. Success has far more to do with creating an engaging methodology that compels learners to want to be there. Our task is not about making them learn. Our goal is to get them to *want* to learn. Without interest and motivation, there will be no learning.

Ask yourself this question: Would learners be in your classroom if they didn't have to be there? The killer app and best 1-to-1 device for 21st century learning is a great teacher: a teacher with a love of learning, an appreciation of the aesthetic, the esoteric, the ethical, and the moral; a teacher who understands Bloom, Gardner, Papert, Piaget, and many other great educational thinkers, a teacher who knows how different children learn in different ways at different times and different rates.

Today's learners are not the same learners for which schools were originally designed, and they are certainly not the learners that many of today's educators were trained to teach. It is crazy to think that 20 years into the 21st century we are still debating what 21st century learning looks like.

We must accept that learners today are different—neurologically different! That's why they see and engage with the world differently.

If we are going to uncover the full intellectual and creative genius of all our nation's learners, it is educators and educational leaders who are going to make it happen. Educators have the hardest job today. They are the beacons for millions of learners in the Knowledge Age. Modern education stands in the gap between their present and their future, between failure and fulfillment, between literacy and fluency, and between the way students traditionally learn and the Modern Fluencies.

The change starts with you. It is your energy, passion, creativity, commitment, and hard work *every day* that builds a bridge so children can cross the gap from the world of today to the world of tomorrow. And as today's children cross the gap, so do entire nations. Educators are a nation's greatest hope and most important professionals. And yes, once again we acknowledge, change is hard. It is easy to become discouraged. But as you finish this book, consider the words of the great anthropologist Margaret Mead, who once wrote: "Never doubt that a small group of thoughtful, committed citizens can change the world; indeed, it's the only thing that ever has" (as cited in Sommers & Dineen, 1984, p. 158).

Fluency Resources 15

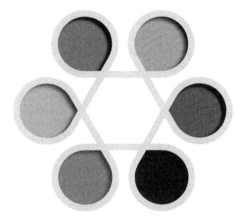

"There's no greater gift than thinking that you had some impact on the world, for the better."

—Gloria Steinem

Fluency Digital Libraries

What is better than purchasing a transformative book? The answer is purchasing a transformative book and getting practically another book for free. In this day and age, digital resources can provide readers (educators in particular) with a rewarding experience filled with classroom takeaways, ideas, and treasures to take the Modern Fluencies from theory into application. Below, we have created a digital library for each book chapter, which can be found on our companion website at **http://www.resources.corwin.com/literacyisstillnotenough**. If you visit a link, you will be transported to a collection of curated resources meant to help readers dive deeper into the content, access chapter-based resources, or simply receive a free gift.

Preface https://bit.ly/LSNEC0-PREAMBLE

Chapter 1: Highly Educated Useless People https://bit.ly/LSNECH1-HEUP

Chapter 2: Education in the Age of Disruption https://bit.ly/LSNECH2-DISRUPTION

Chapter 3: From Literacy to Fluency: The Starting Point https://bit.ly/LSNECH3-FLUENCY

Chapter 4: Modern Learning Pedagogy and the Learning Progression https://bit.ly/LSNECH4-PROGRESSION

Chapter 5: Modern and Future-Ready Learning Environments https://bit.ly/LSNECH5-FUTUREREADY

Chapter 6: Teaching and Learning Using the Modern Fluencies https://bit.ly/LSNECH6-SKILLS

Chapter 7: Solution Fluency: Real-World Problem Solving https://bit.ly/LSNECH7-SOLUTION

Chapter 8: Collaboration Fluency: Global Connections https://bit.ly/LSNECH8-COLLABORATION

Chapter 9: Information Fluency: InfoWhelm and HyperInformation https://bit.ly/LSNECH9-INFORMATION

Chapter 10: Communication Fluency: Text and Multimedia http://bit.ly/lsnech10 https://bit.ly/LSNECH10-COMMUNICATION

Chapter 11: Creativity Fluency: Innovation and Imagination https://bit.ly/LSNECH11-CREATIVITY

Chapter 12: Global Citizenship: Citizenship in the Digital Age https://bit.ly/LSNECH12-CITIZENSHIP

Chapter 13: Authentic Assessment: Techniques and Strategies https://bit.ly/LSNECH13-AUTHENTIC

Chapter 14: The Future of Education Is Now: Are You Ready? https://bit.ly/LSNECH14-FUTUREREADY

Chapter 15: Fluency Resources https://bit.ly/LSNECH15-RESOURCES

Fluency Lesson Sparks

Lesson planning is a very customizable task undertaken in each school. The structure, components, and requirements for a lesson plan vary drastically, making it impossible to provide a perfectly prepared lesson plan for all teachers. However, ideas, or what the authors refer to as *lesson sparks*, can help pique the interest and curiosity of educators and help them embrace the modern fluencies in their classrooms. These lesson sparks provide a real-world scenario to drive instructional planning and allow educators to prepare their instructional materials and delivery for their learners with the Modern Fluencies in mind.

Figure 15.1   Apple

Title: Multiply & Divide: Easy as Apple Pie (Third Grade)

Subjects: Mathematics, Economics, Language Arts

The Essential Question: How can you help save the jobs of the workers in your local area by using your knowledge of math?

The Scenario

Apples can be processed and used for numerous products helping meet the needs for many consumers and generate profit for businesses. There are so many potential apple dishes, desserts, and drinks to sell at a bake sale: apple pie, apple cider, apple vinegar, apple butter, apple fritters, candy apples, caramel apples, and apple sauce to name a few.

The recent weather has jeopardized the apple crops at the local orchard. The apples have ripened earlier than expected, and if the crop is not produced into apple products soon, then the crop will be wasted and the orchard will go out of business. The local orchard employs over 30 people. You must help the local orchard process and sell the food or a lot of people will lose their jobs.

Your school is running a bake sale to collect money to help the struggling apple orchard. The orchard has an abundance of apples, but due to the unseasonal weather they stand to lose a great deal of the crop due to spoilage. Your team must use their knowledge of multiplication and division to portion the apples to produce them into delicious goods for consumers. They must use their knowledge of the production cycle to transform a natural resource like apples into a profitable product to sell to consumers. Finally, the group must produce a bake sale advertisement to spread the word to consumers, volunteers, and community members. The apples do not have long before they rot, so get to work.

Source: Image by AmericanTrails from Pixabay

Figure 15.2   Carnival

Title: Carnival Creations and Calculations (Fourth Grade)

Subjects: Mathematics, Economics, Geography

The Essential Question: How can we improve the profits of a struggling amusement park?

The Scenario

Amusement parks and carnivals are extremely fun, entertaining, and exciting. Many families create wonderful memories when visiting an amusement park or carnival. Parents remember their visits to amusement parks as children and take their families back for their children to experience the same fun. Epcot Center in the United States is known for its cultural diversity and walking tours to explore different countries around the world. Also in the United States, Universal Studios is known for its exciting movie attractions. Finally, La Ronde in eastern Canada boasts incredible rides and roller coasters. The experiences of riding a roller coaster, petting interesting animals, engaging in games of chance, and eating delicious foods is thrilling.

One such amusement park, Algebra Kingdom, is losing its excitement. If nothing is done, Algebra Kingdom will shut down. The reason for this is that attendance is low, and since attendance is low, Algebra Kingdom is not making any money and the people who work for it will lose their jobs. How can we help save Algebra Kingdom?

You must save the amusement park. As fourth graders, you are uniquely qualified in understanding what is fun for families. Your group members have been hired as the new CCOs (Chief Creativity Officers) to redesign some of the park features to attract more people to visit the park and cut down on wait times for the popular features. In preparation for your project, Algebra Kingdom asked its visitors and staff in a survey what areas of the park needed work to improve its profit. The survey identified the roller coaster, petting zoo, aquarium, Algebra Kingdom's banner, the Ferris wheel, admissions, the park map, and the lemonade stand as the areas needing improvements. Using your math skills and knowledge, you are required to redesign the each area on the improvements list. The groups of CCOs will design their park feature and describe it to the Algebra Kingdom staff and visitors for approval.

Source: Image by Jill Wellington from Pixabay

Figure 15.3   Crying Rhinoceros

Title: Our Discovery Channel (Fifth Grade)
Subjects: Language Arts, Science

The Essential Question: What can we do to help save an animal species from extinction?

The Scenario

Earth contains a vast number of animal species. Each year scientists discover 15,000 new species and have predicted that over 8 million species of animals live on Earth. Life on Earth is incredibly diverse and extraordinary: In the foothills of the Andes Mountains scientists have found a bat the size of a raspberry, cockroaches can live up to 9 days without a head, and a snakehead fish can survive for days outside of water.

Human beings are just one of the species living on Earth, but our rapid growth is threatening many habitats and causing the extinction of numerous species daily. Humans are in direct competition with animal species for natural resources and space. People strip forests of trees to produce croplands, houses, or human-occupied spaces and eliminate the habitats of animals in the process. For example, the dodo bird lived with no natural predator on the island of Mauritius until European settlers arrived and hunted the species into extinction. Humans are starting to realize that Planet Earth does not contain an unlimited supply of resources (animal or otherwise) to use.

People must be informed of the risks of extinction for numerous endangered species across the world. The challenge is to inform the local community of the dangers of extinction facing numerous species of animals at the hands of humans by producing informative segments for a television documentary. Educating people of the plight of these endangered species will help promote local and global awareness of this problem.

Your group works for Discovery Geographic, an organization with the mission of informing people about the wonders of the animal kingdom. Your group is made up of animal researchers preparing a documentary about some animal species that are in peril of becoming extinct.

Your group of animal researchers will identify animal species on the brink of extinction and learn about the animal, its habitat, its food, and the specific cause(s) of its endangered status with suggestions to safeguard it from extinction. The viewing audience must have essential information to become active protectors of the endangered species. The animal researchers will place their segments into a documentary titled *Discovery Geographic's Endangered Species*.

Source: Image by AD_Images from Pixabay

Figure 15.4   Data

Title: Business is Booming! (Sixth Grade)
Subjects: Language Arts, Mathematics, Economics

The Essential Question: How do you create a business plan to start your own business?

The Scenario

Having recently inherited $50,000 you are considering opening a sporting goods store. That has been your lifelong dream. You have found a friend willing to invest a similar amount of money in the endeavor. You decide to investigate the possibility of opening the business. You begin to analyze what is needed. To receive additional financing, you must complete a business plan and present it to the bank in 2 weeks.

Source: Image by Gerd Altmann from Pixabay

Figure 15.5   Burger and Fries

Title: Nutrition Mission (Seventh Grade)

Subjects: Health, Mathematics, Language Arts

The Essential Question: How can you use research and your acquired knowledge of nutrition to persuade students and the school to improve the diet of middle schoolers?

The Scenario

As the school dietitian of a local middle school, you are concerned the meals served in the school cafeteria do not conform to the current recommendations for reducing fat to 30% of calories in the diet. While the students love the french fries and hamburgers served by your staff, you realize the high-fat content in these foods may contribute to an increased risk of heart disease as the students get older.

After discussing this with the school principal, you have been asked to conduct a complete study of the nutritional aspects of the school lunches. This study, to be conducted by you and your staff, will analyze current lunch menus for an average school week, calculate the nutrient values of the menu items, and compare this to the U.S. Recommended Daily Allowances (RDAs) for middle school-aged students.

The completed results will be presented to the school board and principal at the next board meeting in 3 weeks. Any recommendations for menu changes should be included in the final report.

Source: Image by RitaE from Pixabay

Figure 15.6   Tree in Broken Globe

Title: Life in a Square Mile (Eighth Grade)

Subjects: Mathematics, Science, Language Arts

Essential Question: What is the importance of biodiversity in your square mile of land?

The Scenario

You are a member of a department of natural resources team. You have been asked to study one square mile area of wilderness and determine what wildlife species live in that area.

Your task is to prepare a report of the current population level and predict the population level for the next 5 years. You will need to present this information to your supervisor in 3 weeks.

Source: Image by Bhargava Marripati from Pixabay

Fluency Lesson Planning Template

Preplanning Steps

1. Choose the target subjects—Select the subjects the lesson will access. Remember, the Modern Fluencies infuse multiple subject areas into each learning journey. Language arts, mathematics, science, social studies, health, and physical education can be combined into real-world, authentic learning experiences.

2. Select the curricular objectives you want to cover—Consult your local curriculums or national standards such as the Common Core State Standards (CCSS) or the Next Generation Science Standards (NGSS).

3. Secret tip: Only select the standards, indicators, objectives, or skills directly explored and assessed during the learning journey. It is a natural tendency to try to select as many objectives as possible. However, it may become difficult to guarantee learners have mastered the selected objectives.

4. Create your scenario—The magic of designing instruction using the fluencies is allowing imagination to pique the interest of students. Educators must create a captivating scenario to draw in students. First, you must craft a compelling introduction to get the students curious. Next, you must introduce a problem, challenge, or task that will provide learners with the opportunity to learn the required learning objectives. After that, engage the learners and openly challenge them to solve the problem, complete the task, or fulfill the challenge.

5. Choose a fun and noticeable title to capture attention—Depending on what skills and scenario you will address, think of a brilliant and splashy title that relates to the topic(s) of the lesson. For instance, if you are crafting a social studies lesson about human, natural, and capital resources and the lesson requires learners to apply these topics in a real-world situation like auditing and analyzing their favorite theme park for human, natural, and capital resources, educators could call it "Resource Roller Coaster" or "The Human, Natural, and Capital Carnival."

Title:

Grade:

Subject(s):

Duration of Learning Unit:

This section includes the preliminary elements of the unit: title, grade level, main content subjects, and estimated class period duration of time.

Content Tags

Tags are the large ideas, concepts, and topics covered in the unit. They should be a single word or brief phrase separated by commas.

Overview

This provides a brief description of the plan's intended outcome.

Essential Question

This is the main question that is the focus of the lesson content derived from the scenario.

Curriculum Objective(s)

These are the academic standards covered by this lesson's content.

Technology Level Integration

High Tech (Technology Integration is high: Explain how technology is used in a meaningful way)

Low Tech (Technology Integration is low: Explain how technology is used in a meaningful way)

No Tech (No Technology Integration)

Scenario

This is the story and context of the learning adventure. The scene is described, the challenge is issued, and the requirements for producing a solution to the problem are detailed. The scenario follows a general strand of ideas that describes everything that should have been accomplished by the students when the journey is over.

Step 1: Define

Step 2: Discover

Step 3: Determine

Step 4: Dream

Step 5: Design

Step 6: Deliver

- o   Produce
- o   Publish

Step 7: Diagnose

Step 8: Debrief

Step 9: Decide

Fluency Integration

- o   Collaboration
- o   Creativity
- o   Communications
- o   Information

References

Adams, L. (2016). Learning a new skill is easier said than done. Gordon Training International. Retrieved from https://www.gordontraining.com /free-workplace-articles/learning-a-new-skill-is-easier-said-than-done/

Amabile, T., & Pratt, M. (2016). The dynamic componential model of creativity and innovation in organizations: Making progress, making meaning. *Research in Organizational Behavior, 36*, 157–183. doi:10.1016/j .riob.2016.10.001

American Academy of Pediatrics. (2016). American Academy of Pediatrics supports childhood sleep guidelines. Retrieved from https://www.aap.org/en -us/about-the-aap/aap-press-room/Pages/American-Academy-of-Pediatrics -Supports-Childhood-Sleep-Guidelines.aspx

Arter J., & Chappuis, J. (2006). *Creating & recognizing quality rubrics.* Saddle River, NJ: Pearson.

Ashton, J., & Newman, L. (2006). An unfinished symphony: 21st century teacher education using knowledge creating heutagogies. *British Journal of Educational Technology, 37*(6), 825–840. doi:10.1111/j.1467-8535 .2006.00662.x

Baer, J. (1993). *Creativity and divergent thinking.* Hillsdale, NJ: Lawrence Erlbaum.

Bandura, A. (2001). Social cognitive theory: An agentic perspective. *Annual Review of Psychology, 52*(1), 1–26.

Bansal, M. (2014). Big data: Creating the power to move heaven and earth. *MIT Technology Review.* Retrieved from https://www.technologyreview.com /s/530371/big-data-creating-the-power-to-move-heaven-and-earth/

Barrett, P., Davies, F., Zhang, Y., & Barrett, L. (2015). The impact of classroom design on pupils' learning: Final results of a holistic, multi-level analysis. *Building and Environment, 89*, 118–133. https://doi.org/10.1016/j .buildenv.2015.02.013

Bartholomew, S., & Strimel, G. (2018). Factors influencing student success on open-ended design problems. *International Journal of Technology and Design Education, 28*(3), 753–770. https://doi.org/10.1007/s10798 -017-9415-2

Benton, J. (2017). Carbohydrates and sugars. *KidsHealth.* Retrieved from: https://kidshealth.org/en/parents/sugar.html

Bilyeu, L. (2017). 40 things the iPhone has replaced. *Turbofuture.* Retrieved from https://turbofuture.com/cell-phones/40-Things-the-iPhone -has-Replaced

Blaschke, L. M. (2012). Heutagogy and lifelong learning: A review of heutagogical practice and self-determined learning. *International Review of Research in Open and Distance Learning, 12*(1), 56–71.

Bloom, B. S., Englehart, M. D., Hill, W. H., Furst, E. J., & Krathwohl, D. R. (1956). *Taxonomy of educational objectives: The classification of educational goals.* New York, NY: Longmans, Green.

Bolat, Y., & Karakus, M. (2017). Design implementation and authentic assessment of a unit according to concept-based interdisciplinary approach. *International Electronic Journal of Elementary Education, 10*(1), 37–47.

Bronson, P., & Merryman, A. (2010). The creativity crisis. *Newsweek.* Retrieved from https://www.newsweek.com/creativity-crisis-74665

Brookhart, S. (2013). *How to create and use rubrics for formative assessment and grading.* Alexandria VA: ASCD. Retrieved from http://www.ascd.org /publications/books/112001/chapters/What-Are-Rubrics-and-Why-Are -They-Important%C2%A2.aspx

Bruner, J. S. (1960). *The process of education.* Ann Arbor, MI: Harvard University Press.

Buchanan, S., Harlan, M. A., Bruce, C., & Edwards, S. (2016). Inquiry based learning models, information literacy, and student engagement: A literature review. *School Libraries Worldwide, 22*(2), 23–39.

Cellitti, J., & Wright, C. (2019). Encouraging student-generated questioning. *Science and Children, 57*(4), 76–79.

Chen, L., & Hseih, H. (2013). The integration of the Big6 information literacy and reading strategies instruction in a fourth grade inquiry-based learning course, "Our aquarium." *Journal of Library and Information Studies, 11*(1), 95–130. doi:10.6182/jlis.2013.11(1).095

Chen, L., Chen, Y., & Ma, Y. (2014). Effects of integrated information literacy on science learning and problem-solving among seventh-grade students. *Malaysian Journal of Library & Information Science, 19*(2), 35–51.

Cheryan, S., Ziegler, S., Plaut, V., & Meltzoff, A. (2014). Designing classrooms to maximize student achievement. *Policy Insights from the Behavioral and Brain Sciences, 1*(1), 4–12. doi:10.1177/2372732214548677

Chick, N. (n.d.). Metacognition. Retrieved from https://cft.vanderbilt.edu /guides-sub-pages/metacognition/

Christensen, C. M., Horn, M. B., & Johnson, C. W. (2008). *Disrupting class: How disruptive innovation will change the way the world learns.* New York, NY: McGraw-Hill.

Clark, C. (1958). *Brainstorming, the dynamic way to create successful ideas.* Garden City, NY: Doubleday.

Cole, R. (2008). *Educating everybody's children: Diverse teaching strategies for diverse learners* (rev. and exp. 2nd ed.). Alexandria, VA: ASCD.

Cooper, J. L. (1995). Cooperative learning and critical thinking. *Teaching of Psychology, 22*(1), 7–9.

Costa, A. L., & Kallick, B. (2008). *Learning and leading with habits of mind: 16 essential characteristics for success.* Alexandria, VA: Association for Supervision and Curriculum Development.

Crockett, L., Jukes, I., & Churches, A. (2011). *Literacy is not enough: 21st-century fluencies for the digital age.* Kelowna, BC: 21st Century Fluency Project.

Danzinger, P. (2018). The fall of the mall and how to make them rise again. *Forbes.* Retrieved from https://www.forbes.com/sites/pamdanziger /2018/10/14/the-fall-of-the-mall-and-three-ways-to-make-them-rise-again /#3fdcda3e2a26

Darling-Hammond, L., & Snyder, J. (2000). Authentic assessment of teaching in context. *Teaching and Teacher Education, 16,* 523–545. doi:10.1.1.511.4676

Dewey, J. (1910). *How we think.* Lexington, MA: D.C. Heath. Retrieved from https://brocku.ca/MeadProject/Dewey/Dewey_1910a/Dewey_1910_ a.html

Dewey, J. (1916). *Democracy and education: An introduction to the philosophy of education.* New York, NY: Macmillan.

Dewey, J. (1938). *Experience and education.* New York, NY: Macmillan.

Dewey, J. (2011). *Democracy and education.* LaVergne, TN: Simon & Brown.

Dias de Figueredo, A. (2005). Learning contexts: A blueprint for research. *Interactive Educational Multimedia, 11,* 127–139. http://www.ub.es /multimedia/iem

Diver, M. (2017). The iPhone changed video gaming forever. *Vice.* Retrieved from https://www.vice.com/en_us/article/8xaagv/the-iphone-changed-video -gaming-forever

Dodge, B. (1997). *Some thoughts about WebQuests.* Retrieved from http:// webquest.org/sdsu/about_webquests.html

Elmore, R. F. (2009). *Improving the instructional core.* Retrieved from http:// www.fpsct.org/uploaded/Teacher_Resource_Center/Instructional_Practices /Resources/20091124152005.pdf

FitzGerald, N. (2018). Why I still buy music in the age of Spotify. *Digital Music News*. Retrieved from https://www.digitalmusicnews.com/2018/01 /03/still-buy-vinyl-music-spotify/

Forbes Communications Council. (2018). Does print still have a place in the future of advertising? 10 experts weigh in. *Forbes*. Retrieved from https:// www.forbes.com/sites/forbescommunicationscouncil/2018/03/02/does -print-still-have-a-place-in-the-future-of-advertising-10-experts-weigh-in /#68c7a39a5fc6

Freire, P. (1972). *Pedagogy of the oppressed*. New York, NY: Herder and Herder.

Fullan, M., Quinn, J., & McEachen, J. (2018). *Deep learning: Engage the world change the world*. Thousand Oaks, CA: Corwin.

Future of Work Institute. (2012). The benefits of flexible working arrangements: A Future of Work report. Retrieved from https://www.bc.edu /content/dam/files/centers/cwf/individuals/pdf/benefitsCEOFlex.pdf

Glasser, W. (1997). "Choice theory" and student success. *Education Digest, 63*(3), 16–21.

Goodwin, T. (2015). The battle is for the customer interface. *TechCrunch*. Retrieved from https://techcrunch.com/2015/03/03/in-the-age-of-disinter mediation-the-battle-is-all-for-the-customer-interface/

Graue, E., Hatch, K., Rao, K., & Oen, D. (2007). The wisdom of class-size reduction. *American Educational Research Journal, 44*(3), 670–700. doi:10.3102/0002831207306755

Grossman, R. (2009). Structures for facilitating student reflection. *College Teaching, 57*(1), 15–22. doi:10.3200/CTCH.57.1.15-22

Gurchiek, K. (2018). 6 steps for building an inclusive workplace. *Society for Human Resource Management*. Retrieved from https://www.shrm.org /hr-today/news/hr-magazine/0418/pages/6-steps-for-building-an-inclusive -workplace.aspx

Hainstock, E. G. (1997). *The essential Montessori*. New York, NY: Plume.

Hase, S., & Kenyon, C. (2013). *Self-determined learning: Heutagogy in action*. New York, NY: Bloomsbury Academics.

Haskell, R. (2001). *Transfer of learning: Cognition, instruction, and reasoning*. San Diego, CA: Academic Press.

Hattie, J. (2008). *Visible learning*. Abingdon, Oxfordshire, UK: Routledge.

Hattie, J. (2012). *Visible learning for teachers: Maximizing impact on learning*. New York, NY: Routledge.

Hattie, J., & Timperley, H. (2007). The power of feedback. *Review of Educational Research, 77*(1), 81–112. doi:10.3102/003465430298487

Heritage, M. (2008). Learning progressions: Supporting instruction and formative assessment. *CiteSeer*. Retrieved from http://citeseerx.ist.psu.edu /viewdoc/summary?doi=10.1.1.518.5999

Hodgkins, K. (2014). Finland prime minister blames iPad and iPhone for country's economic problems. *Engadget*. Retrieved from https://www.engadget.com/2014/10/13/finland-prime-minister-blames-ipad-and-iphone-for-countrys-econ/

Howard, J. (2017). What happened to Google's effort to scan millions of university library books? *EdSurge*. Retrieved from https://www.edsurge.com/news/2017-08-10-what-happened-to-google-s-effort-to-scan-millions-of-university-library-books

Jensen, E. (2005). *Teaching with the brain in mind*. Alexandria, VA: ASCD.

Jensen, E. (2008). *Brain-based learning* (2nd ed.). Thousand Oaks, CA: Corwin.

Johnson, S. (2006). *Everything bad is good for you*. New York, NY: Riverhead.

Jukes, I. (2011). Highly educated useless people. *Allthingslearning*. Retrieved from https://allthingslearning.wordpress.com/2011/02/27/highly-educated-useless-people-from-guest-blogger-ian-jukes/

Jukes, I., & Schaaf, R. (2019). *A brief history of the future of education*. Thousand Oaks, CA: Corwin.

Jukes, I., Schaaf, R., & Mohan, N. (2015). *Reinventing learning for the always-on generation: Strategies and apps that work*. Bloomington, IN: Solution Tree.

Kaplan, J., & Kies, D. (1995). Fostering critical thinking in the middle school by using a quality circle strategy. *Journal of Instructional Psychology, 22*(2), 186–189.

Kariippanon, K., Cliff, D., Okely, A., & Parrish, A. (2019). Flexible learning spaces reduce sedentary time in adolescents. *Journal of Science and Medicine in Sport, 22*(8), 918–923.

Kaye, L. (2013). 95 percent of web traffic goes to sites on page 1 of Google SERPs [study]. Retrieved from https://www.brafton.com/news/95-percent-of-web-traffic-goes-to-sites-on-page-1-of-google-serps-study/

Kerzner, H. (2009). *Project management: A systems approach to planning, scheduling, and controlling*. New York, NY: John Wiley & Sons.

Kieler, A. (2016). 5 things we learned about pay phones & why they continue to exist. *Consumer Reports*. Retrieved from https://www.consumerreports.org/consumerist/5-things-we-learned-about-pay-phones-why-they-continue-to-exist/

Kim, K. H. (2011). The creativity crisis: The decrease in creative thinking scores on the Torrance tests of creative thinking. *Creativity Research Journal, 23*(4), 285–295. doi:10.1080/10400419.2011.627805

Klingberg, T. (2008). *The overflowing brain: Information overload and the limits of working memory*. New York, NY: Oxford University Press.

Kurzweil, R. (2010). 10 questions for Ray Kurzweil. *Time*. Retrieved from http://content.time.com/time/magazine/article/0,9171,2033076,00.html

Land, G., & Jarman, B. (1998). *Breakpoint and beyond: Mastering the future today*. Scottsdale, AZ: Leadership 2000.

Lapus, M. (2018). Tips for modeling responsible tech use and critical thinking. *Common Sense Media*. Retrieved from https://www.commonsense .org/education/articles/3-ways-to-make-digital-citizenship-part-of-your -everyday-teaching

Leinonen, T., Keune, A., Veermans, M., & Toikkanen, T. (2016). Mobile apps for reflection in learning: a design research. *British Journal of Educational Technology, 47*, 184–202. doi:10.1111/bjet.12224

Litchfield, B., & Dempsey, J. (2015). Authentic assessment of knowledge, skills, and attitudes. *New Directions for Teaching & Learning, 142*, 65-80.

Loertscher, D., Koechlin, C., & Rosenfeld, E. (2012). *The virtual learning commons*. Salt Lake City, UT: Learning Commons Press.

Longo, C. (2016). Changing the instructional model: Utilizing blended learning as a tool of inquiry instruction in middle school science. *Middle School Journal, 47*(3), 33–40.

Madoyan, L. (2016). Authenticity and teacher's role in project-based learning. *Armenian Folia Anglistika, Ereván, 2*(16), 109–114.

Malkawi, N., & Smadi, M. (2018). The effectiveness of using brainstorming strategy in the development of academic achievement of sixth grade students in English grammar at public schools in Jordan. *International Education Studies, 11*(3), 92–100.

Mansilla, V., & Jackson, A. (2011). Educating for global competence: Preparing our youth to engage the world. *Council of Chief State School Officers' EdStep Initiatives & Asia Society Partnership for Global Learning*. Retrieved from https://asiasociety.org/files/book-globalcompetence.pdf

Martin, F., & Bolliger, D. (2018). Engagement matters: Student perceptions on the importance of engagement strategies in the online learning environment. *Online Learning, 22* (1), 205–222.

Martin, N. (2018). How social media has changed how we consume news. *Forbes*. Retrieved from https://www.forbes.com/sites/nicolemartin1/2018/11 /30/how-social-media-has-changed-how-we-consume-news/#1f141b503c3c

Martinez, S., & Stager, G. (2019). *Invent to learn* (2nd ed.). Torrence, CA: CMK Press.

Maslow, A. (1943). A theory of human motivation. *Psychological Review, 50*, 370–396.

McArthur, J. (2016). How technology has changed banking industry today? *Engadget*. Retrieved from https://www.engadget.com/2016/10/19/how -technology-has-changed-banking-industry-today/

McCafferty, D. (2014). Surprising statistics about big data. *Baseline*. Retrieved from http://www.baselinemag.com/analytics-big-data/slideshows /surprising-statistics-about-big-data.html

McCain, T., Jukes, I., & Crockett, L. (2010). *Living on the future edge.* Thousand Oaks, CA: Corwin.

McLeod, S. A. (2018, May 21). Maslow's hierarchy of needs. Retrieved from https://www.simplypsychology.org/maslow.html

McLuhan, M. (1964). *Understanding media: The extensions of man.* Boston, MA: MIT Press.

Medina, J. (2008). *Brain rules: 12 principles for surviving and thriving at work, home, and school.* Pear Press.

Mentzer, N., Farrington, S., & Tennenhouse, J. (2015). Strategies for teaching brainstorming in design education. *Technology and Engineering Teacher, 74*(8), 8–13.

Merrill, M. D., Drake, L., Lacy, M. J., & Pratt, J. (1996). Reclaiming instructional design. *Educational Technology, 36*(5), 5–7.

Mohan, N. (2018). Leaders' perception of the influence of SB21 on systemic decision making and persistence on becoming learning organizations (Unpublished doctoral dissertation). Lamar University, Beaumont, TX. Retrieved from https://search.proquest.com/openview/a43bd10ae49337a7c8cd53cadfde77a0/1?%20pq-origsite=gscholar&cbl=18750&diss=y

Monaghan, A. (2013). Nokia: The rise and fall of a mobile phone giant. *The Guardian.* Retrieved from https://www.theguardian.com/technology/2013/sep/03/nokia-rise-fall-mobile-phone-giant

Moran, T. (2010). *Introduction to the history of communication: Evolutions & revolutions.* New York, NY: Peter Lang.

National Governors Association Center for Best Practices & Council of Chief State School Officers. (2010). Common Core State Standards for English language arts and literacy in history/social studies, science, and technical subjects. Washington, DC: Authors.

Neary, L. (2014). Printing Wikipedia would take 1 million pages, but that's sort of the point. *NPR.* Retrieved from https://www.capeandislands.org/post/printing-wikipedia-would-take-1-million-pages-thats-sort-point#stream/0

O'Neal, L. J., Gibson, P., & Cotten, S. R. (2017). Elementary school teachers' beliefs about the role of technology in 21st-century teaching and learning. *Computers in the Schools, 34*(3), 192–206. doi:10.1080/07380569.2017.1347443

OECD/Eurostat. (2018). *Oslo Manual 2018: Guidelines for collecting, reporting and using data on innovation* (4th ed., p. 44). Paris/Luxembourg: Authors. https://doi.org/10.1787/24132764

Ojose, B. (2008). Applying Piaget's Theory of Cognitive Development to mathematics instruction. *Mathematics Educator, 18*(1), 26–30

Palmieri, T. (2007). *Tuchy's Law and other contrarian quotes to help you in life's journey.* North Charleston, SC: Booksurge.

Papert, S., & Harel, I. (1991). *Constructionism.* New York, NY: Ablex.

Partnership for 21st Century Skills. (2009). P21 Framework definitions. Retrieved from https://files.eric.ed.gov/fulltext/ED519462.pdf

Patall, E. A. (2013). Constructing motivation through choice, interest, and interestingness. *Journal of Educational Psychology, 105*(2), 522–534.

Perkins, D. N., & Salomon, G. (1988). Teaching for transfer. *Educational Leadership, 46*(1), 22–32.

Perkins, D. N., & Salomon, G. (1992). Transfer of learning. *Contribution to the International Encyclopedia of Education* (2nd ed.). Oxford, England: Pergamon Press.

Peters, T. (1986). What gets measured gets done. *Tribune Media.* Retrieved from https://tompeters.com/columns/what-gets-measured-gets-done/

Piaget, J. (1973). *The child and reality: Problems of genetic psychology* (A. Rosin, Trans.). New York, NY: Grossman.

Pink, D. H. (2005). *A whole new mind: Moving from the information age to the conceptual age.* New York, NY: Riverhead Books.

Poh, M. Z., Swenson, N. C., & Picard, R.W. (2010). A wearable sensor for unobtrusive, long-term assessment of electrodermal activity. *IEEE Transactions on Biomedical Engineering, 57*(5), 1243–1252. doi:10.1109/TBME.2009.2038487

Popham, W. J. (1997). What's wrong—and what's right—with rubrics. *Educational Leadership, 55*(2), 72–75.

Quinton, S., & Smallbone, T. (2010). Feeding forward: Using feedback to promote student reflection and learning—a teaching model. *Innovations in Education and Teaching International, 47*(1), 125–135. doi:10.1080 /1470329090352591

Rands, M., & Gansemer-Topf, A. (2017). The room itself is active: How classroom design impacts student engagement. *Education Publications, 49,* 26–33. Retrieved from https://lib.dr.iastate.edu/edu_pubs/49

Rau, M. (2016). Conditions for the effectiveness of multiple visual representation in enhancing STEM learning. *Educational Psychology Review, 29*(4), 1–45. doi:10.1007/s10648-016-9365-3

Reeve, J., & Tseng, C. (2011). Agency as a fourth aspect of students' engagement during learning activities. *Contemporary Educational Psychology, 36*(4), 257–267. doi:10.1016/j.cedpsych.2011.05.002

Reichel, C. (2019). The health effects of screen time on children: A research roundup. *Journalist's Resource.* Retrieved from https://journalistsresource.org /studies/society/public-health/screen-time-children-health-research/

Rivero, L. (2012). Be more creative today: Five ways to sustain creativity at home and school. *Psychology Today.* Retrieved from https://www .psychologytoday.com/nz/blog/creative-synthesis/201203/be-more -creative-today

Robinson, K., & Aronica, L. (2015). *Creative schools*. New York, NY: Penguin. Retrieved from https://www.psychologytoday.com/nz/blog/creative -synthesis/201203/be-more-creative-today

Rodrigues, P., & Pandeirada, J. (2018). When visual stimulation of the surrounding environment affects children's cognitive performance. *Journal of Experimental Child Psychology, 176*, 140–149. https://doi.org/10.1016/j .jecp.2018.07.014

Sabtiawan, W., Yuanita, L., & Rahayu, Y. (2019). Effectiveness of authentic assessment: Performance, attitudes, and prohibitive factors. *Journal of Turkish Science Education, 16*(2), 156–175.

Satell, G. (2014). A look back at why Blockbuster really failed and why it didn't have to. *Forbes*. Retrieved from https://www.forbes.com/sites /gregsatell/2014/09/05/a-look-back-at-why-blockbuster-really-failed-and -why-it-didnt-have-to/#347284f51d64

Sato, Y., Hazeyama, A., Miyadera, Y. (2016). Development of a project/ problem-based learning body of knowledge (PBLBOK). 2016 IEEE 8th International Conference on Engineering Education (ICEED) (pp. 181– 186). Kuala Lumpur, Malaysia. doi:10.1109/ICEED.2016.7856068

SINTEF. (2013, May 22). Big data, for better or worse: 90% of world's data generated over last two years. *ScienceDaily*. Retrieved from www.sciencedaily .com/releases/2013/05/130522085217.htm

Small, G., & Vorgan, G. (2008). *iBrain: Surviving the technological alteration of the modern mind*. New York, NY: Collins Living.

Sommers, F., & Dineen, T. (1984). *Curing nuclear madness*. Agincourt, Ontario, Canada: Methuen.

Steiner, G. (2001). Transfer of learning, cognitive psychology of. In N. J. Smelser & P. B. Baltes (Eds.), *Cognitive psychology of international encyclopedia of social & behavioral sciences* (pp. 15845–15851). doi:10.1016/B0-08- 043076-7/01481-0

Sternberg, R. J. (1985). *Beyond IQ: A triarchic theory of intelligence*. New York, NY: Cambridge University Press.

Sternberg, R. J. (1997). *Thinking styles*. New York, NY: Cambridge University Press.

Swartz, R., Costa, A., Beyer, B., Reagan, R., & Kallick, B. (2010). *Thinking- based learning: Promoting quality student achievement in the 21st century*. New York, NY: Teachers College Press.

Tessmer, M., & Richey, R. (1997). The role of context in learning and instructional design. *Educational Technology Research and Development, 45*(2), 85–115. Retrieved from http://www.jstor.org/stable/30221388

Tillema, H. (2010). Formative assessment in teacher education and teacher professional development. In P. Peterson, E. Baker, & B. McGaw (Eds.),

International encyclopedia of education (3rd ed., pp. 563–571). https://doi.org/10.1016/B978-0-08-044894-7.01639-0

Torrance, P. (1974). *The Torrance tests of creative thinking: Verbal tests, forms A and B; figural tests, forms A and B; norms-technical manual* (research ed.). Princeton, NJ: Personnel Press.

Trahan, L. H., Stuebing, K. K., Fletcher, J. M., & Hiscock, M. (2014). The Flynn effect: A meta-analysis. *Psychological Bulletin, 140*(5), 1332–1360. https://doi.org/10.1037/a0037173

University of Exeter. (2019). Chapter 10 - Peer and self-assessment in student work: Principles and criteria. Retrieved from http://as.exeter.ac.uk/academic-policy-standards/tqa-manual/lts/peerselfassessment/

University of Haifa. (2017, August 22). Blue light emitted by screens damages our sleep, study suggests. *ScienceDaily*. Retrieved from http://www.sciencedaily.com/releases/2017/08/170822103434.htm

Vander Ark, T. (2019). Why schools need research and design space. *Forbes*. Retrieved from https://www.forbes.com/sites/tomvanderark/2019/06/03/why-schools-needsresearch-and-development-space/#5e3e06166c46

Vaughn, M. (2014). The role of student agency: Exploring openings during literacy instruction. *Teaching and Learning, 28*(1), 4–16.

Vygotsky, L. S. (1978). *Mind in society: The development of higher psychological processes*. Cambridge, MA: Harvard University Press.

Wagner, T., & Dintersmith, T. (2015). *Most likely to succeed: Preparing our kids for the innovation era*. New York, NY: Scribner.

Walker, M. (2019). Americans favor mobile devices over desktops and laptops for getting news. *Pew Research Center*. Retrieved from https://www.pewresearch.org/fact-tank/2019/11/19/americans-favor-mobile-devices-over-desktops-and-laptops-for-getting-news/

Wallis, C. (2017). Is the U.S. education system producing a society of "smart fools"? *Scientific American*. Retrieved from https://www.scientificamerican.com/article/is-the-u-s-education-system-producing-a-society-of-ldquo-smart-fools-rdquo/?WT.mc_id=send-to-friend

Walsh, J., Barnes, J., Cameron, J., Goldfield, G., Chaput, J., Gunnell, K., Ledoux, A, Zemek, R., & Tremblay, M. (2018). Associations between 24 hour movement behaviours and global cognition in US children: A cross-sectional observational study. *The Lancet*. https://doi.org/10.1016/S2352-4642(18)30278-5

West, R. (2018). *Foundations of learning and instructional design technology*. Retrieved from https://edtechbooks.org/lidtfoundations

Westera, W. (2011). On the changing nature of learning context: Anticipating the virtual extensions of the world. *Educational Technology & Society, 14*(2), 201–212.

Whitefield, J. (2013). The winds are blowing down the door: Preparing for dramatic changes. *Facilities Manager*. Retrieved from http://digital .corporatepress.com/i/208383-facilites-manager-nov-dec-2013/17

Wiggins, G. (1989). A true test: Toward more authentic and equitable assessment. *Phi Delta Kappan, 70*(9), 703–713.

Wiggins, G. (1998). *Educative assessment: Designing assessments to inform and improve student performance*. New York, NY: Jossey-Bass.

Wiggins, G., & McTighe, J. (2005). *Understanding by design* (exp. 2nd ed.). Alexandria, VA: ASCD.

Wikipedia Statistics. (2019). In *Wikipedia*. Retrieved [September 21, 2020] from https://en.wikipedia.org/wiki/Wikipedia:Statistics

Wiseman, L. (2014). *Rookie smarts: Why learning beats knowing in the new game of work*. New York, NY: HarperCollins.

World Economic Forum. (2015). New vision for education: Unlocking the potential of technology. Geneva, Switzerland: Authors. Retrieved from http://www3.weforum.org/docs/WEFUSA_NewVisionforEducation_ Report2015.pdf

World Health Organization. (2019). To grow up healthy, children need to sit less and play more. Retrieved from https://www.who.int/news-room/detail /24-04-2019-to-grow-up-healthy-children-need-to-sit-less-and-play-more

Wurman, R. S. (1989). *Information anxiety*. Garden City, NY: Doubleday.

Yılmaz, F., & Boylan, M. (2016). Multiculturalism and multicultural education: A case study of teacher candidates' perceptions. *Cogent Education, 3*(1), 1172394. doi:10.1080/2331186X.2016.1172394

Ziv, A. (1983). The influence of humorous atmosphere on divergent thinking. *Contemporary Educational Psychology, 8*(1), 68–75.

Zohar, A., & Ben David, A. (2009). Paving a clear path in a thick forest: a conceptual analysis of a metacognitive component. *Metacognition Learning, 4*(3), 177–195.

Index

Leadership That Makes an Impact

MICHAEL FULLAN & MARY JEAN GALLAGHER

With the goal of transforming the culture of learning to develop greater equity, excellence, and student well-being, this book will help you liberate the system and maintain focus.

PETER M. DEWITT

This step-by-step how-to guide presents the six driving forces of instructional leadership within a multistage model for implementation, delivering lasting improvement through small collaborative changes.

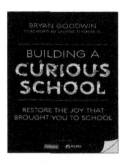

BRYAN GOODWIN

If you've ever wondered anything, really—just out of curiosity—then you have what it takes to lead your school to restored curiosity and your students to well-being and success.

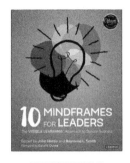

JOHN HATTIE & RAYMOND L. SMITH

Based on the most current Visible Learning® research with contributions from education thought leaders around the world this book includes practical ideas for leaders to implement high-impact strategies to strengthen entire school cultures and advocate for all students.

DAVIS CAMPBELL & MICHAEL FULLAN

The model outlined in this book develops a systems approach to governing local schools collaboratively to become exemplars of highly effective decision-making, leadership, and action.

MICHAEL FULLAN, JOANNE QUINN, & JOANNE MCEACHEN

The comprehensive strategy of deep learning incorporates practical tools and processes to engage educational stakeholders in new partnerships, mobilize whole-system change, and transform learning for all students.

JOANNE QUINN, JOANNE MCEACHEN, MICHAEL FULLAN, MAG GARDNER, & MAX DRUMMY

Dive into deep learning with this hands-on guide to creating learning experiences that give purpose, unleash student potential, and transform not only learning, but life itself.

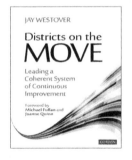

JAY WESTOVER

The transformative framework outlined in this book creates a districtwide approach for changing the culture of learning and creating a coherent system of continuous improvement.

To order your copies, visit **corwin.com/leadership**

ANTHONY KIM, KEARA MASCARENAZ, & KAWAI LAI

This guide provides battle-tested practices to help leaders build better habits for team learning, meetings, and projects, to achieve a more responsive, innovative organization.

EVAN ROBB

Build the foundations of effective leadership despite daily distractions. Learn how to intentionally use ten-minute opportunities to consider and execute your vision.

AMY TEPPER & PATRICK FLYNN

Nineteen strategies help leaders, coaches, and teachers improve their ability to identify desired outcomes, recognize learning in action, collect relevant evidence, and develop effective feedback.

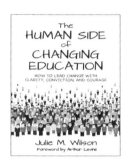

JULIE M. WILSON

Learn to make sense of challenging change journeys and accelerate implementation with this practical framework that includes human-centered tools, resources, and mini case studies.

GRANT LICHTMAN

Our rapidly evolving world is dramatically impacting how we view schools. *Thrive* shows educators how they can help their schools not only survive but thrive during rapid change.

ERIC SHENINGER

The future-forward framework in this book prepares leaders to harness the power of innovative ideas and digital strategies to create relevant, engaging, and intuitive school cultures.

CHRISTINE MASON, PAUL LIABENOW, & MELISSA PATSCHKE

Envision and enact transformative change with an iterative visioning process, thought-provoking vignettes, case studies from exemplary schools, key strategies and tools, and practical implementation ideas.

KIRSTEN RICHERT, JEFFREY IKLER, & MARGARET ZACCHEI

Shifting empowers educational change leaders to proactively and coherently navigate complex, unprecedented change in schools and establish a school culture in which changemakers can thrive.

A SAGE Publishing Company

Helping educators make the greatest impact

CORWIN HAS ONE MISSION: to enhance education through intentional professional learning.

We build long-term relationships with our authors, educators, clients, and associations who partner with us to develop and continuously improve the best evidence-based practices that establish and support lifelong learning.